The Handbook to Literary Research

Edited by Delia da Sousa Correa and W.R. Owens *The Handbook to Literary Research* is a practical guide for students embarking on postgraduate work in Literary Studies. It introduces and explains research techniques, methodologies and approaches to information resources, paying careful attention to the differences between countries and institutions, and providing a range of key examples.

This fully updated second edition is divided into five sections which cover:

- Tools of the trade – a brand new chapter outlining how to make the most of literary resources;
- Textual scholarship and book history – explains key concepts and variations in editing, publishing and bibliography;
- Issues and approaches in literary research – presents a critical overview of theoretical approaches essential to literary studies;
- The dissertation – demonstrates how to approach, plan and write this important research exercise;
- Glossary – provides comprehensive explanations of key terms, and a checklist of resources.

Packed with useful tips and exercises and written by scholars with extensive experience as teachers and researchers in the field, this volume is the ideal handbook for those beginning postgraduate research in literature.

Delia da Sousa Correa is Senior Lecturer in English at The Open University, UK.

W.R. Owens is Professor of English Literature at The Open University, UK.

Contributors: Susan Bassnett, Delia da Sousa Correa, Simon Eliot, Suman Gupta, Sara Haslam, David Johnson, M.A. Katritzky, Derek Neale, W.R. Owens, and Shafquat Towheed.

The Handbook to Literary Research

Edited by

Delia da Sousa Correa and
W.R. Owens

Routledge
Taylor & Francis Group

LONDON AND NEW YORK

The Open University

First published 1998 by Routledge, written and produced by The Open University

This edition 2010 by Routledge
2 Park Square, Milton Park, Abingdon, Oxon OX14 4RN

Simultaneously published in the USA and Canada
by Routledge
711 Third Avenue, New York, NY 10017

Routledge is an imprint of the Taylor & Francis Group, an informa business

© The Open University 1998, 2010

First edition published 1998

Second edition published 2010

Typeset in Goudy by Wearset Ltd, Boldon, Tyne and Wear

British Library Cataloguing in Publication Data
A catalogue record for this book is available from the British Library

Library of Congress Cataloging in Publication Data
A catalog record for this book has been requested

ISBN10: 0-415-49732-9 (hbk)
ISBN10: 0-415-48500-2 (pbk)
ISBN10: 0-203-87333-5 (ebk)

ISBN13: 978-0-415-49732-9 (hbk)
ISBN13: 978-0-415-48500-5 (pbk)
ISBN13: 978-0-203-87333-5 (ebk)

Contents

Contributors

Delia da Sousa Correa is Senior Lecturer in English at The Open University. She is the author of *George Eliot, Music and Victorian Culture* (Palgrave Macmillan, 2003) and editor of *The Nineteenth-Century Novel: Realisms* (Routledge/Open University, 2000) and of *Phrase and Subject: Studies in Literature and Music* (Legenda/MHRA, 2006).

W.R. Owens is Professor of English Literature at The Open University. Among his publications are editions of works by John Bunyan, including *The Pilgrim's Progress* (2003), and, jointly with P.N. Furbank, four books on Defoe. He is joint General Editor of *The Works of Daniel Defoe* (44 vols, Pickering & Chatto, 2000–2009).

Susan Bassnett is Professor of Comparative Literature at the University of Warwick. Recent books include *Exchanging Lives* (2002), a collection of poems and translations; *Sylvia Plath: An Introduction to the Poetry* (2005); *The Translator as Writer* (2006) with Peter Bush; *Ted Hughes* (2008); and *Translation in Global News* (2008) with Esperança Bielsa. She also writes for several national newspapers.

Simon Eliot is Professor of the History of the Book at the School of Advanced Study, University of London, and Director of the London Rare Books School. He has published on quantitative book history, publishing history, the history of reading, and library history. He is General Editor of the new multi-volume *History of Oxford University Press*.

Suman Gupta is Professor of Literature and Cultural History at The Open University. Recent books include: *The Theory and Reality of Democracy: A Case Study in Iraq* (2006); *Social Constructionist Identity Politics and Literary Studies* (2007); *Globalization and Literature* (2008); and a co-edited volume with Tope Omoniyi, *The Cultures of Economic Migration* (2007).

Sara Haslam is Lecturer in English at The Open University. Among her authored works are *Fragmenting Modernism: Ford Madox Ford, the Novel and the Great War* (Manchester University Press, 2002); *Life Writing* (Routledge, 2008) with Derek Neale; and essays on Ford, Thomas Hardy and modernism. Edited works include Ford's *England and the English* (Carcanet, 2003).

David Johnson is Senior Lecturer in English at The Open University. His publications include *Shakespeare and South Africa* (Oxford University Press, 1996), *Jurisprudence: A South African Perspective* (Butterworths Press, 2001) as principal author; and *A Historical Companion to Postcolonial Literatures in English* (Edinburgh/Columbia University Press 2005) as co-editor. He is series editor with Ania Loomba of the Edinburgh University Press series Postcolonial Literary Studies.

M.A. Katritzky is Senior Research Fellow in Theatre Studies at The Open University. Recent publications include *The Art of Commedia: A Study in the Commedia Dell'arte 1560–1620 with Special Reference to the Visual Records* (Rodopi, 2006); and *Women, Medicine and Theatre 1500–1750: Literary Mountebanks and Performing Quacks* (Ashgate, 2007).

Derek Neale is Lecturer in Creative Writing at The Open University. He is editor and co-author of *A Creative Writing Handbook* (A&C Black/Open University, 2009) and co-author of *Life Writing* and *Writing Fiction* (both Routledge/Open University, 2008).

Shafquat Towheed is Lecturer in English at The Open University. He is the editor of *The Correspondence of Edith Wharton and Macmillan, 1901–1930* (Palgrave Macmillan, 2007); *New Readings in the Literature of British India, c.1780–1947* (Ibidem Verlag, 2007); and the Broadview edition of Arthur Conan Doyle's *The Sign of Four* (Broadview, 2010).

1

Introduction to the Handbook

Delia da Sousa Correa and W.R. Owens

Undertaking any programme of postgraduate study or piece of independent research work in literature is both an exciting and a daunting prospect. The aim of this Handbook is to make the whole process of research more exciting and less daunting – and, we might add, more productive and more rewarding.

How are we to do this?

- First, by introducing you to the range of research skills and methods needed by anyone who wants to do the job effectively and productively.

- Second, by offering you a broad survey of the wide variety of intellectual endeavour that now characterises the study of literature at postgraduate level.

- Third, by providing advice and guidance on what is frequently the most tricky (and most postponed) part of research – writing up the dissertation or thesis.

- Fourth, by giving you a substantial quantity of useful and usable information in the form of a glossary and a large bibliographical Checklist.

Although you could certainly gain something by dipping into the book, you may well find it better to start by reading Parts 1–4 in sequence as they build steadily from learning about research resources to writing the final dissertation.

The Handbook is designed to provide guidance on basic techniques for anyone wishing to undertake literary research. In practice, the skills and knowledge required to complete an MA successfully are the same as those needed by students beginning a research degree (an MPhil or PhD) and, indeed, by anyone in or outside higher education wishing to pursue independent research in literature. There are, of course, significant differences in the scope of the projects to which you apply these skills at different levels, and you will find a useful discussion of the transition from a Master's degree to a PhD in Chapter 11 on 'Planning, writing and presenting a dissertation or thesis'.

The chapters in the Handbook have certain characteristics in common: they all include the identification of key ideas and texts within their subject; they all involve discussion of the significant developments in their field; they all discuss the specific nature of research within their subject; and they all include a set of 'Questions and exercises' designed to get you to practise the knowledge and skills to which you have been introduced in each chapter. At the same time the Handbook has a variety of voices because of the wide range of authors who have contributed to it, and we hope that you will find this stimulating and refreshing.

STRUCTURE AND CONTENT OF THE HANDBOOK

Part 1: tools of the trade

Every postgraduate student needs, like any apprentice, to understand and to be able to use effectively the tools of his or her trade. Part 1 is an introduction to the basic research methodologies of literature, and in particular to the range of skills associated with the effective use of research resources. It covers both the use of electronic resources – discussing the impact of digitisation, hypertext and the development of other electronic resources – and of the research libraries which remain crucial to academic research (by 'research library' we mean a university library, or a major city library, or one of the great national libraries). The chapter includes a list of practical exercises which will help you test your growing competence in this set of key skills.

Parts 2 and 3: textual scholarship and book history/issues and approaches in literary research

Over the past half-century or so, literary research has been enriched and complicated by approaches that have broadened our sense of what counts as literary study. At the same time, the increasing availability of electronic resources has contributed to an expansion of the materials and techniques available to literary researchers. The arrival of these new approaches and materials has tended to modify rather than exclude the more traditional forms of study; this has resulted in a rich but potentially confusing range of approaches to literary research from which to choose. One of the aims of this Handbook is to provide a brief guide to what a student might choose in terms of approach, from two broad perspectives.

- Part 2, 'Textual scholarship and book history', is concerned with the more historical and empirical aspects of literary study and deals with classic bibliography in all its variety, with the newer subject of book history, and with the disciplines of scholarly editing. Although these subjects are discussed in discrete chapters, their interconnectedness is made clear.

- Part 3 moves you on to a different set of approaches and issues of relevance to literary research and to the development of 'English' as an academic discipline. The overall emphasis in these chapters is on how an awareness of literary history, critical theory, interdisciplinarity, other media and issues of translation can inform your own research. They aim to help you to develop an awareness of disciplinary history, disciplinary boundaries and issues of translation (in a broad as well as a linguistically specific sense), so that you are equipped to appreciate and engage with the expansion of the discipline of English to encompass work in Comparative and World Literature and its overlapping relationships with other disciplinary areas including Media Studies, Cultural Studies, Linguistics, Philosophy, Sociology, Politics, Music and Fine Arts.

Part 4: planning and completing a research project

When the area of study has been selected, the approach understood and the tools of the trade sharpened, the job itself is still to be done. The ultimate aim of most literary research is to produce some critical, theoretical or historical writing. In most cases such work takes the form of a thesis or dissertation. In Part 4 we offer a sizeable chapter specifically on 'Planning, writing and presenting a dissertation or thesis'. This includes down-to-earth advice on choosing a topic, preparing a research proposal, writing the dissertation or thesis and ensuring that it is properly presented.

In part, learning to write in a scholarly way is about acquiring good writing habits early. For example, you should train yourself, whenever in a piece of writing you refer to the origin of your information, to provide the necessary evidence in terms of a properly referenced source. When making notes, you should always record the exact location of your information – including page numbers so that, if you or anyone else wanted to check that information, it could be done quickly and accurately. None of this is very complicated, but it does require you to understand and use the 'scholarly conventions'. These are discussed in Chapter 11, and you should make sure that you get the hang of them as soon as possible and practise them as much as you can.

Part 5: reference

Any subject, even one that should pride itself on the clarity and exactness of its language, will need occasionally to use specific terminology and abbreviations, and literature is no exception. For this reason we have provided a short Glossary,

Chapter 12, explaining terms used in this book which you are likely to encounter in your further research.

Chapter 13, the 'Checklist of libraries, print, online and other research resources' is perhaps that part of the Handbook to which you will return most frequently throughout your period of research. It is a vital companion piece to Chapter 2. Whereas Chapter 2 discusses methodology, the question of how you go about your research, Chapter 13 is a reference list which helps you to identify what the resources are that you might need to consult. It lists, describes and occasionally discusses the huge variety of databases, catalogues, bibliographies, dictionaries and multifarious other reference works – in printed and electronic versions – without which literary research as a scholarly discipline would hardly be possible. As with every other chapter of this book, the Checklist cannot hope to be comprehensive. But it should provide you with a good introduction to the most important material, and will give you plenty of leads that you can follow up in your own research library or via the Internet.

THE HANDBOOK AND HOW TO USE IT

This Handbook is not designed merely to be read once, as an introduction: it is meant to accompany you from start to finish. For this reason we don't just tell you how to go about literary research, we also *show* you how to do it and provide you with much of the initial material that you will need.

Postgraduate work in literature, as in any subject, is about becoming more intellectually independent. This means that you spend much less time in a seminar room with a prescribed and restricted range of texts, and much more time using research resources and libraries and working through an extended list of texts that you yourself, to a large extent, have compiled. Three features of the Handbook are particularly designed to foster this spirit of independent enquiry and discovery – guided reading, questions and exercises, and textual examples – and it is worth saying a word about each.

Guided reading

One of the Handbook's main functions is to send you off to read extensively and critically. For this reason there is a strong emphasis on what we think of as 'guided reading', and you will find numerous relevant publications cited within the text of each chapter. Each chapter also ends with a list of 'Suggested reading': lists of books, articles and other material relevant to the topic under discussion that you should try to consult. Your choice of further reading will of course be based on what is most relevant to your own field of enquiry. It will also, of necessity, be influenced by what is available. Despite the ever-increasing quantity of digitised material now accessible, students still have to contend with limitations on what they are able to obtain via the combined resources of the Internet and even the best research libraries. This is especially true of printed books, and while electronic journal publication now makes it possible to access articles more easily than book-length texts, books remain a crucial resource for the study of literature.

Questions and exercises

Another recurrent feature of this Handbook is the section entitled 'Questions and exercises' included at the end of each chapter. These sections are designed to give you practice in using the knowledge and skills that you will have just acquired. As with the reading lists, we have tried to offer a range of choices so that, whatever your intellectual interests and library resources, you should be able to find one question that interests you or, at least, is do-able. At the most basic level these 'Questions and exercises' illustrate the sorts of scholarly problem with which specialists in the field are preoccupied.

However, such questions will be much more beneficial if you actually try to answer one or two of them. This is not a trivial point: it is very easy to believe, having read something, that you understand it. But the acid test is whether you are then able to put that understanding and knowledge into your own words. If you are able to do so, then you can move on in the comforting knowledge that you really have grasped the key points of what you have been reading and have made the information your own.

Writing an answer does not necessarily mean producing a full, formal essay: your answer could be in the form of notes or an essay plan. Nevertheless, answering one or two of the questions in the Handbook by means of a formal essay would be a very good idea indeed. You should certainly put pen to paper or fingers to keyboard whenever you can in response to 'Questions and exercises'. As you will learn again and again as you work through the Handbook, the early and frequent practice of good scholarly writing is the key to producing a successful dissertation or thesis.

Textual examples

The final feature that binds the whole Handbook together is the focus on textual examples; you will find a wide variety used to illustrate the discussions within individual chapters. Providing explanations, presenting information and offering practice is what this Handbook is all about. Used properly, it should provide you at the outset with a quick and clear introduction to literary research and, later on, offer you support and guidance as your scholarly confidence grows and your work matures.

ACKNOWLEDGEMENTS

As editors, we would like to record here our warmest thanks to a number of people at The Open University who have helped enormously in the production of this book: Ilona Gingele, course manager; Margrit Bass, Copublishing Department; Michael Thomas, tutor assessor; Christianne Bailey, media project manager; Hazel Coleman, editor; and Joan Crayden, course assistant. We particularly wish to thank members of The Open University library staff, whose contributions have immeasurably improved the book: Helen Clough, Nicola Dowson, Wendy Mears, Katharine Reedy and Christine Tucker. We are also grateful to Professor Martin Priestman, Roehampton University, London, who in his role as external assessor on the MA in English commented on earlier versions of much of the material here. Professor Simon Eliot, now at the School of Advanced Study, University of London, was co-editor with W.R. Owens of the first edition of this Handbook, and we wish to acknowledge his substantial contribution to its initial conception as well as to its present form.

Delia da Sousa Correa and W.R. Owens

Part 1
Tools of the trade

Tools and techniques for literary research: using online and printed sources

2

Tools and techniques for literary research

Using online and printed sources

Shafquat Towheed

INTRODUCTION

You have registered for a taught postgraduate degree, or are contemplating moving on from a taught degree to a programme of research, such as a PhD. You have already completed a first degree in English (or another humanities discipline), and are looking forward to developing your own research interests through the MA dissertation, and after that, perhaps to shaping an original research topic for a potential PhD. Until now, your experience of studying English as a subject will have been mediated through a course of study and directed by the lecturers and tutors at your institution, with relatively little necessity or opportunity for you to undertake substantial primary research on your own. However, one of the key differences at all institutions between undergraduate- and postgraduate-level work will be the much greater emphasis placed on independent research at the higher level. Indeed, the ability to undertake independent research – to identify relevant resources, evaluate them, survey existing scholarship, locate and utilise unpublished archival sources, cite your sources accurately, and remain up to date with current work in the field – is essential to your success in English at a postgraduate level. This chapter is written primarily with British-based postgraduate students in mind, but students located elsewhere in the world will also find valuable information here.

In order to succeed, you will need to acquire and master a set of key attributes and skills that you will be able to deploy with confidence on a regular basis. These include:

- having an overview of the main online and printed sources relevant to your research;

- getting to know a range of available online sources, and being able to evaluate these sources comparatively;

- gaining confidence in using online resources to identify, evaluate and retrieve relevant primary material and secondary scholarship for your research topic;

- using online and printed sources to identify and locate material archives;

- participating in online information networks and becoming part of a research community;

- and finally, being able to keep up to date with developments in the subject.

Equipped with these key skills and resources, you will find that independently forging your own research will become progressively more rewarding and less time consuming.

Contents of this chapter

This chapter is divided into two sections. Section 1 looks briefly at the general principles of postgraduate literary research using largely electronic resources. Section 2 concentrates more systematically on the type of materials available (online, printed and archival), and how they might be used. The overall trajectory of the chapter will therefore be from conducting general online searches, to identifying specific, material sources. When you have read through this chapter, you may want to look through the accompanying 'Checklist of libraries, print, online and other research resources' in the reference section at the end of this Handbook (Chapter 13), noting particularly how it is arranged under *headings* which point you to reference works on various *topics*.

The constantly evolving tools and techniques needed for successful research work in literary studies have changed considerably over the last few decades. Two decades ago, a newly enrolled postgraduate researcher needed to have the ability to create and use a double-indexed card cataloguing system, order a book manually by finding the class mark and filling out a request form, skim through voluminous printed sources, make rapid and accurate manual transcriptions of archival material, and learn to use a manual typewriter. A decade ago, a new postgraduate student would be expected to be able to use the first generation of CD-ROM-based databases accessible only from public-access terminals inside libraries, use internal electronic library catalogues to identify books which then needed to be ordered manually, mark and print search results from first-generation scholarly databases, and have sufficient familiarity with a computer-based word processing package in order to submit their written work.

Today's postgraduate students need to be able to acquire, use and evaluate a wide range of electronic resources, mark, export and store electronic records, participate in discussion forums, and identify and order books remotely. They will most likely have their own laptops with Wi-Fi, enabling continuous and uninterrupted high-speed Internet access, will be able to multitask across a range of open windows, and use email to maintain links with their tutors and each other. The postgraduate student of the future will have access to information through a variety of Internet web-browsing devices, will be more actively engaged in the social construction and dissemination of knowledge (the wiki model), will have access to remote archives that they have never physically visited, and will be supervised largely through a virtual research environment. The tools and techniques for literary research are constantly changing; the challenge for any postgraduate research student is to adapt accordingly.

Some of the information offered in this chapter is inherently time sensitive and will be superseded. The chapter reflects best practice in research at the time of writing, with a full awareness that much of this information (and many key skills) will change significantly with time. As well as using the Handbook, you should refer to additional resources offered by your home institution, to ensure that your research skills are current and effective.

SECTION 1: GENERAL PRINCIPLES OF POSTGRADUATE LITERARY RESEARCH

This section aims to familiarise you with how to use electronic and printed resources in your literary research. A basic level of computing expertise, such as operating Microsoft Word, the ability to use a web browser to access, browse and bookmark websites, and an awareness of how to mark, download and export database search results, is assumed. This section will offer you some basic principles to underpin your research, which you can then apply to the sources discussed in section 2.

Best practice

In undertaking any research project, *always record the route you take*, whether via online or printed sources. This process is important, as you will benefit greatly by logging your research trail. The majority of online sources will require you to enter their websites through your own institution's authenticated gateway, i.e. after entering your user ID and password to log on to your university account.

Simply typing or pasting the URL into your web-browser address window won't always offer you access or full benefits from online resources. Your university library will usually have an institutional subscription to a variety of online resources, and so you need to log in through its site in order fully to benefit from a range of access rights (such as full text and exporting search results).

Preparation is key to effectiveness in scholarly research. Survey what is available online before you arrange a visit to a library, as a large number of scholarly journals, books (both primary sources and criticism) and reference works are now available online. Start your research by finding out what is easily available online and focus on what else you need to locate before visiting a library. You should therefore create a hierarchy in your approach to research:

- First, *identify what is available online*. Familiarise yourself with the main digital resources that are available to you through public-access sites, as well as those offered through your home institution.

- Second, *visit your own university library*, either in person or via its website, and familiarise yourself with both the available electronic and material holdings.

- Third, *identify your nearest major research library*. This may well be your own university library if you are a graduate of Oxford or Cambridge, but the other most important research libraries in the UK include the British Library and the National Libraries of Scotland, Wales and Ireland. In advance of your visit, identify specific sources (books, journal articles, etc.) that you have not been able to find (either online or in your university library's print collections) and organise your research trip around this.

This hierarchy offers an effective plan for action which you can then deploy each time you start work on a research project, providing you with a reliable, systematic and time-effective research methodology.

It is important to find out where to get help. There will be instances when you won't know how to access the material you need to see, or how to negotiate a particularly unwieldy cataloguing system. In the first instance, your university library helpdesk will be the best place to go; increasingly, helpdesks are staffed seven days a week, and can be contacted through a range of methods: email, phone, post, fax and web chat. Most university libraries offer skills training or induction courses, which you can attend; in addition, they may offer dedicated research support for postgraduate research students.

Getting started with the Internet

Using the Internet will be essential to postgraduate research. You need to be aware of what you can find there, and develop key skills so that you can get the most out of it. The Internet is a multimedia resource – you will find not just text, but images, video clips, audio material and so on. Make sure that you are aware of basic search skills, can manage your web browser and understand the terminology in common usage before you start research. You can develop your Internet and searching skills competence by utilising the **Skills in Accessing, Finding and Reviewing Information (SAFARI)** (www.open.ac.uk/safari). This open-access resource offers an online information skills tutorial with seven sections (14 hours in total), but you can work through any of the sections individually; the sections on 'Planning a Search', 'Searching for Information' and 'Evaluating Information' will be of greatest use to you.

At postgraduate level, you need to develop specific subject skills to optimise your research time. While not specifically aimed at postgraduates, the best subject-specific introduction on how to use the Internet for literary studies is Intute's Virtual Training Suite on the Internet for English website (www.vts. intute.ac.uk/he/tutorial/english). If you complete the online tutorial and answer the tour quiz at the end of it, you will have gained an excellent overview of planning and conducting searches and evaluating data.

Using Google

Although it is only a decade old, **Google** (www.google.com) has become an indispensable research tool. As a postgraduate literary researcher, you will use it frequently, but it does pay to understand what it does and doesn't do. The biggest problem you will face when conducting a Google search is the sheer number of hits returned. There are a number of ways in which you can delimit search fields and maximise the retrieval of relevant information. You can restrict your search by language, domain, national territory, date-range, type of material and file format. Using the advanced search function and entering a specific phrase or combination of words by placing it in double speech marks ("...") will greatly improve the accuracy of your search, as it will search for only that particular combination. You can also undertake a synonym search by placing a tilde (~) mark before your search term, specifically exclude something by placing a minus (−) before it, or conversely include it by placing a plus (+) mark before it. All of these can be used together to refine your search.

Remember that Google lists items based on the relationships between search terms, and that there are web pages that will remain either invisible or buried very far down the returned search hits. Using the advanced search functions will greatly increase your chances of returning the hits that you want, while significantly reducing the volume of retrieved information, thereby saving you valuable research time.

Google also offers some specific search functions which are of great benefit to literary researchers. **Google Scholar** (http://scholar.google.com) allows you to search for scholarly publications (books, articles, reviews, etc.) across a range of disciplines. Generally, you cannot access these publications directly from Google Scholar (unless your institution's library has enabled access: to check this click on Scholar Preferences and enter your library name in the library links box), but there will be links to digital or material holdings (journal websites, library catalogues, etc.) to follow up; your institutional access may allow you to view them. Entries are partly weighted by how often they are cited in scholarship, so the ranking of individual articles might reflect their relative importance.

Google Book Search (http://books.google.com) offers a remarkable and constantly growing virtual library; copyright material is available in limited preview or 'snippet' mode (a page range or excerpt only), while non-copyright books can sometimes be read, downloaded and printed in their entirety. Google Book Search is often an excellent resource for accessing difficult to acquire, pre-1900 primary sources, but there are two things that you should always bear in mind when using it:

1   as a matter of routine, always note the exact bibliographical details of the book (including edition details) accessed through Google Book Search, as you need to be systematic and consistent in your citations from it; and

2   always record the precise URL for the digitised source, so that you can find it again without having to repeat the original search. Accurate citation of digitised books is every bit as vital as with a material printed source, and it is wise to get into the habit of accurate and full citation of online sources as quickly as possible.

Finally, a caveat: the image quality of scanned books available on Google Book Search varies immensely, and you may find that you will need to access a physical hard copy of the book you have just found after all. While Google will often be a rewarding first port of call in starting literary research, don't treat it as a one-stop panacea for your research needs.

Wikipedia and evaluating data

Wikipedia (www.wikipedia.org) is the world's largest open-access encyclopaedia, founded on the collaborative social knowledge construction or 'wiki' model; it is a useful tool for literary researchers. Wikipedia provides a helpful first port of call, providing author biographies, indicative bibliographies, links to relevant external sites, and discussion forums. An excellent guide on how to use the resource is available at www.howwikipediaworks.com; you might want to look specifically at chapter 3, 'Finding Wikipedia's Content', for detailed advice on effective searching.

There are some key advantages to using Wikipedia. Unlike other printed (or some online) sources, the frequency of editing and updating of information is extremely high; Wikipedia will often reflect recent events or developments before other sources (this is particularly helpful for researchers in contemporary literature). Creating a username and password to access Wikipedia will allow you to contribute to the social construction of knowledge by joining relevant discussion forums, suggesting useful external links for specific pages and checking content accuracy and (if needed) suggesting changes. Be sure to cite any page accessed from Wikipedia accurately; clicking on the 'cite this page' link in the toolbox on the left-hand margin of each page will automatically generate the correct citation in a range of bibliographic styles (MHRA, MLA, Chicago, etc.). Make sure that you maintain a consistent system of citation.

The wiki model presents many opportunities, but also some challenges. There is far more data on the Internet than any of us can process either individually or collectively, and not all of it is subject to rigorous scrutiny. A small proportion of the material that you will encounter on Wikipedia will be inaccurate, out of date, poorly referenced or incorrect. This is not to say that you should not use Wikipedia, just that you need to exercise your own comparative evaluative skills in order to assess whether the information is useful to you in your research or not. As the social networking of knowledge increases, these evaluative skills will become increasingly important.

As best practice, where possible use websites and databases that clearly show a named editor or editorial team, and evidence of quality assurance (all websites that are attached to academic projects will have this quality certification). Always corroborate information that you find online, either with reference to another independent website, or else against a printed source. Never cite from a website that is not accurate, systematic and transparent about its own sources; this runs the risk of simply replicating those errors in your own work. In order to develop further your evaluative skills, complete the 'Judge' section from Intute's **Internet for English** website (www.vts.intute.ac.uk/he/tutorial/english).

Bookmarking and managing references

A number of Web 2.0 tools will help you record and manage references to both electronic and printed matter. Social-networking-based Internet bookmarking tools such as **Delicious** (http://delicious.com), **digg** (http://digg.com), **reddit** (http://ww.reddit.com), **Facebook** (www.facebook.com) and **StumbleUpon** (www.stumbleupon.com) will store web pages and also allow you to share these pages with others. Your own university's virtual-learning environment may have its own bookmarking tool as well. Online bibliographic-management tools such as **RefWorks** (www.refworks.com) can help you to produce and keep updated bibliographies, thereby keeping a real-time record of your research (you must register on RefWorks before you can use it). You might also be able to acquire commercial bibliographic-management software, such as **EndNote** (www.endnote.com), through your institution at a discounted rate.

Citing sources

There is a serious ethical and legal imperative that shapes how you use your research. Remember that *all sources, whether online, printed or unpublished, need to be cited as fully and as accurately as possible.* Do not, for example, assume that a quotation from an electronic source does not need to be cited as fully as one from a printed book; each needs to be cited in full. If you are in any doubt about how to cite Internet sources, look first at your prescribed style guide. (For more information on the use of scholarly conventions, including citing sources correctly, see Chapter 11, 'Planning, writing and presenting a dissertation or thesis'.)

SECTION 2: TYPES OF MATERIAL

This section provides an overview of the main types of material with which you will need to be familiar as a postgraduate literary researcher. It will provide (1) a survey of the most important reference works, catalogues and guides to materials; (2) guidance on finding and using British libraries; and (3) advice on locating and using archives. It ends with some suggestions about participating in scholarly communities, and keeping up to date with developments in your field. It focuses on some of the key printed and electronic sources, rather than offering an exhaustive catalogue. (For a more comprehensive list, see the Checklist, Chapter 13.) As best practice, wherever online resources are listed, you will need to access them through your own institution's password-protected gateway, in order to benefit from institutional authentication.

General guides and reference works

There are a number of extremely useful biographical dictionaries available online. **The Oxford Dictionary of National Biography** (www.oxforddnb.com) is the single most useful online biographical source for the literary researcher; you can print or download entries, or export them to your own email account. Each entry provides an excellent summary of primary sources, including the bibliographical details of important scholarship on the subject; the provenance and location of extant archives; likenesses; and wealth at the time of death, from probate records. There are also direct links in the left-hand column to other online resources for the subject, such as the National Register of Archives (for more on the NRA, see the section on 'Identifying archives: using electronic tools' below). As a subscription site, in order to gain access you must enter the Oxford DNB through your home institution's authenticated gateway. For American subjects, you should consult the **American National Biography** online (www. anb.org). General encyclopaedias and reference works available online that you might find useful include **Encyclopaedia Britannica** (www.britannica.com), the complete **Oxford Reference Online** suite (www.oxfordreference.com), and the second edition (1989) of the **Oxford English Dictionary** (http://dictionary. oed.com). These sources will give you a general flavour of the scope of literary research, but in order to progress further, you will need to be able to use key online tools to narrow your focus to a specific topic.

Indexes and abstracts
One skill that you will have to acquire is the ability to use available online indexes and find abstracts of books and journal articles, thereby mapping out the scope of existing scholarship in a given field. In order to do this, you will need to become familiar with the following four online databases:

- the **Modern Language Association International Bibliography** of books and articles on the modern languages and literatures (MLA, available through the OCLC First Search website, http://firstsearch.oclc.org – simply select 'MLA' from the list of databases);

- the **Annual Bibliography of English Language and Literature** (ABELL, available via LION at http://lion.chadwyck.co.uk);

- the Routledge **Annotated Bibliography of English Studies** (ABES, http:// abe.informaworld.com);

- the **British Humanities Index** (BHI, available through www-md4.csa. com).

All four of these key databases can be searched in order to find the extent of existing scholarship on a given subject, and all four will allow you to tag, email, export bibliographic software, or print your search results.

Library catalogues
For British-based researchers, the most important library catalogue for you to negotiate is the **British Library's Integrated Catalogue** (http://catalogue.bl.uk). If you have a reader's pass or are a registered user, you can order items remotely

in advance of your visit. There is a comprehensive FAQ and a help screen available to support your use of the integrated catalogue. Note that books need to be ordered in advance (at least two hours for most material and up to 48 hours for selected Document Supply Centre material) and that you can only consult them *in situ* in one of the nominated reading rooms.

COPAC (http://copac.ac.uk) is the best British cumulative catalogue; it can save you a great deal of time if you want to know which libraries hold copies of a particular book you need to access. Bear in mind, however, that COPAC will not be able to find material that has not been entered into individual institutional integrated catalogues, so that if a particular library still has material which is only listed through its card cataloguing system, then it will be invisible on COPAC.

Although far from being comprehensive, **WorldCat** (available through the OCLC website, http://firstsearch.oclc.org) is the world's largest bibliographic database. The advantage of WorldCat is that you can instantly find the international holdings (together with reference numbers) of any given publication.

Primary sources and eBooks
There are a large number of primary literary texts online, as well as considerable numbers of scholarly titles available as eBooks. **Bartleby** (http://bartleby.com) offers a range of verse and fiction, as well as a considerable reference suite, all of which can be read online, or downloaded (Bartleby supports Amazon's eBook reader system, Kindle). **Project Gutenberg** (www.gutenberg.org/catalog) offers more than 27,000 titles (largely fiction published before c.1935); you can browse the alphabetical author list, or search for a specific title. **Literature Online** (LION; http://lion.chadwyck.co.uk) offers the most comprehensive single source available (LION has incorporated earlier full-text databases, such as the English Poetry database). You can search as well as browse, and every entry will link to an author page (giving you brief biographical details), a full list of the holdings of that particular author, as well as criticism written about them. See the section below on 'Full-text journal articles' to see how you can integrate your reading of primary sources with research on existing criticism. Your ability to freely access primary sources (such as fiction and poetry) through these sites will largely be determined by copyright restrictions. However, it's worth bearing in mind that accessing rarer primary sources online can be a time-effective way of researching and reading in your subject, and may save you the effort and expense of a trip to a research library.

Newspapers: electronic and printed sources
Whether your research is historical or contemporary, newspapers provide an important source of book and performance reviews, publishers' advertising, serialisations, editorial comments and author interviews. Increasingly, some of

the most important newspaper collections, such as **The Times Digital Archive 1785–1985** (http://archive.timesonline.co.uk) have been digitised. Be sure to enter this database through your institutional gateway in order to obtain full access. Content can be searched, downloaded and printed for academic research. The even larger **Nineteenth Century British Library Newspapers Website** (www.gale.cengage.com/DigitalCollections/products/britlib) can be accessed from within the British Library's reading rooms in St Pancras and Colindale, or remotely if your institution has access. On a smaller scale, the open-access **Nineteenth-Century Serials Edition** website (www.ncse.ac.uk/index.html) offers full facsimiles of six different British serials. If your research involves late-nineteenth-century book history, you will find the *Publishers' Circular* (1880–90) especially useful. For more contemporary news media sources, the subscription site **NexisUK** (www.lexisnexis.com) has a wide geographical and linguistic reach. Note that many of these digitised newspaper databases are extremely graphically intensive and the images may take some time to load.

While digitisation has been progressing apace, many newspapers are still only available in hard copy or microfilm. The best single UK resource is the British Library's **Newspapers Reading Room in Colindale** (www.bl.uk/reshelp/inrooms/blnewspapers/newsrr.html). To search for items, you must select the Newspapers subset in the British Library's Integrated Catalogue (http://catalogue.bl.uk) by clicking on 'Catalogue subset search' in the blue bar under the Integrated Catalogue logo, and then click on 'Newspapers'. The Basic Search screen appears; the banner title changes, confirming the Newspapers catalogue subset. You can remotely order material online, preferably 48 hours in advance of your visit. An equivalent US resource is the Library of Congress Newspaper and Current Periodical Reading Room, www.loc.gov/rr/news. In most countries, the largest newspaper collection is likely to be housed in the National library.

Full-text journal articles
There is a wealth of scholarship available in ejournals, offered directly through the electronic publisher, or mediated through one of the cumulative subject-specific resources. You should already be familiar with conducting a search for abstracts by using resources such as the MLA, ECO (Electronic Collections Online) or ABELL databases. A preliminary search for abstracts on a given author, title, topic or search keyword should enable you to sketch out the extant scholarship in any given field; it is good research practice to save a copy of your abstract search for reference for the next stage of your research. You now have to populate the field that you have sketched out by accessing full-text journals, so that you can read and evaluate current scholarship, and refer to it in your own work. One of the best sources for full-text journals is **Literature Online** (LION; http://lion.chadwyck.co.uk). You can search for scholarly articles by author,

keyword or title of article, and the retrieved results will be flagged with this symbol 2 if the full text of the article is available. Articles can be downloaded, printed or exported to your email address; search results can also be marked up and saved for future reference.

Another major resource that you will use is **JSTOR** (www.jstor.org). Unlike LION, JSTOR is both interdisciplinary (only a small percentage of the journals are literary) and entirely full-text; its historical reach is bigger, with some nineteenth-century journals included. Unlike LION, JSTOR presents the text as a facsimile in PDF format, which may make it more difficult to read or use. A more important restriction is the fact that JSTOR has a 'moving wall', i.e., the most recent few years' worth of a journal will not be available (this wall varies from one to ten years, but usually averages around five years). This means that JSTOR is inherently better for finding older scholarship, while LION is much better for locating, identifying and reading the newest scholarly articles.

Finally, **Project Muse** (http://muse.jhu.edu), although a smaller and newer database, manages to combine some of the best features of both JSTOR and LION. It offers full-text journal articles only, but unlike JSTOR, gives you the choice of viewing your selected article or journal in PDF or HTML format; there is no 'moving wall'. The only disadvantage is that there is little archival depth; most of the journals are post-2000 issues. Project Muse is good for current research, but poor at filling in the gaps of earlier scholarship; you might find that your search will not demonstrate the successive (and often mutually interrogative) nature of scholarly debates in journals.

You should always see if you can locate and read full-text journal articles remotely, but there will be some journals which are not available in electronic form. In order to consult these, you will need to access the print periodicals holdings of one of the major libraries.

Relevant multimedia material available online
There are a number of multimedia sources, offering a range of audio-visual material, to support your research in literary studies. **Poets on Screen**, which is available through Literature Online (LION; http://lion.chadwyck.co.uk), offers video clips of contemporary poets reading their own work, or reading the work of other poets, playable in either Real Player™ or Windows Media Player ™. As the performances themselves are copyright material (even if some of the verse is not), you cannot download or reproduce these audio-visual clips; however, you can download a shortcut link for each clip on to your desktop (right click on your mouse, and choose 'save target as...') and create your own list of easily accessible clips. This database requires subscriber authentication, so you must access it through your institutional gateway. **Poetry Archive** (www. poetryarchive.org) offers freely accessible poetry readings by poets themselves,

ranging from Alfred Tennyson reading 'The Charge of the Light Brigade' to Stevie Smith reading 'Not Waving but Drowning'. The **British Film Institute's** open-access website offers the excellent BFI **Film and TV database** (www.bfi. org.uk/filmtvinfo/ftvdb).

You might also want to utilise resources in the visual arts, such as the excellent **Bridgeman Education** database (www.bridgemaneducation.com); as with Poets on Screen, access this through your institutional gateway. You can search or browse thematically (use the search indexes option), exploring the extensive list of book covers, illustrated frontispieces or book illustrations, create a personalised slideshow of images for use in a presentation, and download images, providing it is for your own research (not for publication). A photographic equivalent is the **Education Image Gallery** (http://edina.ac.uk/eig); there is a great deal of material here relevant to research in literary studies (book covers, photographs of book launches, etc.). Its sister database, **Film and Sound Online** (www.filmandsound.ac.uk) offers hundreds of hours of film and television documentary footage for you to use.

Finally, the video-sharing site **YouTube** (www.youtube.com) offers a remarkably rich resource for the literary researcher. You can find video clips of interviews with authors, film directors and artists, recent dramatic productions and eyewitness news footage which may be unavailable elsewhere. You can delimit your search by national domain, language, channel (i.e. topic), and special-interest community; you can flag selected clips, add them to your playlist, and create a customised multimedia resource which you can share with others.

The list above is a sample of some of the more useful multimedia resources available online. It is worth bearing in mind that only a fraction of extant multimedia content has been digitised and made available through open-access searchable databases and much of this material is still only available in physical archives; see the section on 'Identifying archives: using electronic tools' later in this chapter.

Finding and using libraries

Your first recourse should always be to the library of your home institution, but you may need to have access to other university, national, public or private libraries in the UK and further afield. Perhaps the single most useful tool to help you gain access to UK university libraries is **SCONUL, the Society of College, National and University Libraries** (www.sconul.ac.uk), which coordinates access rights between reciprocal British institutions. If you are a registered student on either a taught postgraduate course, or a programme of research (such as a PhD) on either a full-time or part-time basis, you will be eligible to apply for a SCONUL Access card, which will give you borrowing rights at a range of university libraries for up to three years. You can determine your eligibility on the SCONUL website (www.access.sconul.ac.uk/members); you will then need to complete an application form and send this to your home institution's library for authorisation. You must be registered as a member of your home institution's library to make use of this. Your home institution will then issue you with a SCONUL Access card, granting you entrance and limited borrowing rights for up to 170 university libraries across the UK (this will vary according to your status and whether your institution has entered into reciprocal agreements). Note that SCONUL does not provide any access rights for students registered at institutions outside the UK.

COPAC (http://copac.ac.uk, see description earlier in this chapter) can provide you with very precise information about library holdings for a particular work, if it is held in any of the participating university libraries. This is an excellent way of identifying where the nearest copy of a particularly difficult to find work might be held, before you make a trip to the particular university library (or order an interlibrary loan). As it is a cumulative catalogue, it will save you having to make separate searches of individual university library catalogues.

HERO, the Higher Education and Research Opportunities in the UK website (www.hero.ac.uk), offers a comprehensive, searchable listing of all universities and further education institutions in the UK. You can use HERO to find the universities or further education institutions closest to you by entering your town or city and conducting a location search. All universities and further education institutions will have libraries, and you can use HERO to conduct a primary evaluation of how useful their specific libraries might be for your research (there are links provided to each individual institution).

Major national libraries

The discussion has so far concentrated on the use of British libraries and their online catalogues, but a familiarity with some of the other major national libraries, and an understanding of how to use their online resources, can be of great benefit to your research. Remember that while the British Library's integrated catalogue will list every single British publication since the institution of copyright and deposition in 1711 (as the nominated copyright deposit library), it does not hold every title printed in the USA, France, Russia or India, for example. The **United States Library of Congress** (http://catalog.loc.gov), the official US copyright deposit library is the world's largest library, holding more than 32 million printed books and some 61 million manuscripts items. Because the Library of Congress holds at least one copy of every title printed in the USA since 1800, there are hundreds of thousands of titles in the Library of Congress that are not in the British Library's holdings. This has particularly interesting implications in the post-1800 Anglo-American world of print. You will find American editions of British books listed in the Library of Congress Online Catalogue that have no existence in the British Library's integrated catalogue, for instance. The Library of Congress website also offers a wealth of publicly accessible information, including a virtual reference shelf (www.loc. gov/rr/askalib/virtualref.html).

Sometimes, national library integrated catalogues are useful not only for the bibliographical information that they yield, but also the additional author information that they may offer. The French **Bibliothèque Nationale's** online search catalogue, **BN-OPALE PLUS** (http://catalogue.bnf.fr), offers some author information that the equivalent British Library integrated catalogue lacks (including a list of pseudonyms and other names for the author, their gender and usually their dates as well). You can use **Libdex** (http://wwwlibdex. com) or **IFLANET's National Libraries of the World** (www.ifla.org/VI/2/p2/ national-libraries.htm) to identify relevant national libraries across the world, and **The European Library** (www.theeuropeanlibrary.org) to cumulatively search 43 European national libraries and collections. Should you need to access a national library as part of your programme of research you should bear in mind the key skills of identification, familiarisation and evaluation detailed above. Preparation, as ever, is the key to the successful utilisation of library resources, and the more time and effort you put into this, the more effective will be your time spent in the library itself.

Finding your way around a library
Now that you have used your electronic resources to find your specific library, and have identified what you want to consult, you will need to find your way around it. The majority of UK libraries classify their open-access reference books according to the Dewey Decimal Classification system (invented by Melvil Dewey in America in 1876). DDC divides knowledge into ten classes with three digit headings, from 000 for general works (bibliographies, encyclopaedias, etc.) to 900 for general geography and history (including biography and genealogy); the section for literature was given the 800 class mark. Within each class, ten divisions were determined in equal decimal divisions; thus American literature is under 810, English and Anglo-Saxon under 820, and the literature of the Germanic languages under 830. Within the 820 division, there are another ten sections, with English poetry classified as 821, drama as 822, and fiction as 823 etc. The 821–3 section range is therefore likely to be of most use to you, with occasional forays into the 000 class (reference works), 900 (biography and genealogy), and 600 (history of the book, printing and publishing).

A full listing of Dewey class marks is available on the **OCLC** website (www. oclc.org/dewey/resources/summaries/default.htm); for an overview of how the Dewey Decimal Classification system works, have a look at the animated tour and self-assessment (www.oclc.org/dewey/resources/tour). Dewey funnels information from a broad division to increasingly specialised categories; for this reason it is an excellent browsing tool. A working knowledge of the Dewey system (and its logical idiosyncrasies) can be of great use in finding books on library shelves. Works in the history of the book are classified under the number 655 (600 is the general title for technology and the applied sciences) and not under literature and the 800 heading. This means that they are often shelved on completely different floors.

The other important classification system is the **Library of Congress Classification system** (www.loc.gov/catdir/cpso/lcc.html), which divides titles into 21 categories. It is important to remember that the majority of any particular library's holdings will be in closed shelving or stacks, and therefore invisible (because unavailable) to any physical browsing by visitors. Given the possibilities of technology, libraries are increasingly offering virtual tours of their facilities through their websites. As best practice, always take a virtual tour of a library (should it be available) in advance of any visit.

Archives and preparation for future research

Archival sources can offer a wealth of information for you to draw upon as your research topic develops during the course of study for the MA, and more importantly, in looking forward towards PhD-level research. Archives (both material and electronic) can contain rare printed books, unpublished material (handwritten drafts, manuscripts, correspondence, etc.), personal library collections, ephemera and unpublished scholarship (such as MA dissertations and PhD theses). The official national archives, public records offices, national, regional and university library special collections, and various private institutions and corporations (such as publishers) will have archival material that you might want to access and consult as part of your postgraduate research. Because of the trade in rare books and manuscripts, and the effect of the bequests of various literary estates, the archived items that you most want to access may well be geographically remote from you. For example, the page proofs of George Eliot's *Middlemarch* (1871–2) are found not in the British Library, which is where the manuscript of the novel is housed, but in the Harry Ransom Research Center at the University of Texas at Austin. It is therefore essential to know where relevant archives might be located, and how you might access them. There are several strategies that you might want to adopt in order to identify archives, and a number of key skills that you need to develop.

Identifying archives: using electronic tools
There are a number of electronic tools that can help you locate specific archives. One of the best single resources to offer location and description advice for

the UK is **Archives Hub** (www.archiveshub.ac.uk). Archives Hub is a national descriptive database of UK archive holdings; it does not reproduce in digital form any of the contents of these archives, but instead offers a searchable database of descriptions of these holdings, allowing you to identify their relevance to your work. **Access to Archives** (www.nationalarchives.gov.uk/a2a), also known by its acronym **A2A**, allows you to search a larger number of collections in England and Wales only (about 30% of the total extant archives); over 400 repositories are covered, and where available, a descriptive catalogue can be called up. Note once again that A2A does not reproduce digitised archival content, and in addition, it does not include the holdings of the National Archives at Kew.

The **National Archives** website (www.nationalarchives.gov.uk) offers a comprehensive survey of the UK government's archival resources that are available in the public domain through a series of searchable databases. When you access the site, click on the drop-down menu under 'research and learning', and then choose 'starting your research'. You will find six separate categories from which to choose, ranging from military history to academic research. There is a useful explanation of how to go about using the website to best effect. One of the most useful databases housed on the National Archives website for literary scholars is the **National Register of Archives** (www.nationalarchives.gov.uk/ nra). Note that the National Register is just that; it does not provide either a descriptive catalogue of each individual archive (or of a specific repository), or reproduce the contents of the archives listed (although usually there is an external weblink for you to click to get the required information).

The electronic tools I have listed above should give you more than enough information to identify archives relevant to your particular research topic in literary studies. Sometimes, however, it is better to go directly to a specialist tool. For those working in the early modern period (Renaissance and seventeenth century), Peter Beal's forthcoming **Catalogue of English Literary Manuscripts** 1450–1700 (CELM; http://ies.sas.ac.uk/cmps/Projects/CELM/ index.htm) will be particularly helpful; this will be available as an open-access, online resource, and will largely supersede the first two volumes of the Index to Literary Manuscripts (see below) that he had compiled earlier. Researchers in the Victorian period might want to move directly to Patrick Leary's judicious list of archival sources on **Victoria Research Web** (http://victorianre-search.org/archive.html). Likewise, if your area of research includes Caribbean, Black and Asian history in the UK, you might want to look at **Casbah** (www. casbah.ac.uk), which offers a detailed, browsable and searchable descriptive catalogue of relevant repositories.

Some archival research can be conducted safely, efficiently and in totality from your own home. Increasingly, archives are digitising their material and making it available for you to consult online or download, often for a small charge; your own institution may have a special arrangement to allow for free downloads for registered students, so check the terms of access with your university library. A good example of this is the **British National Archives' Documents Online site** (www.nationalarchives.gov.uk/documentsonline), which allows you to access a range of digitised public records, including all recorded wills (more than one million records) from 1384 to 1858, military service records and alien registration cards for Greater London. All of this data is vital if you are, for example, trying to establish accurate biographical details for a little-known writer. Where electronic access to a fully digitised archive is available, try to make the most of this; for both environmental and pragmatic reasons (the loss of research time and expense through travelling, etc.), this is preferable to making a trip to the archive.

If your particular research topic has an international dimension, there are a number of national archives that you might want to consult. In Australia, the **National Archives of Australia** (www.naa.gov.au); in France, the **Archives Nationales** (www.archivesnationales.culture.gouv.fr); in Germany, the **Bundesarchiv** (www.bundesarchiv.de); in India, the **National Archives of India** (http://nationalarchives.gov.in); in Italy, the **Amministrazione Archivistica Italiana** (www.archivi.beniculturali.it) which collects the various Italian Archivi di Stato (state archives); and in the USA, the **National Archives and Records Administration** (www.archives.gov) are among the most important. A highly useful list of foreign archival repositories is available through the **ARCHON** directory, accessible through the National Archives website (www.nationalarchives.gov.uk/archon/searches/foreign.asp).

My focus in this survey has been entirely on archives that are of direct relevance to researchers working in English Literature. If your particular research topic has an interdisciplinary (or multidisciplinary) remit, you may need to look at subject-specific archival databases as well. For example, for a full archival register of music collections (instruments, sheet music, manuscripts, scores, ephemera, etc.) in Britain and Ireland, you might want to consult **Cecilia** (www.cecilia-uk.org), or if your work has an aural or oral dimension, you may need to use the British Library's excellent **Archival Sound Recordings** (http://sounds.bl.uk). Likewise if your topic stretches to the performing arts, you will need to look at **Backstage** (www.backstage.ac.uk), and if your interest is in cinema, film and television, you might want to explore both **Moving History** (www.movinghistory.ac.uk) and the extensive **British Film Institute's National Archive** (www.bfi.org.uk/nftva).

There are also a number of printed resources for finding literary archives that will be useful to you. The four-volume Index of *English Literary Manuscripts*

(London: Mansell, 1980–93) compiled by Peter Beal *et al.* is a detailed location register of English literary manuscripts from 1450 to 1900, and is available as an open-access reference resource in major libraries. The eleventh edition of the Royal Commission on Historical Manuscripts' *Record Repositories in Great Britain* (National Archives, Kew: PRO, 1999) lists archives with (relatively) up-to-date contact details. The fourth edition of Janet Foster and Julia Sheppard's *A Guide to Archive Resources in the United Kingdom* (Basingstoke: Palgrave, 2002) is the most comprehensive single-volume guide to British archives. Alexis Weedon and Michael Bott's *British Book Trade Archives, 1830–1939: A Location Register* (Reading: History of the Book on Demand Series, 1996) is also available as an electronic resource (http://meanwhile.beds.ac.uk/dav/british-book) and provides an excellent guide to British publishers' archives.

Accessing and using archives: practical advice
Of course, once you have found the particular archive that you want to investigate, you have then to negotiate the specific conditions of access and practicalities of organisation. While archiving is increasingly coherent in terms of best practice, you might well find that different special collections in research libraries have particular ways in which they organise their material (archiving policy has of course changed considerably over the last century). Private archives (such as those held by families) may or may not conform to any accepted archiving procedures at all. In order to make the most of any archival trip, it is worth the effort to do as much preparation as possible in advance. You might want to consider the following steps:

- Visit the **Archives Research Techniques & Skills** website (http://arts-scheme.co.uk) and complete the online tutorial offered. Also read through the information on the four main national archives in the UK – the National Archives; the British Library; the National Archive of Scotland; and the National Library of Wales.

- Contact the archivist as soon as convenient, to establish the date(s) of your visit, find out about the terms of access (such as opening hours, whether you can take in a laptop, etc.), and whether there are any *restrictions on the material* that you want to consult. Some archives have specific, timed restrictions on access, i.e. you may be able to view the material, but not reproduce it, or quote directly from it. Most special collections will require that postgraduate students *supply a letter of recommendation* from their supervisor (either sent in advance, or brought on the day) in order to be admitted, so make sure that you ask your tutor or supervisor to do this before your visit.

- If the archive has a specific finding aid or annotated register, available either electronically or in print, *consult this before* your trip; you will get much more from your visit if you have a clear idea of what you're going to be seeing on site. Consulting an annotated guide will allow you to identify exactly which manuscripts or documents you need to see.

- An archival visit may entail transcribing or reproducing a large amount of holograph (handwritten) material. Consider the logistics of how you might approach this. A laptop will of course be essential for rapid and accurate transcription. If it is allowed, you might also want to consider either having the material reproduced for you (photocopy, digital scanning or microfilm) by the archivist, or else you might want to use a digital camera to photograph the material, and then transcribe it at your leisure. This has the benefit of being a more efficient use of time in the archive; the disadvantage is that you will need to spend much longer transcribing the material once you return home. As it is a non-invasive form of reproduction, digital capture (without flash) is often less damaging to fragile books or manuscript material. If you are planning to reproduce any material in any form, make sure that you have the permission of the archivist first.

- Carefully consider the copyright implications of any work that you undertake in the archive. According to the current UK Copyright, Designs and Patents Act (1988) which was modified by an EU directive in 1993, the copyright for all published material remains with the author for 70 years after their death, i.e. if an author died in 1950, his or her work remains protected by copyright law until 1 January 2021. For unpublished material, the terms are even more stringent; the period of protection is 125 years for material written (but not published) after 1988; material composed (but not published) before the Act came into force is protected until 1 January 2040. If you are planning to make extensive use of unpublished archival material in your dissertation or thesis, it is essential that you obtain the written formal permission of both the archive holding the material and the copyright holder (usually a nominated literary agency, but sometimes a descendent of the author). A fairly comprehensive list of copyright holders is available through the **Writers and their Copyright Holders (WATCH)** database at the University of Texas (http://tyler.hrc.utexas.edu) which you should consult. Generally, archivists and estates are very happy to grant permission to quote from material if it is used for MA or PhD dissertations, as this does not entail any commercial loss of earnings to the parties involved.

- If for any reason you find yourself working on archival material that has not been catalogued (e.g. loose papers in a box without a descriptive index), you might want, as a courtesy, to index the material as you work through it, and leave a copy with the archivist. This will save you time should you need to revisit the material, and will also benefit future researchers.

This checklist should provide you with a solid basis for approaching research in archives and equipping yourself with the skill set needed to make the most of the documents they hold. The ability to identify and effectively utilise unpublished archival material is an essential part of most PhD-level research work, so this is a skill that you must acquire if you want to progress at post-graduate level.

Finally, a word of both caution and encouragement: there are few scholarly activities that are potentially more time-consuming, frustrating and sometimes demoralising than working in the archive (poor cataloguing, missing and/or damaged material and restrictive access are just some of the pitfalls to negoti-ate). However, at the same time, nowhere are you more likely to have that ser-endipitous moment of discovery in your research than in the archive. New material is still being unearthed, and despite the legions of scholars working on the various special collections, the cumulative archival material of the world's leading libraries is still far from being exhausted. Recovering underused archival material is an essential part of ensuring that your research topic has genuine intellectual credibility; for the very best research work, there is simply no substitute for time productively spent in the archive.

Participating in a research community, and keeping up to date

As you develop your research skills and gain confidence, you may find that your supervisors and peers mention the term 'research community' with increasing frequency. But what exactly is a 'research community'? How do you identify the particular community that is relevant to you, and how do you participate in its activities? What expenses might be incurred, and benefits gained, from belonging to a research community or communities? And how might participation contribute towards your own development as an effective scholar?

Your own institution will have a research community relevant to you, usually supported by the research school and centred on the academic staff in your department, and the postgraduate students working towards higher degrees in English Literature. There will be specific seminars (often with invited speak-ers) to attend, and events to encourage the exchange of ideas. However, being part of a wider research community involves more than attending the requisite sessions on research skills offered by your university as part of its system of skills training, or participating in the research seminars organised for postgrad-uate students, although these will be invaluable as part of your training. It will involve actively identifying the wider community (or communities) of researchers outside your institution, city or even country. How do you go about doing this, and how might you benefit from it?

In a literal sense, the wider research community will include scholars at all levels, from young graduate students to emeritus professors, who are actively engaged in primary research and scholarship that contributes to knowledge in the field. Invariably, the research community will also include librarians and archivists, bibliographers, members of author societies, managers of specialist websites and online discussion forums, and highly knowledgeable non-professionals (such as members of author societies) who are interested in the topic. Usually, a specific research community is organised by historical period (i.e., eighteenth century, Renaissance, Victorian, etc.), perspective (theory, postcolonial studies, book history, etc.), or topic (popular fiction, women's reading, underground drama, etc.). Often, research communities are defined by their membership of particular scholarly bodies. The largest ones for English Literature are the **Modern Humanities Research Association** (MHRA, www.mhra.org.uk) in the UK, and the **Modern Language Association** (MLA, www.mla.org) in the USA. You should be familiar with both these names already, as they are the official bodies in their respective countries defining the system of scholarly citation and presentation (they produce style guides that academics are required to follow).

For a much fuller discussion of the ongoing development of English Literature as a discipline, and the implications that this may have in planning your own research and choosing which research communities to engage with, have a look at Chapter 6 of the Handbook, 'Institutional histories of literary disciplines'.

On a practical level, the 'research community' for your particular area will become more self-evident as your research becomes more specialised. The research community of literary scholars working in nineteenth-century literature, for example, is vast, but the number of those working on say, Thomas Hardy, are going to be smaller, and those working on a particular approach (Hardy and music, for example), smaller still. Try to think of research communities as a series of sometimes (though not always) overlapping Venn diagrams of different sizes. You may need to identify and participate in more than one research community for your particular area of research.

For example, I am interested in the American expatriate novelist Edith Wharton's relationship with her publishers on both sides of the Atlantic (she lived mainly in Europe, but her novels were usually published first in America). As this is a broadly speaking book historical approach to a specific author, I need to belong to, and actively participate in, two different research communities: a scholarly book historical research community, exemplified by the Society of the History of Authorship, Reading and Publishing (SHARP; www.sharpweb. org), and an author society, in this case, the Edith Wharton Society (www. wsu.edu/~campbelld/wharton/index.html), which is the leading organisation for scholarship on Edith Wharton. As a member of both organisations and engaging in both research communities, I am in the intersection of the Venn diagram, and count myself in the overlap between the two. In addition, as Edith Wharton's dates (1862–1937) straddle the division between two generally agreed historical periods for literary scholarship (the Victorian and the Modern, or the nineteenth and twentieth centuries) I need to stay informed more generally about new scholarship in both those fields. And finally, as she was an American expatriate writer based in Europe, I need to be aware of scholarship on both sides of the Atlantic, which means that as a scholar based in Britain, I need to be aware of recent developments in the wider field of American literary studies. Membership of research communities can therefore be complementary, supporting your research in a number of different ways.

Participating in a research community: expenses and benefits
So what are the benefits from joining scholarly learned societies, and what expenses are you likely to incur? Scholarly bodies almost without exception will offer postgraduate students heavily discounted rates of membership; some, such as the MHRA, will offer all registered, British postgraduate students three years' free membership of the organisation, a copy of their excellent style guide and three years' free online access to one of their leading journals, such as *The Modern Language Review* or *The Yearbook of English Studies*. Where there is a charge, the annual membership cost of joining a learned society is very modest, compared to the possible benefits. For example, joining the Society for the History of Authorship, Reading and Publishing (SHARP) costs a mere $20 for students, and includes access to their excellent online discussion forum, SHARP-List, as well as subscription to their quarterly newsletter, *SHARP News*. Reading the newsletter and looking at the discussion threads would keep you more than adequately up to date about events in the field of book history.

Many scholarly bodies also help support postgraduate students attend conferences through a bursary scheme. **The British Society for Eighteenth Century Studies** (BSECS, www.bsecs.org.uk) offers up to 12 bursaries of £100 each for graduate students to attend its annual conference and give papers, while the membership charge for joining the organisation is a mere £20 per year, and includes subscription to the *Journal for Eighteenth-Century Studies*.

Joining the **North American Victorian Studies Association** (NAVSA, www. purdue.edu/navsa) as a student costs only $40, but offers you an annual subscription to the journal *Victorian Studies* (widely considered to be the most influential journal in nineteenth-century studies) and access to the 'members-only' section of the website, which includes working papers from their most recent conference (which always take place in North America). Membership of NAVSA is therefore a very cost-effective way of staying informed about the best recent scholarship as well as learning about papers delivered at conferences that you might not be able to attend. In summary: selective membership of scholarly and learned bodies is a highly cost- and time-effective way of participating in research activity relevant to your course of study or research project. Do not be indiscriminate, joining every scholarly body and learned society that you come across; instead, in order to maximise the effectiveness of your participation, think carefully about which research communities you want to join, and proceed accordingly.

Presentations, workshops, networking
As you develop your expertise as a researcher and scholar, you will find that there will be a requirement, both on a personal and an institutional basis, to discuss your work beyond the immediate orbit of your tutors or your supervision team. Part of good practice in academic research is to test your ideas in front of your peers, informally through the circulation of draft essays and chapters, more formally in the form of presentations at conferences or seminars, and eventually through publication. This is a type of collective quality assurance, and you would do well to engage in it as soon as your research project is sufficiently developed. Conferences, seminars, workshops and symposia are also the venues where academics meet one another – so if you are thinking of graduate study and research as a part of career, this is an essential part of your career development.

Attending relevant workshops, research seminars and conferences will give you a more immediate sense of scholarship in your area of study, as these are often the first venues of the dissemination of work in progress. Remember that there is a time lag, often of several years, between a piece being offered at a conference, and being published as a journal article or as part of a scholarly monograph. Regularly attending conferences and research seminars will ensure that you remain up to date about the major trends and developments in your area of research.

Attending conferences and seminar series is also an excellent way to network with fellow postgraduate students and introduce yourself to the wider scholarly community. There may be other researchers or academics who are interested in your work – but the only way that you will know this is by engaging in the academic circuit, and through effective networking.

The importance of making presentations at conferences and seminars, attending workshops and networking with peers cannot be stressed highly enough. Again, as with joining scholarly bodies, you need to be selective about your commitment, and consider the implications it might have in terms of time otherwise allocated for research or writing.

Keeping abreast of developments: best practice

As the discussion in the previous pages indicate, keeping abreast of developments in English generally, and your own area of research specifically, is a key skill to develop as an effective research student. In order to do this, you need to be aware of new developments in your subject, and you can make sure of this through a number of strategies.

Subscribe to a good 'call for papers' site, such as the American-based, but fairly globally representative **University of Pennsylvania's English Call for Papers site** (http://cfp.english.upenn.edu) or an active British listserv, such as the **Lit-Lang-Culture-Events List** housed at **JISC** (www.jiscmail.ac.uk/cgi-bin/ webadmin?A0=LIT-LANG-CULTURE-EVENTS). This is administered by the Higher Education Academy English Subject Centre, and therefore offers a pretty comprehensive survey of recent calls for papers at conferences, as well as details of other events, taking place in the UK.

Look out for conferences, workshops, seminars or electronic publications specifically aimed at postgraduate students. There is a growing awareness throughout the tertiary-education sector that students learn and acquire skills very effectively from one another. Events organised specifically for postgraduate students will offer an excellent venue for networking with fellow researchers, allow you to exchange ideas in a less intimidating setting, and perhaps shape your first publication – all of these are key skills for a good researcher to acquire.

Many major conferences will now have specific workshops targeted at postgraduate students as part of their event, which will effectively offer you additional skills training. These sessions are often led by leading practitioners, and may give you the opportunity to enter special collections and handle rare archival material, as well ask questions. They are well worth attending.

When you join a scholarly body, be sure to sign up to their email list so that you can be notified in advance of forthcoming events that might be of interest to you.

If you have access to a discussion forum attached to a specific scholarly body (such as SHARP-List), monitor any threads that are relevant to your work, and save these in a specific email folder (this will provide an excellent archive for posterity, and a great source for recommendations or leads that might not crop up elsewhere).

Finally, for those of you working on contemporary literature, it is certainly appropriate to look at authors' own websites, which often have regularly updated information about their work, as well as biographical and bibliographical information, and sometimes personal weblogs as well. Literary prize websites such as the **Man Booker Prize** (www.themanbookerprize.com) or the **Nobel Prize for Literature** (http://nobelprize.org/nobel_prizes/literature) often commission interviews with shortlisted or prize-winning authors, as well as offer accurate bibliographies of their work.

QUESTIONS AND EXERCISES

1   Connect to the Internet for the English tour on the Intute: Virtual Training Suite website (www.vts.intute.ac.uk/he/tutorial/english). Take the online tour and then complete the quiz.

2   Take the online tour of the Dewey Decimal Classification System on the OCLC website (www.oclc.org/dewey/resources/tour), and complete the 'test your knowledge of DDC' section.

3   Using the University of London's Senate House Library online catalogue (www.ull.ac.uk) as your reference, conduct a class-mark search for Dewey decimal number 655.45. What is the specialist subject that this class mark brings up, and where are these books physically located inside Senate House Library?

4   If you are a UK-based student, access the HERO website (www.hero.ac.uk) and click on 'university finder'. Conduct a location search of university and further education college libraries within 15 miles of your town/city, evaluate the results and identify the three potentially most useful university or further education college libraries for your research.

5   For UK-registered students, use SCONUL Access (www.access.sconul.ac.uk), enter your current status (taught postgraduate student, registered PhD student, etc.) and your institutional affiliation and find out which university libraries will offer you full lending rights. Download and complete the online application form, and send this to your home institution for validation, in order to gain access (your home institution's library, of which you will need to be a registered member, will process the application and send you an access card).

6   Conduct comparative searches of the British Library's Integrated Catalogue (http://catalogue.bl.uk) and the United States Library of Congress Online Catalogue (http://catalog.loc.gov) for any one specific book title published after 1800 (you might want to pick a particular novel, for example). How do the two library catalogues compare in the results that they yield?

7   Conduct comparative searches of the British Library's Integrated Catalogue (http://catalogue.bl.uk) and the Bibliotheque Nationale's BN-OPALE PLUS (http://catalogue.bnf.fr) for the author Marc Hélys. See if you can find out the gender of this author, their dates and their published names.

8   Visit the Archives Research Techniques & Skills website (http://arts-scheme.co.uk) and complete the online tutorial offered.

9   On the Archives Hub website, find the guided tour for the Unity Theatre collection, GB0394UNITY (www.archiveshub.ac.uk/tour/index.html) and complete it. Then see if you can answer the following questions: where exactly is the Unity Theatre's archive located? How many boxes does it contain? How much shelf space does it occupy? Where are the Unity Theatre's ephemera and photographs held?

10 Utilising the search facilities available on the ARCHON website (www.nationalar-chives.gov.uk/archon), see if you can identify exactly how many items relating to Alfred, Lord Tennyson (1809–92) are currently held in the special collections archive of Indiana University's Lilly Library in Indiana, USA.

11 Using the 'Making of America Books' website at the University of Michigan, http://quod.lib.umich.edu/cgi/t/text/text-idx?page=simple&c=moa, search for the Edith Wharton short story 'The Pelican', which was published in *Scribner's Magazine*, vol. 24, November 1898, pp. 620–9. Once you have located this story, either print it off or electronically download the text.

SELECTED READING

Phoebe Ayres, Charles Matthews and Ben Yates, *How Wikipedia Works, and How You Can Be a Part of It* (San Francisco: No Starch Press, 2008), also available as an open-access resource at http://howwikipediaworks.com.

Tara Brabazon, *The University of Google: Education in the (Post) Information Age* (Aldershot. Ashgate, 2007).

Pat Cryer, *The Research Student's Guide to Success*, third edn (Maidenhead: The Open University Press, 2006).

Stephen Potter, *Doing Postgraduate Research*, second edn (London: Sage Publications, 2006).

Gordon Rugg and Marian Petre, *A Gentle Guide to Research Methods* (Maidenhead: The Open University Press, 2006).

Part 2
Textual scholarship and book history

Bibliography: enumerative, analytical, descriptive, historical

History of the book

Editing literary texts

3
Bibliography

Simon Eliot

INTRODUCTION

One of the founding principles of this Handbook is that scholars cannot regard themselves as adequately educated unless they have some understanding of both the intellectual and the material history of literature. It is this history that provides the rich soil out of which even the most recent and radical piece of literature grows. If you do research in literature, it is likely that most of your time will be spent studying the 'meaning' or 'significance' of texts. In order to do this you will have to make assumptions about the integrity of that text, assumptions about the way in which the author wrote (or 'produced') it, and assumptions about the way in which the author's contemporaries read (or 'consumed') it. Even if you are not worried about the historical context, you will need to know something about how your texts are produced and consumed today.

For instance, the fact that *Tristram Shandy* was published in nine volumes over a number of years (1760–7) must have had an effect on how Sterne's contemporaries responded to the work as a whole. (How, for instance, would they know when it was complete? Did readers feel that, as later volumes were being written as they read the earlier ones, they had a chance to influence the author?) The fact that it is now available as a single volume in the Oxford World's Classics series, with a critical introduction – a volume that can be read in a few days or weeks (as a whole, as a 'classic') – is bound to give the modern reader a different attitude to it.

To take another example: the fact that Tennyson's 'Charge of the Light Brigade' was first published in the pages of a magazine (*The Examiner* on 9 December 1854) only a week after Tennyson had read an account of the charge in the *Times* must have coloured contemporaries' attitudes to it. (Even the famous line 'Some one had blundered' was based on a phrase used in the *Times* article.) Surrounded by ephemeral political and social comment, the poem must have seemed to some readers like an editorial in verse.

It is not just the physical form of the publication that affects meaning. The very way in which literature gets put into print can change the meaning of a text. For instance, when a compositor's hand misses the correct section of his type tray (or 'case'), or when his assistant puts the type in the wrong section of the case, or when he misreads the manuscript copy from which he is setting the book, then Hamlet's 'too, too solid flesh' becomes 'sullied' or 'sallied'. (For other examples of this, see Bruce Harkness, 'Bibliography and the Novelistic Fallacy', in *Bibliography and Textual Criticism*, ed. O.M. Brack, Jr and Warner Barnes, Chicago and London: University of Chicago Press, 1969.) Never forget that texts are material objects – written, printed, advertised, sold (or borrowed or stolen) and used by fallible human beings, many of whom would not have had a particularly reverential attitude towards the materials they were dealing in.

The arrival of the electronic book in the last two decades of the twentieth century, and the subsequent development of hypermedia, is in the process of transforming the book just as much as the development of the codex in the first–fourth centuries or the introduction of printing in the fifteenth century. It is certainly having an affect on bibliography: a whole range of searchable catalogues is revolutionising the way in which quantitative and historical bibliography is practised. Digitised images of early books provide a remarkable resource and can save a huge amount of time. But such resources cannot be an adequate substitute for a bibliographer who needs to see many copies of the apparently same book, and needs to handle them in order to observe, for instance, the quality of, and watermarks in, the paper; the results of worn type; and the structure of the binding. Developments in electronic text also raise considerable practical problems, and problems of definition. Unlike physical books, whose construction can provide evidence for their origins and history, electronic texts rarely exhibit a recoverable history. Earlier forms of book from clay tablet to the printed codex may have exhibited huge variations in text, but at least the given copy or copies that you were studying had a fixity and a longevity on which the bibliographer could base his or her work. The electronic text has no such fixity or solidity: it can vary from day to day and place to place. It can exist at a particular address on the Web one day and have moved or even disappeared by the next. The Web also has the opposite power: its users can generate textual variations at an unprecedented rate and then spread these variants far and wide. A few years ago I ran a search on Google for Kipling's poem 'If'. The first ten hits presented seven variant texts. If the Web provides the bibliographer with a chance to wander electronically through a library greater than the Alexandrian Library, it also threatens to turn that library into a Tower of Babel.

We could summarise all this by saying simply that the meaning and nature of a literary work (indeed, of any text) can be significantly affected by the various processes that enable its transmission from the author's original manuscript to a reader. Even if we cannot agree with Marshall McLuhan that the medium is all of the message, nevertheless we might well accept that it constitutes a significant part of it. It is therefore important to study the text as a physical object, as a product of the material world and as a result of a series of manufacturing processes, most of which can, intentionally or unintentionally, alter the nature of the text being transmitted. The study of the book as a material object is called 'bibliography'. Various types of bibliography are used by other scholarly disciplines for their own purposes, and two such disciplines are examined in later chapters: the history of the book (Chapter 4) and scholarly editing (Chapter 5).

Although you will find a wide range of books in 'Selected reading', you will find the following two books particularly useful:

- Philip Gaskell, A New Introduction to Bibliography (Oxford: Clarendon Press, 1972).

- D.C. Greetham, Textual Scholarship: An Introduction (New York and London: Garland, 1994).

Both books are to be dipped into rather than read from cover to cover. In 'Selected reading' I give page references to one or other of them so that you can look up specific subjects in greater detail if you want to.

WHAT IS BIBLIOGRAPHY?

> Books are the material means by which literature is transmitted; therefore bibliography, the study of books, is essentially the science of the transmission of literary documents.
> (W.W. Greg, The Library, fourth series, 13 (1932–3), 115)

To most students, a 'bibliography' is probably just a 'list of books consulted' which is usually given at the end of a scholarly work. This is certainly the most common meaning of the word, but it is not the only one, nor is it the most important. In many ways, using 'bibliography' to mean a selected list of books is a partial contradiction of its other meanings. The discipline of bibliography, in treating books and other printed matter as physical objects, is much less evaluative than most other forms of literary study. In essence, bibliographers are not at all concerned with the contents of a book: the volume before them could be the works of Shakespeare, an atlas, a book of recipes or a collection of the most tedious sermons imaginable. As products of the scribe or printing press, these would all be of equal interest and value to a bibliographer. Of course, this is not to say that there is no relationship between the textual content of a book and its structure. Indeed, as we shall see, the way in which the material book is created and distributed can have a substantial impact on the meaning of the text, but a bibliographer as such is not obliged to pursue that link. This can be left to a book historian or a literary critic.

Most authorities distinguish a number of types of bibliography, as does Greetham. In some ways these distinctions are rather spurious, because in practice one type merges into another. Nevertheless, for the purpose of this introduction, we shall respect the divisions.

Enumerative bibliography

Essentially, enumerative bibliography enumerates – it lists and counts all books produced over a given period or in a given country, or defined by some other large and, as far as possible, value-free category. Typically, each entry will contain details of the author, the title, the printer, the year of publication and a list of libraries in which copies can be found. What is lost in detail, however, is made up for in quantity. Most major enumerative bibliographies draw on the collections of some, and sometimes many, of the great library collections of the world, so their listings can be very comprehensive.

Perhaps the clearest examples of the enumerative bibliographer's art in the twentieth century were the sequence of printed short-title catalogues. These included *The Incunable Short Title Catalogue* (London: The British Library); usually known as ISTC, which lists books printed before 1501, and is most easily accessed through the Web at http://138.253.81.72/~cheshire/istc/about.html. ISTC is an international database, but the ones that follow concentrate on books in English mostly published in the UK and the USA. The first of these is A.W. Pollard and G.R. Redgrave, *A Short Title Catalogue of Books Printed in England, Scotland, and Ireland, and of English Books Printed Abroad, 1475–1640* (London: Bibliographical Society, 1926; rev. 1976–89), known as STC. The STC was continued by Donald G. Wing, *Short Title Catalogue of Books Printed in England, Scotland, Ireland, Wales, and British America and of English Books printed in Other Countries, 1641–1700* (New York: MLA, 1945–51), and known as 'Wing'. Both these works set a standard which was followed by *The Eighteenth Century Short Title Catalogue* (London: British Library, 1983–), known as ESTC. From a rather different tradition comes *The Nineteenth Century Short Title Catalogue* (Newcastle upon Tyne: Avero, 1984–), known as NSTC. The NSTC is divided into three series (Series I: 1801–15; Series II: 1816–70; Series III: 1871–1919). All three series are available in printed form and on CD-ROM. NSTC was not compiled on the same rigorous bibliographical principles as the ESTC (it would have been too expensive to do so); nevertheless, it is for the time being the best we have for this period.

The *STC*, Wing and the *ESTC* have now for most purposes been superseded by the *English Short Title Catalogue* (also confusingly shortened to ESTC) which lists printed material published mostly in the UK and USA in the period 1473–1800. This is available online at www.bl.uk/collections/early/estc1.html.

The chance to search an entire enumerative bibliography quickly and cheaply allows the scholar, for the first time, to answer very broad questions about book production in earlier centuries. How many books were printed in Oxford in 1688? How many books of poetry did Moxon publish in the 1840s? How many books that referred to 'magistrates' in their titles were published between 1730 and 1750? These questions are not, of course, exclusively bibliographical; but we have bibliography to thank for providing the means to answer them.

Analytical bibliography

Analytical bibliography concerns itself mostly with the manufacture of the printed book. (Study of the manufacturing processes involved in producing manuscript books is known as codicology, but we shall not concern ourselves with that here.) The analytical bibliographer would begin by discussing and describing the ways in which an author's manuscript might have been put into type, how many compositors might have been used, and which compositors were responsible for which sheets, and what sort of mistakes they might have made in putting the manuscript into type. The bibliographer would then go on to consider how the type, once set, would have been used to print the pages of the book, and how corrections to the text might have been introduced during printing (thus leaving, for instance, half of the copies of a given book with a number of pages in an uncorrected state, and the other half of the copies with some or all of the corrected pages). If many of the printed sheets that made up a book were corrected at some stage during their printing, this would mean that it was highly likely that any given copy might be different in some way from most, if not all, other surviving copies.

The bibliographer would then describe how the printed sheets of paper were folded, cut and bound together to produce the final copy, how some of those printed sheets had, perhaps, been kept back as surplus to current requirements, and how those sheets might then have been used in a second edition – thus creating a hybrid in which some of the pages were from a new edition and some were from the old.

All this knowledge would be derived from two sources. First, information comes from the close physical investigation of the book itself – its physical dimensions; the nature of its paper (colour, texture, watermarks, etc.); the typeface(s) and ornaments used; the way in which the signatures were arranged; page layout and design; and so on. Second, bibliographers can call on the knowledge derived from historical investigations into how printing was and is carried out. (For example, our knowledge of the sort of subdivided trays used by type compositors – and thus which letters were next to which other letters – allows us to detect errors in printing created when a compositor picked up a letter adjacent to the one he actually wanted.)

Descriptive bibliography

Analytical bibliography, as we have just seen, is concerned with the close analysis of individual copies of books in the light of our knowledge of how books were produced. However, for many reasons we should not assume that one copy of a book from a given edition is going to be identical to another copy from the same edition. This is particularly true of books published in the earlier centuries of printing when there were many more variations and inconsistencies in printing practices. For instance, when in 1968 Charlton Hinman published a facsimile 'ideal copy' of Shakespeare's First Folio, he had to photograph pages from no fewer than 30 copies of that work.

You meet a potential problem if you analyse just one copy of a book: not only may it be unlike the other copies from the same edition, it may also be incomplete. Until you have analysed a number of copies, you will not know whether your first copy was complete. From these doubts – as to whether single copies provide a sound basis for generalisation about a particular edition – came the idea of the 'ideal copy'. Now the 'ideal copy' of a given edition does not mean a 'perfect copy' (few if any editions have ever come out of any printing works without a single error, misprinting or blemish). To use Roy Stokes's definition:

> Ideal copy is not concerned with matters governing the correctness of the text, or freedom from misprints, but simply with an assessment of the physical details of the book and their exact relationship to the state in which the book was planned to appear at the time of its initial publication.
>
> (*The Function of Bibliography*, Aldershot: Gower, 1982, p. 72)

This concept is quite a tricky one, and many modern bibliographers would want in one way or another to qualify it. For instance, our knowledge of the ways in which printing houses were run lead us to believe that any 'planning', if that was what it was, would have included the inevitability of variations in the output. Nevertheless, this need to pursue and record the 'ideal copy' gave rise to a third type of bibliography – descriptive bibliography.

Descriptive bibliography is concerned with taking the information derived from analysis of a number of copies of the same work, creating out of these a description of an ideal copy, and then recording the bibliographical details of this ideal copy as precisely and as consistently as possible. The final product of an exercise in descriptive bibliography is commonly a comprehensive and exhaustive, not to say exhausting, account of all the editions in a particular area. The three most common areas are:

a   the works of a single author (for example, A *Bibliography of Elizabeth Barrett Browning*);

b   all the works within a particular genre (for example, A *Bibliography of the English Printed Drama to the Restoration*);

c   all the works produced by a single press or, if the publisher was a large one and long-flourishing, the production of that press over a particular period (for example, *The Cambridge University Press, 1696–1712*).

As you will appreciate, descriptive bibliographies are products of very slow and painstaking work. It would be impossible to record more than a fraction of the books produced by printing presses since the 1450s if all bibliographers were expected to be so thoroughly analytical and so comprehensively descriptive.

Historical bibliography

Greetham, in *Textual Scholarship*, says that historical bibliography is sometimes described as 'the biology of books' (p. 7); but his second epithet, 'Darwinian', is in fact more accurate. Historical bibliography is strongly 'developmental': it is concerned with the way in which the various processes and materials involved in the construction of a book (themselves subjects of analytical bibliography) developed over time, and the way in which those developments affected the form and contents of the book. For example:

a   the gradual introduction of paper; the spread of paper mills; the evolution of watermarks (as a means of dating undated or wrongly dated books); the development of paper-making machinery; the introduction of different paper-making materials in the nineteenth century (esparto grass, wood pulp, etc.);

b   the evolution of typecasting; the development of the three main forms of typeface (gothic, roman, italic);

c   the development of the techniques of composing and imposing type; the evolution of work practices governing composition and printing; the evolution in the nineteenth century of type-composing machinery;

d   the technical development of printing machinery; the change from wood to metal construction; the change from human-powered to steam-powered presses;

e   the development of the techniques of gathering, folding and sewing of the printed sheets;

f   the development of the different techniques of book illustration;

g   the evolution of different binding techniques and styles; the emergence of the publisher's standard casing in the nineteenth century.

All the above are examples of the sorts of study that historical bibliographers have to undertake if they are to understand the structure of the book and the changes it underwent through time. These historical studies, as you can imagine, feed back into all other forms of bibliography, particularly into analytical bibliography. Indeed, it would be a mistake to assert that any of the types of bibliography described above is an independent study: all of them are inextricably intermixed and interdependent. One sort of bibliographer will put a greater emphasis on one type of bibliography than on another, but that does not mean that he or she can ignore the others. Bibliography provides a basic methodological tool for History of the Book and, indeed, shades into the latter subject.

If you are interested in bibliography and its related disciplines, you should think of joining a bibliographical society. There are many local ones, but the two most important national ones are:

• **The Bibliographical Society** (www.bibsoc.org.uk/index.htm), whose journal, *The Library*, is one of the foremost publications in the field.

• **The Bibliographical Society of America** (www.bibsocamer.org/default. htm), which is the equivalent organisation in the USA, and publishes *Papers of the Bibliographical Society of America*.

QUESTIONS AND EXERCISES

1   Identify Fredson Bower's four 'systems' that can be used for organising a systematic bibliography. Using a research library, find your own examples of each of these systems.

2   Using your local reference library, find a subject bibliography that covers your own locale or, alternatively, an author or a subject in which you are interested. Write a

brief critique of it: comment on its coverage, in its organising principles, and on its possible usefulness (or otherwise) as a research tool.

3   Distinguish between the three main methods of printing – relief (for example, letterpress), intaglio (for example, copper engraving) and planographic (for example, lithography) – and suggest a rough date when each process was first used in Western Europe. Describe one of the processes in detail.

4   How was paper made in Europe before 1800? What is the significance of chain lines and watermarks? How can you use them to work out the format of a given book?

5   Take one change in book-production technology that occurred in the period 1800–1900, describe the changes involved and evaluate the impact these changes had on the production of books.

6   Select a book printed before 1850 and produce a collation formula for it.

7   Discuss the concept of an 'ideal copy'. Identify and discuss some of the problems raised by this concept.

8   Before the nineteenth century, most reprints were separate editions; during and after the nineteenth century, most reprints were probably impressions. Why? And what significance has this fact for the bibliographer, the editor and the literary critic?

SELECTED READING

Introduction

O.M. Brack, Jr and Warner Barnes (eds), *Bibliography and Textual Criticism* (Chicago and London: University of Chicago Press, 1969).

John Carter, *ABC for Book Collectors* (1952; London: British Library, 2004); also available online at www.ilab-lila.com/images/abcforbookcollectors.pdf.

Martin Coyle, Peter Garside, Malcolm Kelsall and John Peck (eds), *The Encyclopaedia of Literature and Criticism* (London: Routledge, 1990); see especially Section VII, 'Production and Reception', pp. 809–940.

Peter Davison (ed.), *The Book Encompassed* (Cambridge: Cambridge University Press, 1992).

D.F. McKenzie, *Bibliography and the Sociology of Texts* (Cambridge: Cambridge University Press, 1999).

D.F. McKenzie, *Making Meaning: Printers of the Mind and Other Essays* (Amherst: University of Massachusetts Press, 2002).

Roy Stokes, *The Function of Bibliography* (Aldershot: Gower, 1982 [1969]).

G. Thomas Tanselle, *Selected Studies in Bibliography* (Charlottesville: University of Virginia Press, 1985).

G. Thomas Tanselle, *Literature and Artifacts* (Charlottesville: Bibliographical Society of the University of Virginia, 1998).

William Proctor Williams and Craig S. Abbott, *An Introduction to Bibliographical and Textual Studies*, third edn (New York: MLA, 1999).
Hugh Williamson, *Methods of Book Design* (London: Oxford University Press, 1966).

Enumerative bibliography

D.C. Greetham, *Textual Scholarship*: *An Introduction* (New York and London: Garland, 1994), chapter 1.
Martin Coyle, Peter Garside, Malcolm Kelsall and John Peck (eds), *The Encyclopaedia of Literature and Criticism* (London: Routledge, 1990), 'The Bibliographical Record', pp. 915–25.
Roy Stokes, *The Function of Bibliography* (Aldershot: Gower, 1982 [1969]), chapter 2, pp. 17–44.

Analytical bibliography

David Diringer, *The Book Before Printing* (New York: Dover Publications, 1982).
D.C. Greetham, *Textual Scholarship*: *An Introduction* (New York and London: Garland, 1994), chapters 2, 3, 5, 6.

Descriptive bibliography

Fredson Bowers, *Principles of Bibliographical Description* (Winchester: St Paul's Bibliographies, 1986 [1949]).
Philip Gaskell, *A New Introduction to Bibliography* (Oxford: Clarendon Press, 1972), pp. 321–35, 368–80.
D.C. Greetham, *Textual Scholarship*: *An Introduction* (New York and London: Garland, 1994), chapter 4.
E.W. Padwick, *Bibliographical Method* (Cambridge and London: James Clark, 1969).
G. Thomas Tanselle, 'The Bibliographical Description of Paper', *Studies in Bibliography*, 24 (1971), 27–67.

4
History of the book

Simon Eliot

INTRODUCTION

This relatively new discipline extends some of the techniques of bibliography, which were discussed in Chapter 3, into a very large and stimulating subject indeed. This is the historical study of the book in its economic, social and cultural contexts.

The questions asked by this discipline are commonly much broader than those posed by conventional bibliography. For instance, how did the economic, technical and social context in which the book was produced affect its development, its content, its appearance and its reception? How did the book as a communicator of ideas, values and experience affect the society in which it operated? Such questions highlight a fundamental distinction between books and almost any other artefact produced by society, a distinction which makes the historical study of books such a pressing and important subject. Unlike tables, toys, bread, guns, shoes, carpets or cars, books are intended to have specific intellectual and emotional effects on those who read them. Books can be designed to influence, and sometimes to change, the economic, social or cultural circumstances in which they were produced. There is thus a feedback loop built into the relationship between society and its books which ensures that one generation of books will have an influence on the context in which the next generation of books appears, and so on.

The 'history of the book' is, perhaps, something of a misnomer, for the discipline could not, and does not, restrict itself to the study of books alone. Any printed text – whether it be a book, pamphlet, newspaper, magazine, handbill, broadsheet, printed form or raffle ticket – can come within the notice of the book historian. Some of these examples may sound trivial until one begins to realise, for instance, how much of a local printer's time in the eighteenth century would have been taken up with the printing of legal forms for the local magistrate, or how much of a nineteenth-century jobbing printer's output would be in the form of programmes for events and advertising posters. The study of these printed ephemera, themselves an important aspect of the 'history of the book', has much to tell us of the way in which print intruded into the daily life of people who wouldn't even have thought of picking up novel or reading a poem.

The historian of the book is interested in any sort of text that takes a recoverable form and once it gets disseminated in whatever way society and technology allow – by writing, by printing, by photocopying, by CD-ROM, by solid state memory cards or by the Web.

Nevertheless, even with this broad perspective of the discipline, the historian of the book still runs the risk of being parochial. We must, for instance, take a wider view geographically. Printing was developed in Europe in the mid fifteenth century, but it had existed in the East for many centuries before that. Printing from 'movable type' (that is, individual pieces of type designed to print one letter or sign – usually called 'typography') had been used in Korea as early as the fourteenth century, while printing whole pages from carved wooden blocks (called 'xylography') had been used in China since at least the seventh century. In other words, the book historian must be able to take a global perspective.

A broader chronological perspective is also required. Even before the earliest printing, books written by hand – manuscript books – were a major means of transmitting information and, sometimes, entertainment. In Europe any time between the twelfth and fifteenth centuries, major cities (particularly those that had universities or law courts) would have workshops that employed secular scribes to produce copies of books either to specific order or as 'off the peg' books to be sold in bookshops. Before the twelfth century the majority of books would have been made by monks in monasteries either for their own consumption or for swapping with other monastery libraries, or for gifts to dignitaries at home and abroad. Until the later medieval period (when paper became more widely available), most of these books would have been written on parchment which was usually the skin of cows, sheep or goats which had been cleaned, de-haired, stretched and scraped to produce a durable – but quite expensive – writing surface.

Nor should we think of the subject as merely concerned with marks made on paper or parchment. There are references to parchment as early as the fifth century BCE, but it was probably not used widely until the first few centuries CE. Before parchment, papyrus was the main writing surface used by the Egyptians, the Greeks and the Romans. Papyrus is made by slicing up the pith of a large reed into strips, laying these strips vertically, one slightly overlapping the next, and then laying another set of strips horizontally over the top. These two layers are then beaten together and allowed to dry. The rectangular sheet made by this process can then be used individually or, more likely, stuck to other sheets to make a long roll. An average papyrus 'book' normally consisted of a roll 25–33 cm wide and 6–8 m long (though high-status rolls could be much bigger and much longer). A standard roll was long enough to contain a 'book' of the Bible or a 'book' of Homer. Large works, such as the New Testament or the Iliad, were thus not single entities, but collections of individual rolls which could be grouped together in various ways and various orders. The earliest surviving sheet of papyrus in Egypt can be dated to around 3000 BCE. Even before this, 'books' existed in the Sumerian civilisation (occupying what is now part of Iraq) in the form of small clay tablets with marks on them inscribed with a stylus made of wood or bone. The manuscript book thus has a hugely longer history than the printed book, stretching from c.3500 BCE to c.1450 CE; in comparison, the printed book in the West has only been around for about 550 years.

There is always a danger of adopting a 'whiggish' view of book history, that is, of assuming that the story is of a steady rise of technology and sophistication in which earlier forms are swept aside by newer and better ones. This in practice is no truer in book history than any other form of history. New developments, new technologies, frequently do not completely replace older versions, but only partially displace them, creating a new environment in which old and new technologies coexist in some way. In India, for instance, despite the introduction of printing, the oral and manuscript cultures remained vigorous and productive for centuries, and were preferred to print by many readers. In the West, the production of manuscript books did not suddenly stop when the printed book arrived. For a number of decades the printed book was regarded as a vulgar upstart, and the most affluent book collectors still preferred the manuscript book. Even when the printed book became wholly accepted, people still kept commonplace books and journals in which they wrote, and they still exchanged letters; collections of poems might be circulated among the cultured in the form of handwritten copies. Then as now, printed books might have approving or critical comments written in their margins, or births and deaths within a family written on the flyleaf of a bible. In other words, manuscript and printed forms do not just coexist, they inter-react.

Apart from writing and printing, there is another form of human communication that must also be acknowledged by book history, and that is the oral tradition, the mode that pre-dates writing but that then accompanies both writing and printing up to the present day. The problem here is that book history deals with 'recoverable evidence' and, of course, until the invention of audio recording in the late nineteenth century, oral exchange or performance in the past didn't leave much evidence that was recoverable. If we are dealing with current oral performances, or ones that were recent enough to be recorded, this is not a problem. If we are dealing with oral performance before the late nineteenth century, then things are more difficult. However, as writing and print inter-react, so does the oral and the written, and that interaction does leaves recoverable evidence. For instance, the earliest epic poems such as the Sumerian poem *Gilgamesh* or Homer's *Iliad* and *Odyssey* were originally oral performances and retain, even in their modern and revised forms, evidence of their earlier state. The standard descriptive phrases (e.g. 'the wine-dark sea', 'rosy-fingered dawn') and lists of heroes or deeds are characteristic of oral performances where standard and repeated verbal patterns assist the memory. Even when literacy is fully established, oral and written or printed traditions frequently run in parallel and exchange material. For instance, those collecting English folk songs in the early twentieth century found that they were transcribing not a purely oral tradition, but one that had picked up material from printed sources along the way.

One further expansion of the subject is required. In the following pages you will be reminded frequently that book history is, rather like archaeology, a material-based subject. Whatever else it is, the book is an object in the material world that is made, transported and used. When we think of a book we have also to think of pack animals, roads, waterways, ocean-going ships, railways, aircraft – and the Internet: all those means of getting the books out. But not just those things. The introduction of paper (a Chinese invention of the first or second century CE) into Europe in the twelfth century allowed, over the next few centuries, a huge increase in text production that would not have been possible with parchment alone. Gutenberg would not have been able to make his 42-line Bible the success it was had Mainz not been on the Rhine which gave the printer easy access to a large European market for his expensive book. International copyright laws in the later nineteenth century would have been difficult if not impossible to enforce had it not been for the international telegraphic system that allowed nearly instantaneous coordination of a publishing event. The global mass distribution of electronic texts in the twenty-first century would not have been feasible without cheap personal computers, the infrastructure of the Internet, and the user-friendliness of the World Wide Web. In other words, the History of the Book is just part of a much larger history: the history of communication.

Two books that can be particularly recommended as overall introductions to the subject of book history are *The Blackwell Companion to the History of the Book*, ed. Simon Eliot and Jonathan Rose (Oxford: Blackwell, 2007), and *The Book History Reader*, ed. David Finkelstein and Alistair McCleery (London: Routledge, 2006). In the list of 'Selected reading' below I give page references to one or other of these, so that you can explore specific subjects in greater detail.

Useful bibliographies covering the subject include 'Book History Online: International Bibliography of the History of the Printed Book and Libraries' (available at www.kb.nl/bho/index.html), and *The British Book Trade from Caxton to the Present Day*, ed. Robin Myers (London: André Deutsch, 1973), which includes works on individual publishers and publishing houses.

ASPECTS OF BOOK HISTORY

Being a rich and extensive subject, various scholars have attempted to subdivide book history into a number of more manageable sections. Perhaps the most successful – and certainly the most widely used – is what is known as the 'communications circuit' model. This was first proposed by the distinguished historian of French Book History, Robert Darnton, in his essay, 'What is the History of Books?' (first published in 1982; reprinted in *The Book History Reader*, chapter 2). The model has been adjusted and adapted by various historians but in essence it survives. A composite version would read something like this: it views the text as having a life cycle which begins with its creation by an author or authors (known or unknown); its copying or multiplication via scribes, publishers and printers; its distribution and selling via water, road or rail, and through wholesalers, booksellers and pedlars; its consumption or reception by readers (who buy, borrow, steal, listen, or read over someone's shoulder); and, finally, its long-term survival in libraries, archives, etc. This is called a circuit because, of course, the texts that are read and preserved create a context in which the next generation of texts are written, and so the feedback loop mentioned above is created and sustained.

Of course, in practice, one would have to create a slightly different sort of circuit to describe the life cycle of a book in, say, Imperial Rome, twelfth-century Europe or twentieth-century USA, but this rough model does allow us to see book history as consisting of distinct though thoroughly inter-related parts:

1   History of authorship;

2   History of publishing;

3   History of book production;

4   History of distribution;

5   History of reading;

6   History of libraries and archives.

1 History of authorship

Studies in this part of the circuit should not be confused with biographical studies of authors, although nowadays such biographies often do include information on the way in which authors worked in relation to the book trade. Authorship studies foreground this relationship and frequently concentrate on the way an author's work is influenced by his or her sense of how the publishing trade operates and what the readers want or expect.

Authorship studies on the whole tend to concentrate mostly but not exclusively on the last 300 years or so. This is because the concept of 'author' as we understand it in the twentieth century is a relatively recent invention. There were always authors but, in the past, for most readers, it was the text that was of primary interest, not the producer of the text. Before the late fifteenth century, most books did not have a title page, so there was no obvious place for the author to feature. The modern interest in the author as a significant figure associated with creative individuality has emerged in the last few hundred years and was given a considerable boost by two developments in the eighteenth century. The first was Romanticism with its stress upon the importance and distinctiveness of the individual, and particularly the creative individual. The second was the development of the concept of 'copyright' from 1710 when the first Copyright Act in the world was passed in England.

Before that time ownership of a literary property was a slippery idea. Once an author had allowed the original text to be copied in some way it was usually a free-for-all. In the manuscript period this was not too much of a problem because multiplication of texts was usually a slow and expensive process. However, with the arrival of printing which allowed rapid and large-scale copying, it became more of a problem. In some cultures at some times an author or a work might be granted a 'privilege' by the state, and this would allow the writer (or, more likely the person who arranged for the printing of text) to have a monopoly, but this was not a right and was only granted for particular reasons to particular titles. In England such privileges had emerged in the sixteenth century. By the mid sixteenth century the Stationers' Company in London had been given a Royal Charter and had begun to provide the state with a means of licensing publications that at once kept them under control and gave those that printed them some sort of protection against unauthorised copying. This was achieved by entering details of each title in the Company's 'Entry Books'. This provided a form of 'copyright' that developed and gained strength (with a notable interruption during the 1640s and 1650s) until the end of the seventeenth century. The odd thing to our eyes was that literary property was regarded as being perpetual – that is, those who owned a copyright had a permanent monopoly (unlike modern copyright which lasts only for a specified time before the book enters the public domain). For various reasons this system broke down at the end of the seventeenth century and was finally replaced by the Copyright Act of 1710.

However, it was only with a series of court cases in the early 1770s that the full meaning of the 1710 Act became clear. This new copyright was limited: it lasted for 14 years with the opportunity of renewal for another 14 years. After a maximum of 28 years a book was no longer copyright and anyone could reproduce it with impunity. Since that time there have been many copyright Acts, and they have tended to extend the length of copyright (in the EU it now lasts for 70 years after the author's death) but the idea of 'perpetual copyright' has never been restored. These changes in the eighteenth century resulted in two things. Before the abolition of perpetual copyright there was little incentive for those publishers who owned valuable literary properties (say, the collected works of Shakespeare) to publish cheap editions because they had a monopoly and could keep prices high. Nor was there any strong incentive to publish lots of new books when publishers could make comfortable living re-publishing popular old books. After the 1770s there was a need to find new books to publish because older books wouldn't stay yours for long. The result was that production of new printed material expanded hugely (just think of the growth of novels and newspapers at the end of the eighteenth century – both of which, it was assumed, you would read once and then move on to something new), and more and cheaper reprints became available as other publishers issued out-of-copyright books.

As the literary market expanded in terms of titles and print-runs, so the demand for new and cheaper books increased, and this had a tendency to increase the demand for certain authors' works. Higher demand meant that copyrights, which in law were initially owned by authors, became more valuable. This tended to raise the status and income of the most successful authors. The age of the author as economically successful celebrity had arrived. Of course, for every Scott, Byron, Dickens or Miss Braddon, there were thousands of authors whose copyrights weren't worth much or, even if they were, they had to be sold outright, often for a low price to the publisher, to make enough money to live.

Some literary theorists, most notably Roland Barthes, have declared that the author is dead. However, anyone who has studied the anguished correspondence between an author and publisher about copyright or royalty income will find this difficult to believe. Book history and bibliography have a different take: in the light of the work of scholars such as D.F. McKenzie, Jerome McGann and Roger Chartier, we are more likely to argue that books are shaped not only by the author but also by all those involved in the process of book production from the publisher (think about the influence of 'house style' on a book) to the printer (think of how different printers' spelling conventions influence meaning in Shakespeare's First Folio), and beyond.

2 History of publishing

'Publishing' in this context describes a series of functions: (1) finding a text to publish and, if there is an author of the text, negotiating with the author; (2) arranging for the text to be prepared for reproduction and then reproducing it (normally by printing); (3) arranging for the resulting book to be advertised and for it to be distributed to places where it might be bought. 'Publisher' is a term that was used more and more frequently from the late eighteenth century on; before that time the publishing function might be carried out by the printer or, more commonly, by a bookseller. In the manuscript age these functions would frequently be carried out by the owner of the scribal workshop.

The history of publishing thus involves the study of the relationships between those performing the publishing function and authors on the one side and printers and binders on the other (see section 3). It concerns itself, among many other things, with the way in which publishers chose books to publish (the rise of the publisher's reader in the nineteenth century was important here), how contracts were negotiated and relations maintained (or lost) with authors, how profits were divided, and with how publishers competed or cooperated with each other. It is also concerned with the marketing of books (in particular advertising and distribution, see section 4).

Histories of publishing can take many forms from great national histories down to specific studies of individual publishing houses and the relationships between a particular author and the publisher he or she used, or even the history of one particular book. Such studies can give not only an account of the origin, publication and success of a book, but can also explore the impact that it had on contemporary readers and the ways in which it provided a context for later publications. For instance, James Secord's study of the publication and subsequent history of *Vestiges of the Natural History of Creation* in his *Victorian Sensation* (Chicago and London: University of Chicago Press, 2000) explores both the history of this work of popular science and also explains the impact that it had on Tennyson and the ways in which it provided an intellectual context for Darwin's *The Origin of Species*.

As with the history of authorship, the nature of publishing history studies changes according to whether you are studying the period before or after copyright legislation started to have a major effect. Prior to the eighteenth century, author–publisher relations were generally less important than the relationships between booksellers. In part this was because in the seventeenth and eighteenth centuries it was common for different booksellers to own a share in the rights to reproduce, say, Shakespeare's plays, so such a book would be published by many booksellers working together (often called a 'conger'). In this earlier period relationships between booksellers and the state, and the way in which the individual booksellers related to the Stationers' Company, were also very important. Later, as modern publishing firms emerged at the end of the eighteenth century, as the Stationers' Company diminished in importance and as copyright began to assume its modern significance, relations with authors became more important.

Another factor that enters in the later nineteenth century, and one that complicates the author–publisher relationship, is the rise of the 'literary agent'. As the value of certain sorts of literary property increased in the nineteenth century (see section 1), and the ways in which an author might make money out of the copyright multiplied (e.g. serialisation rights, reprint rights for North American and Empire markets, dramatisation rights, translation rights and, in the twentieth century, film rights), so the need for someone who could negotiate with publishers and others to maximise an author's profits became more pressing.

3 History of book production

As this deals with such subjects as quantitative and statistical surveys of book production, the analysis of the types of scribal practice and descriptions of the manual and powered technology of papermaking, typesetting, printing and binding, it can appear to be one of the more daunting aspects of book history. This is a shame, because it can actually bring us closer to the day-to-day material life of the past than most other studies.

The errors made by medieval copyists are products of the same weariness and eye-skipping we know today; the need to save money and use what you've got explains the fact that virtually every surviving copy of the First Folio of Shakespeare is different. These are things we can understand. The impact of powered machinery and mass production on the availability and cheapness of printed goods from the mid nineteenth century onwards is something that has parallels in our mass-produced world.

In the twenty-first century the latest developments in the way a book is produced and delivered create particular problems for the book historian. As bibliographers know, the apparent stability of text in printed form is something of an illusion. Compositors make errors, sheets are wrongly bound – even stereoplates get damaged: their punctuation marks get detached and wander across the page. But such instability is as nothing when compared with the multitude of easy and quick ways in which digital text can be changed. The elusiveness, the malleability and the potential vulnerability of texts in digital form will provide new challenges to the modern book historian, particularly when so much of the evidence may not be preserved. To give two examples: (1) unlike manuscript letters, emails are rarely consistently archived so publishers' records may be less informative; (2) the various editorial stages a book passes through may be recorded when each stage is represented by a marked-up physical text, but not when one electronic file is simply over-written by a newer one.

Another aspect of this area is quantitative book history. This concerns itself with collecting data about print-runs, costs, prices, and sales of books, periodicals, etc. Work on the statistics of book production continues, and there is at least one project that is aiming to assemble the surviving data of British book production from the fifteenth to the twentieth centuries. Most work in this area has so far been done on the nineteenth and early twentieth centuries. On the quantitative side, statistical studies of book prices can tell us a huge amount about who could afford to buy certain sorts of books and newspapers – and who could not. This alone leads to fascinating questions such as: what was the average price someone from the working class could afford to spend on print? (The answer is almost certainly no more than a few old ['d' not 'p'] pennies.) Or, if you couldn't buy a book in the past, how could you get to read it? (This leads us on to sections 5 and 6.)

William St Clair's study *The Reading Nation in the Romantic Period* (Cambridge: Cambridge University Press, 2003) explores the impact of the changes in copyright and, later, the modes of production in the eighteenth and nineteenth centuries on the sorts of literature that would have been cheaply available to readers. It turns out that in the late eighteenth and early nineteenth centuries, the period of the great Romantic poets, few of those poets would have been available cheaply to readers, most of whom would have been brought up on writers who had flourished in the early eighteenth century or before and who were thus by that time out of copyright. By the mid nineteenth century, matters were different. The works of poets such as Scott, Byron, Wordsworth, Shelley, Keats and Coleridge were coming out of copyright but, equally importantly, a new technology was widely available: stereotype. Until the late eighteenth century, books were printed from movable type. Many printers did not have enough type to set an entire book, so the type for the first few sheets would be set up (books are, of course, printed on sheets of paper that are then folded and cut to produce individual leaves and pages) and the sheets printed off. The type would then be broken up, cleaned and used to set the second group of sheets, and so on. Even if the printer had sufficient type for the whole book, it would be unlikely that he would leave this amount of type set up in the hope that a second impression would be called for. This meant that if a book were popular and a second printing was needed, the whole typesetting process had to be gone through again – with all the costs in time, labour and materials that represented. Stereotype (or 'solid type') – developed in the eighteenth century but used in the UK from about 1805 onwards – changed all that. The type for each page would be set up as usual but then plaster-of-Paris (later a laminate material made of paper called 'flong' replaced the brittle plaster) would be used to take an impression of the whole page. Into the plaster-of-Paris mould would then be poured molten type metal, which would then set. This created a single sheet, or 'stereoplate', of metal from which a page could be printed. These plates could then be stored and reused whenever a reprint was required. This revolutionised reprinting and made it much cheaper.

Although stereotype solved one problem, there was still the difficulty that most printers could not afford to set a whole book in one go. This meant that an author could only correct his or her text in stages: the first few sheets, and then the next few sheets. If an author detected an inconsistency in later sheets, the early sheets could not be corrected because the type used to print them had been broken up and reused. Unless the publisher was very confident that a reprint would be called for, no stereotype would have been made (and anyway correcting stereotype was difficult). This led to novels, for instance, that had inconsistencies in plotting and characterisation and seemed to lack rigorous organisation and formal control – 'huge baggy monsters', Henry James called them. However, in the UK from the 1860s and 1870s onwards (in the USA it happened earlier), new typecasting machines began to replace the skilled human typecaster. This meant that type could be produced faster and more cheaply, and in turn this meant that the whole text of a novel could be set up so that the author could revise the first pages in the light of later ones. This produced more tightly organised and consistent novels – novels like those of Henry James himself. Here is an example of a technical and economic change having an immediate impact on a cultural product and the expectations that go with it. For more information on this subject see Allan C. Dooley, *Author and Printer in Victorian England* (Charlottesville and London: University Press of Virginia, 1992).

4 History of distribution

This involves the study of how books were moved from their place of production to the point at which they would be sold or used. In the pre-print era this might have simply involved transporting a single copy from the monastery or workshop in which it was made to its place of use. Nevertheless, it is worth remembering that there were manuscript-based cultures – such as that in the early Roman Empire – that produced (by using workshops manned by a multitude of literate slaves) many hundreds of copies that would have been distributed to bookshops around Italy and further afield. Certainly after the invention of printing, distribution almost always tended to involve bulk transport of many copies (and books, usually in the form of printed sheets – binding would come later – were bulky) to customers or sellers. This transport might use road, river and even sea and represent a long and uncertain link between printer and reader that could involve shipmen, waggoners, agents – and even smugglers if the books were regarded as dangerous, as was the case of Protestant pamphlets in England in the early sixteenth century or the *Encyclopédie* in eighteenth-century France. See, for instance, Robert Darnton's *The Business of Enlightenment* (Cambridge, MA: Harvard University Press, 1979) which explores the racy history – including smuggling – of the *Encyclopédie* between 1775 and 1800.

In the early modern period most books would end up with booksellers who might sell copies on or exchange them for other books with other booksellers at national and international fairs. In the nineteenth century the books might first go to wholesalers such as Simpkin, Marshall or W.H. Smith who would then supply individual bookshops with mixed orders from a range of printers and booksellers. In the nineteenth and twentieth centuries, wholesaling was a very important part of the trade, and one that allowed small and sometimes provincial publishers and printers to get access to national markets. In the twenty-first century the wholesaling function has been partly taken over by Internet-based firms such as Amazon, although in this case the roles of wholesaler and bookseller have been combined.

The process did not end with the bookshop. The bookseller has to display and promote his wares and encourage customers to browse and buy, so advertising, in the form of display pages and cards, might be important. There were relatively few specialist bookshops in the past; most sold other (and often faster-moving and more profitable) goods such as stationery, fancy goods or medicines (there is a close link in the UK and elsewhere between books and medicines – hence the large number of advertisements for patent medicines you find in cheap popular books in the nineteenth century). In addition, from the 1840s onwards, station bookstalls were becoming an important outlet for books and periodicals. Long before the nineteenth century, however, the cheapest books designed for the lower orders would never see the shelves of bookshops, but would be sold in the street or at fairs by pedlars and chapmen (chapbooks were low-priced, usually 1d or 2d pamphlets that were sold in markets).

The Internet and the digital revolution have transformed this area, as they have done many others. Not only has the Web allowed book-buyers to circumvent the bookshop when ordering books, it has also provided free access to many out-of-copyright texts through such systems as the Gutenberg Project (www.gutenberg.org/catalog) and the more recent initiatives by Google and

Microsoft. It has allowed the introduction of 'print-on-demand' systems to keep specialist and low-demand books 'in print'. Indeed, some have argued that such systems will allow any and every title, however obscure, to remain available on the publisher's backlist. There have always been printers and publishers whose aim was not mass production or mass distribution, but the selling of very high quality specialist books in small numbers to discerning (and usually affluent) readers. The private-press movement since the late nineteenth century is one such example, as is the work of certain Italian printers in the sixteenth century, and William Morris with his Kelmscott Press in the 1890s. The Internet gives such private and specialist producers a particularly cost-effective means of targeting their particular clientele.

The Web has also revolutionised second-hand and antiquarian bookselling, providing catalogues that can be searched by keywords, thus escaping from the tyranny of alphabetical listings of author or titles when, as a book historian, one might want to look for publishers' names or dates of publication. The specialist search engines such as AbeBooks or AddALL enable the user to search thousands of book dealers' catalogues simultaneously, and allow the dealers and potential buyers to compare prices. At a less-exalted level, systems such as eBay have encouraged all sorts of people to set up as sellers of their own books. Such systems allow the book historian the chance to search for publications, particularly popular publications of the last few centuries, that have escaped the great libraries (mostly because they were cheap reprints).

5 History of reading

Books have performed many functions in society. They are a major manufactured and traded good out of which a lot of people can make money for, as long as enough books are sold, authors, publishers, printers, shippers, wholesalers and retailers will make money whether those books are read or not. Books are used in secular and religious rituals (think of the Bible in a court of law or in a church). Books can be a means of displaying wealth (think of all those libraries created by eighteenth-century gentlemen who used them, if they used them at all, to fall asleep in after dinner). They can also be a demonstration of the owner's knowledge and learning. However, most buyers or borrowers of books do read them, or parts of them, and without reading the cultural feedback loop described in the introduction to this chapter would not be possible. The history of reading is thus of considerable importance in book history and, indeed, has become one of the most popular aspects of the subject.

By history of reading we do not mean some literary critic's idea of what a reader in the past thought: in these circumstances it is too easy for the critic to invent an ideal reader who, unsurprisingly, turns out to read in exactly the way that the critic expected and hoped. Nor do we mean a study of 'the implied reader' which, as the critic or theorist usually does the inferring, may come down to the same thing. Nor is the historian of reading wholly devoted to what the great writers and critics of the past read. That is interesting, of course, and it has its part to play, but what the historian is really trying to get at is what the unfamous, the ordinary and, if there is such a thing, the average reader read, and how he or she responded to what they read.

This is a difficult job for, overwhelmingly, reading experience in the past (as now) left no trace. What we can find, however, are references in diaries, letters, reading lists, commonplace books, scrap books and in the marginal marks and comments left by readers in the books themselves. Biographies and autobiographies can also be used but, when drawing on the latter, the historian has to be alert to the likelihood that authors will adjust their accounts so as to present the best possible image of themselves as serious and disciplined readers.

Studies of particular readers are useful in that they remind us of the dangers of generalisation, and of the quirkiness of individuals at any time in history. For instance, John Brewer, in *The Practice and Representation of Reading in England*, ed. James Raven, Helen Small and Naomi Tadmor (Cambridge: Cambridge University Press, 1996), explores the reading life of Anna Larpent through her diaries which covered the years 1773–1828. She was a well-educated, enthusiastic and pious reader who nevertheless had a broad taste which included history, biography, social science, science, travel writing, sermons, works of piety – and novels, poems and plays (her husband was the 'Inspector of Plays' for the Lord Chamberlain's Office – a sort of censor). Interestingly, in her accounts of novel-reading she presented herself, not as reading for the passionate emotions or for escapism, but to appreciate those characters (particularly women) who endured suffering and misuse with heroic stoicism. For Anna Larpent, unlike most modern readers, a novel was there to provide a moral education.

By the later nineteenth and earlier twentieth centuries it is possible to find enough evidence, although it still needs careful interpretation, for historians to look at groups of readers and to start to detect patterns of reading in different parts of society. In Jonathan Rose's *The Intellectual Life of the British Working Classes* (New Haven and London: Yale University Press, 2001), for instance, there is a table listing the favourite reading of the early Labour MPs in 1906. Bunyan, Burns, Cobbett and Darwin are all there, but the top three places are occupied (in ascending order) by the Bible, Dickens and Ruskin. This choice of reading can tell us a lot about the nature and intellectual background of the Left in Britain at the time.

6 History of libraries and archives

This final aspect of book history is concerned with the ways in which books are accumulated in libraries, archives and other public or private collections, and by being so are preserved for contemporary and future readers and writers. At this level library history is closely associated with the history of scholarship and, more generally, with the history of communication. On the other side, the history of libraries also relates to the distribution of books (given that books tended to be expensive in the past, users were more likely to borrow than buy their books) and to the history of reading.

Libraries and archives seem to have arrived soon after the clay-tablet book in ancient Sumeria. By 2000 BCE there is evidence for the first primitive library 'catalogue'. Most of what was stored and catalogued was what was of the first importance to any state: lists of production, lists of taxes gathered, legal contracts of all sorts – and the appropriate hymns, incantations and rituals to secure to the king and his country the approval of the gods. Literature and learning, although it was there from quite early on, took up only a very small proportion of the material housed in the first libraries.

Subsequently, great libraries were commonly associated not only with book collections, but scholarship and book-making as well. This is particularly true of the period between the fall of the Roman Empire in the West and the twelfth century, during which monastic libraries and their associated scriptoria were virtually the only source of texts. Indeed without them, and particularly the work of the Carolingian monasteries in the ninth and tenth centuries, very few classical texts would have survived to the Renaissance. From the twelfth century, universities began to emerge in Europe, and gradually these and their associated libraries, and the secular scribal workshops found close by, took over the majority of book-making and scholarship from monastic libraries.

From the eighteenth century on, most libraries were not grand places but usually small institutions, frequently commercial in nature that provided their users with useful or entertaining books. Over 50 per cent of known libraries in the UK before 1850 were circulating libraries which were commercial organisations providing readers with what they wanted (which from the late eighteenth century was mostly novels). The great national libraries, such the Library of Congress, the British Library or the Bibliothèque nationale, have reasonably stable collections; most commercial and public libraries do not. Like Heraclitus's river, the average library never stayed the same: new books were being acquired and old ones 'de-accessioned', as the jargon has it. When such libraries failed, and most commercial libraries did eventually fail, their remaining stock was sold off and thus they ceased to exist in the historical

record. It is thus much easier to write the histories of long-lasting great libraries than the local commercial libraries as these rarely leave a wrack behind. At
best one has the occasional catalogue and, if you are very fortunate, a list of
borrowers and what they borrowed, but such survivals are very rare.

QUESTIONS AND EXERCISES

1   'It is not that the author is dead, but rather that he or she can no longer be thought
of as the sole creator of a given text.' Choose a favourite author and consider his or
her publishing career in the light of this statement.

2   Choose a book, and see if you can find out how much the book earned during the
author's lifetime, and how the profit was shared between publisher and author.

3   Select an early literary agency (one founded before 1914). What services did it
offer, and which authors did it represent in the first full decade of its operations?

4   Why did the introduction of wood engravings (as opposed to woodcuts) in the
early nineteenth century have such an impact on the way books and newspapers
were illustrated?

5   Taking one date (such as 1650, or 1750, or 1850) and one country, describe the
sorts of cheap printed publications that would be available to readers who did not
visit booksellers; explain how these publications got to their readers.

6   What were the main factors that contributed to the rapid rise in literacy rates in
industrialising countries during the nineteenth century?

7   Choose a favourite book published before 1900. Using the **Reading Experience
Database** (see under 'Selected reading' below), survey readers' reactions to that
book. Are there any common factors in their reactions?

8   Select a country or a region with a public library system, and discuss the changes
that system has undergone over the period 1960–2000.

SELECTED READING

Introduction

Elizabeth L. Eisenstein, *The Printing Press as an Agent of Change* (Cambridge: Cambridge
University Press, 1979).
Simon Eliot and Jonathan Rose (eds), *Blackwell Companion to the History of the Book*
(Oxford: Blackwell, 2007), chapters 5–12.
Simon Eliot, Andrew Nash and Ian Willison (eds), *Literary Cultures and the Material Book*
(London: British Library Publications, 2007).

Lucien Febvre and Henri-Jean Martin, *The Coming of the Book*, trans. David Gerard (London: Verso, 1984).

David Finkelstein and Alistair McCleery (eds), *The Book History Reader* (London: Routledge, 2006), chapters 2–9.

D.C. Greetham, *Textual Scholarship* (New York and London: Garland Publishing, 1994).

Leslie Howsam, *Old Books & New Histories* (Toronto: University of Toronto Press, 2006).

Frederick G. Kilgour, *The Evolution of the Book* (New York: Oxford University Press, 1998).

More detailed studies can be found in the various national histories of the book that have been published or are being published. Foremost for readers of English are:

A History of the Book in America (Chapel Hill: University of North Carolina Press, 2000–present); planned for five volumes.

A History of the Book in Australia (St Lucia: University of Queensland Press, 2001–present).

History of the Book in Canada (Toronto: University of Toronto Press, 2004–7); all three volumes published.

Oxford History of the Irish Book (Oxford: Oxford University Press, 2006–present).

The Edinburgh History of the Book in Scotland (Edinburgh: Edinburgh University Press, 2007–present); planned for four volumes.

The History of the Book in Britain (Cambridge: Cambridge University Press, 1999–present); planned in seven volumes, most of which should be published by 2012.

The international scholarly society that covers the whole span of book history is the Society for the History of Authorship, Reading and Publishing (SHARP), which issues a quarterly newsletter, *SHARP News* and a yearly journal, *Book History*. It holds an annual summer conference, alternating (usually) between Europe and North America, and also smaller, specialist conferences at other times in the year. Its website, which includes a useful list of teaching, research and other resources, can be found at www.sharpweb.org.

History of authorship

Nigel Cross, *The Common Writer* (Cambridge: Cambridge University Press, 1985).

Simon Eliot and Jonathan Rose (eds), *Blackwell Companion to the History of the Book* (Oxford: Blackwell, 2007), chapters 17, 29, 38.

John Feather, *Publishing, Piracy and Politics* (London: Mansell, 1994).

David Finkelstein and Alistair McCleery (eds), *The Book History Reader* (London: Routledge, 2006), chapters 14–17.

Alvin Kernan, *Samuel Johnson & the Impact of Print* (Princeton: Princeton University Press, 1989).

Robert L. Patten, *Charles Dickens & His Publishers* (Oxford: Oxford University Press, 1978).

Catherine Seville, *Literary Copyright Reform in Early Victorian England* (Cambridge: Cambridge University Press, 1999).

Catherine Seville, *The Internationalisation of Copyright Law: Books, Buccaneers and the Black Flag in the Nineteenth Century* (Cambridge: Cambridge University Press, 2006).

Peter L. Shillingsburg, *Pegasus in Harness: Victorian Publishing and W.M. Thackeray* (Charlottesville, VA and London: University Press of Virginia, 1992).
John Sutherland, *Victorian Novelists and Publishers* (London: The Athlone Press, 1976).
Eva Hemmungs Wirtén, *No Trespassing* (Toronto: University of Toronto Press, 2004).

History of publishing

Asa Briggs, *History of Longman* (London: British Library, 2008).
Simon Eliot and Jonathan Rose (eds), *Blackwell Companion to the History of the Book* (Oxford: Blackwell, 2007), chapters 17–27.
John Feather, *A History of British Publishing* (Beckenham: Croom Helm, 1988).
David Finkelstein and Alistair McCleery (eds), *The Book History Reader* (London: Routledge, 2006), chapters 17–21.
Albert N. Greco, *The Book Publishing Industry*, second edn (Mahwah: Erlbaum, 2005).
Elizabeth James (ed.), *Macmillan: A Publishing Tradition* (London: Palgrave Macmillan, 2002).
David McKitterick, *A History of Cambridge University Press* (Cambridge: Cambridge University Press, 1992–2004).
Ian Norrie, *Mumby's Publishing and Bookselling in the Twentieth Century*, sixth edn (London: Bell & Hyman, 1984).
John Tebbel, *A History of Book Publishing in the United States* (New York and London: R.R. Bowker, 1972–81, four vols).
Michael Winship, *American Literary Publishing in the Mid-Nineteenth Century: The Business of Ticknor and Fields* (Cambridge: Cambridge University Press, 1995).
William Zachs, *The First John Murray and the Late Eighteenth-century London Book Trade* (Oxford: Oxford University Press, 1998).

History of book production

J.J.G. Alexander, *Medieval Illuminators and their Methods of Work* (New Haven, CT and London: Yale University Press, 1992).
Colin Clair, *A Chronology of Printing* (London: Cassell, 1969).
C. de Hamel, *Scribes and Illuminators* (London: British Museum, 1992).
Simon Eliot, *Some Patterns and Trends in British Publishing 1800–1919* (London: The Bibliographical Society, 1994).
Simon Eliot and Jonathan Rose (eds), *Blackwell Companion to the History of the Book* (Oxford: Blackwell, 2007), chapters 3, 5–6, 13, 20, 28.
Mirjam Foot, *The History of Bookbinding as a Mirror of Society* (London: British Library, 1998).
Philip Gaskell, *A New Introduction to Bibliography* (Oxford: Oxford University Press, 1972).
Richard L. Hills, *Papermaking in Britain 1488–1988* (London: The Athlone Press, 1988).
S.H. Steinberg, *Five Hundred Years of Printing* (London: British Library, 1996 [1955]).
Michael Twyman, *Printing 1770–1970* (London: British Library, 1998).
Alexis Weedon, *Victorian Publishing 1836–1916* (Aldershot: Ashgate, 2003).

History of distribution

Robert Darnton, *The Kiss of Lamourette: Reflections in Cultural History* (London: Faber and Faber, 1990).
Simon Eliot and Jonathan Rose (eds), *Blackwell Companion to the History of the Book* (Oxford: Blackwell, 2007), chapters 24–7, 29–30.

John Feather, *The Provincial Book Trade in Eighteenth-Century England* (Cambridge: Cambridge University Press, 1985).

Laura J. Miller, *Reluctant Capitalists* (Chicago, IL and London: University of Chicago Press, 2007).

James Raven, *London Booksellers and American Customers* (Columbia: University of South Carolina Press, 2002).

James Raven, *The Business of Books: Booksellers and the English Book Trade 1450–1850* (New Haven, CT and London: Yale University Press, 2007).

Charles Wilson, *First with the News* (London: Jonathan Cape, 1985).

The **British Book Trade Index (BBTI)** is a very useful online resource at www.bbti.bham.ac.uk. It provides details of all those who worked in the English and Welsh book and related trades up to 1851. There is a similar resource for Scotland run by the National Library of Scotland at www.nls.uk/catalogues/resources/sbti/index.html.

History of reading

R. D. Altick, *The English Common Reader* (Chicago: University of Chicago Press, 1957).

Guglielmo Cavallo and Roger Chartier (eds), *A History of Reading in the West*, trans. Lydia G. Cochrane (Cambridge: Polity Press, 1999).

C.M. Cipola, *Literacy and Development in the West* (Harmondsworth: Penguin, 1969).

Stephen Colclough, *Consuming Texts: Readers and Reading Communities, 1695–1870* (London: Palgrave Macmillan, 2007).

David Cressy, *Literacy and the Social Order* (Cambridge: Cambridge University Press, 1980).

Robert Darnton, *The Forbidden Best-Sellers of Pre-Revolutionary France* (London: HarperCollins, 1996).

Simon Eliot and Jonathan Rose (eds), *Blackwell Companion to the History of the Book* (Oxford: Blackwell, 2007), chapters 4, 34.

David Finkelstein and Alistair McCleery (eds), *The Book History Reader* (London: Routledge, 2006), chapters 22–8.

Heather Jackson, *Marginalia: Readers Writing in Books* (New Haven: Yale University Press, 2001).

Joseph McAleer, *Popular Reading and Publishing in Britain 1914–1950* (Oxford: Oxford University Press, 1992).

Alberto Manguel, *A History of Reading* (London: HarperCollins, 1996).

David Vincent, *Literacy and Popular Culture: England 1750–1914* (Cambridge: Cambridge University Press, 1989).

One of the major research resources for the history of reading is the **Reading Experience Database (RED)** at The Open University. This aims to record reading experiences of those in the British Isles and those born in the British Isles between 1450 and 1945. Currently RED contains about 25,000 records but is expanding all the time. It is available at www.open.ac.uk/Arts/RED/index.html. If you visit the page you will see that you can not only use it but also contribute to it. If you are working on a piece of reading-history research you should certainly think of contributing your discoveries to RED.

History of libraries and archives

Alistair Black, *The Public Library in Britain 1914–2000* (London: British Library, 2000).
Lionel Casson, *Libraries in the Ancient World* (New Haven: Yale University Press, 2001).
Simon Eliot and Jonathan Rose (eds), *Blackwell Companion to the History of the Book* (Oxford: Blackwell, 2007), chapters 35, 36, 39.
P.R. Harris, *A History of the British Museum Library* (London: The British Library, 1998).
Peter Hoare (ed.), *The Cambridge History of Libraries in Britain and Ireland* (Cambridge: Cambridge University Press, 2006, three vols).
G.L. Griest, *Mudie's Circulating Library and the Victorian Novel* (Bloomington and London: David and Charles, 1970).
Paul Kaufman, *Libraries and Their Users* (London: Library Association, 1969).
Thomas Kelly, *A History of Public Libraries in Great Britain 1845–1975*, second edn (London: Library Association, 1977).
James Raven, *Lost Libraries* (London: Palgrave Macmillan, 2004).

The **Library History Database**, set up by Professor Robin Alston, contains information on more than 27,000 libraries established in the British Isles before 1850 and can be found at www.r-alston.co.uk/contents.htm. It provides the most comprehensive listings of libraries of all types up to 1850.

5

Editing literary texts

W.R. Owens

The preparation of reliable texts of literary works is one of the most valuable tasks a scholar can undertake. General readers as well as professional literary critics depend on the accuracy of texts, and their work of interpretation or evaluation will be damaged if these are corrupt or imperfect. The more detailed a critic's attention to the words of a text, the more important it is that the text be accurate. The US critic F.O. Matthiessen was famously caught out when he wrote admiringly of what he took to be a brilliantly incongruous image in Herman Melville's *White Jacket* – the 'soiled fish' of the sea. Unfortunately for Matthiessen, 'soiled' was the printer's invention; Melville had actually written 'coiled'.

The job of scholarly editors is to remove errors such as these, and to work towards the production of more accurate editions of literary texts. This can be a highly complex and laborious task, requiring specialised skills, but it can also be very enjoyable and rewarding, and if you are attracted to it there may be opportunities for you to edit a text, or part of a text, yourself. In any case, as a postgraduate student it is important that you have some general knowledge of the methods and aims of editors and textual scholars, so that, if for no other reason, you are able to assess the relative authority of the various available texts of the works you will be studying.

WHY LITERARY TEXTS NEED TO BE EDITED

Many important literary works are still read and studied in woefully undependable texts. The reasons why texts become corrupt are manifold. Consider some of the processes that an author's work may have gone through before its final publication. In the days before word processing, the manuscript or typescript will very likely have been full of scribbled deletions or additions, in near-indecipherable handwriting or wretched typing. This document will then have been prepared for the press by a 'copy-editor' at the publishers who will have made various changes, including applying a 'house style' in matters of spelling and punctuation. When this copy-edited text comes before a compositor to be set in type, there are almost limitless opportunities for mistakes to creep in – in misreading the manuscript; in well-meant but mistaken attempts to 'correct' the author; or in setting wrong types. Words or whole sections may be left out, added, or set in the wrong order. Some of these mistakes may be corrected at proof-reading stage, but the author may also take this opportunity to change or add to the original text; and, in setting this fresh material, further errors may occur. All this means that even the first edition of a book seldom presents to readers the exact words as intended by its author. When it goes through subsequent editions, the errors of the first edition are often reproduced, and more errors introduced when it is reset, so that the longer texts are in print, the more corrupt they may become.

The problems faced by an editor seeking to establish an authoritative text are, however, much larger and more difficult than the correction of fairly obvious errors. To show you what I mean, let us explore briefly a couple of specific examples. The first is from one of the most famous works in literature, Shakespeare's *Hamlet*. Three distinct early editions of *Hamlet* were published, known to scholars as the First Quarto or Q1 (1603), the Second Quarto or Q2 (1604/5) and the First Folio or F1 (1623). The first two appeared during Shakespeare's lifetime, in the form of small books (the size of a modern paperback) known as 'quartos' from the fact that they were made up of printed sheets folded twice to make four leaves. The third was included in the great folio collection of Shakespeare's works published, after his death, in 1623 (a folio being a large volume made up of printed sheets folded once). In Figures 5.1(a), 5.1(b) and 5.1(c) you will find, reproduced in facsimile, Hamlet's 'To be, or not to be' soliloquy as it appears in each of these early editions.

Hamlet facsimiles

As you can immediately see, the Q1 version differs markedly from the others, but the two later versions also differ in their wording and punctuation. These differences have posed difficult questions for the editors of *Hamlet*. Why does the earliest printed version differ so markedly from the two other early printed editions? Why do the second and third editions also differ from each other? What text should be reproduced in modern editions?

Until fairly recently it was generally agreed by scholars that Q1 is defective in many respects, the most widely accepted explanation for this being that its text had been reconstructed from memory by an actor, or group of actors, and written down in this form by a scribe to be set by the printer. Not having been set from a manuscript in Shakespeare's own handwriting, it lacked 'authority'

Ham. To be, or not to be, I there's the point,
To Die, to sleepe, is that all? I all:
No, to sleepe, to dreame, I mary there it goes,
For in that dreame of death, when wee awake,
And borne before an euerlasting Iudge,
From whence no paßenger euer retur'nd,
The vndiscouered country, at whose sight
The happy smile, and the accursed damn'd.
But for this, the ioyfull hope of this,
Whol'd beare the scornes and flattery of the world,
Scorned by the right rich, the rich curßed of the poore?

The widow being oppreßed, the orphan wrong'd,
The taste of hunger, or a tirants raigne,
And thousand more calamities besides;
To grunt and sweate vnder this weary life,
When that he may his full *Quietus* make,
With a bare bodkin, who would this indure,
But for a hope of something after death?
Which pußles the braine, and doth confound the sence,
Which makes vs rather beare those euilles we haue,
Than flie to others that we know not of.
I that, O this conscience makes cowardes of vs all,
Lady in thy orizons, be all my sinnes remembred.

Figure 5.1(a) Hamlet: 'To be, or not to be' from the First Quarto (1603).

Ham. To be, or not to be, that is the queſtion,
Whether tis nobler in the minde to ſuffer
The ſlings and arrowes of outragious fortune,
Or to take Armes againſt a ſea of troubles,
And by oppoſing, end them, to die to ſleepe
No more, and by a ſleepe, to ſay we end
The hart-ake, and the thouſand naturall ſhocks
That fleſh is heire to; tis a conſumaticn
Deuoutly to be wiſht to die to ſleepe,
To ſleepe, perchance to dreame, I there's the rub,
For in that ſleepe of death what dreames may come
When we haue ſhuffled off this mortall coyle
Muſt giue vs pauſe, there's the reſpect
That makes calamitie of ſo long life:
For who would beare the whips and ſcornes of time,
Th'oppreſſors wrong, the proude mans contumely,
The pangs of deſpiz'd loue, the lawes delay,
The inſolence of office, and the ſpurnes
That patient merrit of th'vnworthy takes,
When he himſelfe might his quietas make
With a bare bodkin; who would fardels beare,
To grunt and ſweat vnder a wearie life,
But that the dread of ſomething after death,
The vndiſcouer'd country, from whoſe borne
No trauiler returnes, puzzels the will,
And makes vs rather beare thoſe ills we haue,
Then flie to others that we know not of.
Thus conſcience does make cowards,
And thus the natiue hiew of reſolution
Is ſickled ore with the pale caſt of thought,
And enterpriſes of great pitch and moment,
With this regard theyr currents turne awry,
And looſe the name of action. Soft you now,
The faire *Ophelia*, Nimph in thy orizons
Be all my ſinnes remembred.

Figure 5.1(b) Hamlet: 'To be, or not to be' from the Second Quarto (1604/5).

Ham. To be, or not to be, that is the Queſtion:
Whether 'tis Nobler in the minde to ſuffer
The Slings and Arrowes of outragious Fortune,
Or to take Armes againſt a Sea of troubles,
And by oppoſing end them : to dye,to ſleepe
No more; and by a ſleepe, to ſay we end
The Heart-ake, and the thouſand Naturall ſhockes
That Fleſh is heyre too? 'Tis a conſummation
Deuoutly to be wiſh'd. To dye to ſleepe,
To ſleepe, perchance to Dreame ; I, there's the rub,
For in that ſleepe of death, what dreames may come,
When we haue ſhuffiel'd off this mortall coile,
Muſt giue vs pawſe. There's the reſpeĉt
That makes Calamity of ſo long life :
For who would beare the Whips and Scornes of time,
The Oppreſſors wrong, the poore mans Contumely,
The pangs of diſpriz'd Loue, the Lawes delay,
The inſolence of Office,and the Spurnes
That patient merit of the vnworthy takes, -
When he himſelfe might his *Quietus* make
With a bare Bodkin? Who would theſe Fardles beare
To grunt and ſweat vnder a weary life,
But that the dread of ſomething after death,
The vndiſcouered Countrey, from whoſe Borne
No Traueller returnes, Puzels the will,
And makes vs rather beare thoſe illes we haue,
Then flye to others that we know not of.
Thus Conſcience does make Cowards of vs all,
And thus the Natiue hew of Reſolution
Is ſicklied o're, with the pale caſt of Thought,
And enterprizes of great pith and moment,
With this regard their Currants turne away,
And looſe the name of Aĉtion. Soft you now,
The faire *Ophelia?* Nimph, in thy Orizons
Be all my ſinnes remembred.

Figure 5.1(c) Hamlet: 'To be, or not to be' from the First Folio (1623).

as a text. By contrast, Q2 explicitly claimed to be authoritative, declaring on its title page that it was 'Newly imprinted and enlarged to almost as much againe as it was, according to the true and perfect Coppie'. The claim to enlargement is supported by the fact that it is about 1,600 type lines longer than Q1, and scholars have generally taken the reference to the 'true and perfect Coppie' to mean that it was printed from Shakespeare's own handwritten draft. The 1623 Folio also claimed on its title page to be 'Published according to the True Originall Copies'. In the case of *Hamlet*, however, most scholars believed that the text set by the printer was not Shakespeare's original draft, but was a transcript of this prepared by a scribe, probably for use as a prompt-book when the play was being performed. It differs in significant ways from Q2, including not only the kinds of small changes we have noticed in the 'To be or not to be' speech, but lengthy omissions and additions. No very satisfactory answer could be given as to why Q2 did not include passages that appeared in F1, or why F1 did not include passages that had appeared in Q2. It was assumed, however, that since these passages all seemed to be authentically Shakespearean, they must have been intended by him to be included in the play. Editors therefore conflated (blended) the Q2 and F1 texts to produce a single text containing as many of these passages as possible.

More recently, a number of scholars have begun to question the assumption that there was only a single version of *Hamlet*, arguing instead that the changes in F1 may represent deliberate revision by Shakespeare. The case for regarding these changes as authorial revision was argued at length by the team of scholars (Stanley Wells, Gary Taylor, John Jowett and William Montgomery) who edited the Oxford University Press *Complete Works of Shakespeare* in 1986, in their accompanying *Textual Companion* which appeared in 1987. On the assumption that F1 represents the fruits of Shakespeare's own revision of his play, in which he cut passages that had been published in Q2 and added new passages, they based the Oxford text on F1 alone. The more than 200 lines that only appear in Q2 are not incorporated into the Oxford text, but are reprinted in an appendix. A different approach was taken by Ann Thompson and Neil Taylor, editors of the third edition of the Arden *Hamlet*, published in 2006. They based their main text on Q2, on the grounds that it derives more certainly from an authorial manuscript, one published during Shakespeare's lifetime and perhaps with his knowledge. However, recognising that all three early texts are of great interest in their own right, they also published, in a separate volume, fully edited, modernised texts of Q1 and F1.

We will return to this example from *Hamlet* later, but for the moment it can stand as a notable (perhaps extreme) example of some of the complex problems encountered by scholarly editors. For a second, somewhat less complicated example of a textual problem, let us turn to Daniel Defoe's novel *Moll Flanders*.

In Figures 5.2(a) and 5.2(b) you will see facsimiles of an extract from the first edition, which was published in January 1722, followed by the same extract as it appeared in the 'second edition, corrected', which was published in July 1722. Please examine these facsimiles carefully, noting differences between them.

Moll Flanders facsimiles

As you can see, there are a number of small, but significant, differences between these early versions of *Moll Flanders*. Quite a few words and phrases are cut in the second edition, but there are also one or two additions. If you imagine that you are preparing a scholarly edition of *Moll Flanders*, the question you would have to consider is whether there is any reason to believe that Defoe himself was responsible for introducing the changes in the second edition. If you came to the conclusion that he was, you might decide to base your new edition on the text of this later edition, rather than on the first, on the grounds that it represents the text of the novel as revised by the author.

In fact, editors of modern scholarly editions of *Moll Flanders* such as G.A. Starr (Oxford University Press, 1971; rep. Oxford World's Classics series, 1981), Edward Kelly (Norton Critical Edition, 1973) and Liz Bellamy (vol. 6 in *The Novels of Daniel Defoe*, Pickering & Chatto, 2009) have unanimously come to the view that there is no reason to suppose that Defoe had any hand in editions published after the first one. Detailed study indicates that the main reason for the numerous small changes in the second and subsequent editions was simply to shorten the text and thus reduce the cost of reprinting the book. The second edition is 63 pages shorter than the first, and given that over half the expense of printing a book at this time was the cost of the paper, this represented a significant saving.

The fact that Defoe had no involvement in the production of the second edition does not, however, mean that it can be ignored by an editor of *Moll Flanders*. It is true that in compressing the text a number of manifest errors have been introduced, through carelessness, or due to misunderstanding of Defoe's text. Nevertheless, the second edition also contains a small number of important corrections to the first edition text, and it is possible that either the compositor or the corrector of the second edition had access to Defoe's manuscript. There is a good example of this in the facsimiles you have just been looking at. The sentence in the first edition (p. 14) beginning 'But my new generous Mistress...' is obviously incomplete, and makes no grammatical sense as it stands. What seems likely to have happened is that the compositor's eye skipped over a line in the manuscript ('had better Thoughts for me, I call her generous'). This error is corrected in the second edition (p. 12), almost certainly by reference back to the manuscript.

(14)

the Neighbours who had known my Circumstances, took such Compassion of me, as to acquaint the Lady in whose Family I had been a Week, as I mention'd above; and immediately she sent her Maid to fetch me away, and two of her Daughters came with the Maid tho' unsent; so I went with them Bag and Baggage, and with a glad Heart you may be sure: The fright of my Condition had made such an Impression upon me, that I did not want now to be a Gentlewoman, but was very willing to be a Servant, and that any kind of Servant they thought fit to have me be.

BUT my new generous Mistress, for she exceeded the good Woman I was with before, in every Thing, as well as in the matter of Estate, I say in every Thing except Honesty; and for that, tho' this was a Lady most exactly Just, yet I must not forget to say on all Occasions, that the First tho' Poor, was as uprightly Honest as it was possible for any One to be.

I was no sooner carried away as I have said by this good Gentlewoman, but the first Lady, *that is to say,* the *Mayoress* that was, sent her two Daughters to take Care of me; and another Family which had taken Notice of me, when I was the little Gentlewoman, and had given me Work to do, sent for me after her, so that I was mightily made of, as we say; nay, and they were not a little Angry, especially, Madam the *Mayoress,* that her Friend had taken me away from her, as she call'd it; for as she said, I was Hers by Right, she having been the first that took any Notice of me; but they that had me, wou'd not part with me; and as for me, tho' I shou'd have been very well Treated with any of the other, yet I could not be better than where I was.

(15)

HERE I contin'd till I was between 18 Years old, and here I had all the Advantages for my Education that could be imagin'd; the Lady had Masters home to the House to teach her Daughters to Dance, and to speak *French,* and to Write, and others to teach them Musick; and as I was always with them, I learn'd as fast as they; and tho' the Masters were not appointed to teach me, yet I learn'd by Imitation and enquiry, all that they learn'd by Instruction and Direction. So that in short, I learn'd to Dance, and speak *French* as well as any of them, and to Sing much better, for I had a better Voice than any of them; I could not so readily come at playing on the Harpsicord or Spinnet, because I had no Instrument of my own to Practice on, and could only come at theirs in the intervals, when they left it, which was uncertain, but yet I learn'd tollerably well too, and the young Ladies at length got two Instruments, that is to say, a Harpsicord, and a Spinnet too, and then they Taught me themselves; But as to Dancing they could hardly help my learning Country Dances, because they always wanted me to make up even Number, and on the other Hand, they were as heartily willing to learn me every thing that they had been Taught themselves; as I could be to take the Learning.

BY this Means I had, as I have said above, all the Advantages of Education that I could have had, if I had been as much a Gentlewoman as they were, with whom I liv'd, and in some things, I had the Advantage of my Ladies, tho' they were my Superiors; but, they were all the Gifts of Nature, and which all their Fortunes could not furnish. First, I was apparently Handsomer than any.

HERE

Figure 5.2(a) Moll Flanders: extract from the first edition.

(12)

was all the Estate the little Gentlewoman had in the World; and when I ask'd the Daughter for it; she hust me, and told me, she had nothing to do with it.

IT was true the good poor Woman had told her Daughter of it, and that it lay in such a Place, that it was the Child's Money, and had call'd once or twice for me to give it me, but I was unhappily out of the way, and when I came back she was past being in a Condition to speak of it: However, the Daughter was so Honest afterwards, as to give it me, tho' at first she us'd me Cruely about it.

Now was I a poor Gentlewoman indeed, and I was just that very Night to be turn'd into the wide World; for the Daughter remov'd all the Goods, and I had not so much as a Lodging to go to, or a bit of Bread to Eat: But it seems some of the Neighbours took so much Compassion of me, as to acquaint the Lady in whose Family I had been; and immediately she sent her Maid to fetch me; and away I went with them Bag and Baggage, and with a glad Heart you may be sure: The fright of my Condition had made such an Impression upon me, that I did not want now to be a Gentlewoman, but was very willing to be a Servant, and that any kind of Servant they thought fit to have me be.

BUT my new generous Mistress had better Thoughts for me, I call her generous, for she exceeded the good Woman I was with before in every Thing, as in Estate; I say, in every Thing except Honesty; and for that, tho' this was a Lady almost Honest, yet I must not forget to say on all Occasions, that the first, tho' Poor, was as uprightly Honest as it was possible.

I was no sooner carried away as I have said by this good Gentlewoman, but the first Lady, that is

(13)

to say, the Mayoress that was, sent her Daughters to take care of me; and another Family which had taken Notice of me when I was the little Gentlewoman, sent for me after her, so that I was mightily made of; nay, and they were not a little Angry, especially the Mayoress, that her Friend had taken me away from her; for as she said, I was hers by Right, she having been the first that took any Notice of me; but they that had me, would not part with me; and as for me I could not be better than where I was.

HERE I continued till I was between 17 and 18 Years old, and here I had all the Advantages for my Education, that could be imagined; the Lady had Masters home to teach her Daughters to Dance, and to speak French, and to Write, and others to teach them Musick; and as I was always with them, I learn'd as fast as they; and tho' the Masters were not appointed to teach me, yet I learn'd by Imitation and Enquiry, all that they learn'd by Instruction and Direction. So that in short, I learned to Dance, and speak French as well any of them, and to Sing much better, for I had a better Voice than any of them; I could not so readily come at playing the Harpsicord or Spinnet, because I had no Instrument of my own to Practise on, and could only come at theirs in the intervals when they left it; but yet I learned tollerably well, and the young Ladies at length got two Instruments, that is to say, a Harpsicord and a Spinnet too, and then they Taught me themselves; but as to Dancing they could hardly help my learning Country Dances, because they always wanted me to make up even Number; and on the other Hand, they were as heartily willing to learn me every thing that they had been Taught themselves, as I could be to take the Learning.

BY

Figure 5.2(b) Moll Flanders: extract from the second edition.

HOW EDITORS PREPARE SCHOLARLY EDITIONS

Having considered some of the complicated textual problems thrown up by the examples we have just been looking at, I want now to take you through the traditional procedures followed by editors. These can be grouped under four main headings:

- *collation* of the relevant manuscript and/or printed texts of the work to be edited;

- *selection* of a 'copy-text' on which the edition will be based;

- *emendation* of the copy-text, and the provision of textual notes listing all significant emendations;

- *explanation* (in an introduction and explanatory notes to the text) of the circumstances of authorship, publication, distribution and reception of the text, in its own historical period and subsequently.

Collation of texts

From our consideration of passages from *Hamlet* and *Moll Flanders*, we have learned that the first thing scholarly editors have to do is collect together copies of all the texts that may reasonably be thought to have any authority in order to 'collate' them, that is, to analyse and compare them to identify variants between them. Often this will only involve texts written or published in the author's lifetime, but sometimes, as we have seen with the Shakespeare Folio, texts published after an author's death may also have to be considered. Another example of this is Samuel Richardson's famous novel *Pamela*, first published in 1740 (though dated on the title page 1741). Richardson had his own printing business, and not only printed his own novels but was continually revising them, so that there are changes in the text of nearly every edition published in his lifetime. Some important late changes, however, remained unpublished until they were incorporated in an edition of 1801, 40 years after Richardson's death in 1761. The changes in this posthumously published edition affect the presentation of the leading characters significantly. The actions of Pamela's master in trying to take advantage of his position of power to rape her now seem less reprehensible than they did in the first edition, while Pamela herself has become much more refined and lady-like and less like a young servant who would have been unfit to marry her master. (For an account of the textual history of *Pamela*, see Philip Gaskell, *From Writer to Reader: Studies in Editorial Method*, Oxford: Clarendon Press, 1978; rep. Winchester and New Castle, DE: St Paul's Bibliographies and Oak Knoll Press, 1999, pp. 63–79.)

Selection of a copy-text

The purpose of collation is to try to determine the relationship between a series of texts, and then to decide which one should be selected as the 'copy-text' upon which a scholarly edition can be based. The question of how to select copy-text is a highly contentious one, and has been much debated. There was a long-standing tradition that the last text to be published in an author's lifetime should be adopted as the text that would most faithfully represent his or her 'final' intentions for the work. This was challenged in a famous essay by W.W. Greg, 'The Rationale of Copy-Text', first published in *Studies in Bibliography*, 3 (1950–1), 19–36, where he drew a distinction between the 'substantives', that is the words of a text, and the 'accidentals' – the punctuation, spelling, capitalisation and such typographical matters as the use of italics. In the majority of cases, Greg argued, while an author may change words and whole passages in editions after the first, he or she is unlikely to scrutinise the accidentals in subsequent editions. In such cases, assuming that the manuscript has not survived and that there is no convincing evidence that the author substantially changed the punctuation and other accidentals in a later edition, the editor will usually choose as copy-text the first published edition, since it will transmit most accurately the accidentals of the manuscript from which it was set. There will almost certainly be errors in the first edition, but in the absence of other evidence to the contrary it must, according to Greg, be regarded 'within reason' as the basic authority because it represents more completely and reliably the writer's intentions.

Greg's editorial principles have been extremely influential, particularly through the work of the US scholar Fredson Bowers. Indeed what has come to be called the 'Greg–Bowers' approach to textual scholarship may be said to have dominated the practice of Anglo-American scholarly editing for most of the twentieth century. It would, however, be a mistake to regard it as an unquestioned orthodoxy. Scholars such as James Thorpe, Philip Gaskell and Thomas Tanselle have variously questioned and modified aspects of Greg's theory. More recently, as we shall see, the whole theoretical basis of the copy-text method of editing has been challenged.

Emendation of the copy-text

Having decided upon a copy-text, the editor will then 'emend' (alter) this in various ways. These emendations would include not only the correction of obvious errors, but could also include the restoration of words or passages omitted in the copy-text due to the intervention of a censor, or through a misreading by the printer, or for some other reason. They could also include changes to wording, or deletion or addition of words or whole passages, where such alterations seem likely to have been introduced or sanctioned by the author in later editions. This is what is known as an 'eclectic' approach to editing, where variant readings which seem likely to have authorial sanction are incorporated into the copy-text.

Sometimes emendations are made where the editor believes that what is written or printed in the copy-text is simply wrong, and cannot have been what the author intended. These are often described as 'conjectural emenda-tions', in the sense that they have no *textual* authority, but are made on the authority of the editor alone. The most famous conjectural emendation is probably the one made to the text of *Henry V* (at Act 2, scene 3, line 15) by an eighteenth-century editor of Shakespeare, Lewis Theobald. In the Folio text, where Mistress Quickly is reporting Falstaff's death, her speech includes some words that make no sense at all: 'and a Table of green fields'. Theobald's inspired conjecture was that what Shakespeare must have written (or intended to write) was 'and 'a babbled of green fields'. This reading has been adopted in virtually every subsequent edition of the play, and is usually explained as the dying Falstaff reciting words from Psalm 23:2.

A third important way in which editors emend the copy-text is by altering the punctuation. There is a particular problem here, because it is often difficult to know what an author's intentions in the matter of punctuation may have been. Often, for example, authors *expected* their manuscripts to be provided with punctuation by the printer, and indeed may be said to have intended this to happen. In other cases authors may have had very definite ideas about punctu-ation, but a publisher's house style has been applied in contravention of autho-rial wishes. An example of this is D.H. Lawrence's novel *Sons and Lovers*, where the first edition of 1913 made thousands of changes to Lawrence's punc-tuation, often to deleterious effect (see further Helen Baron, 'Some Theoret-ical Issues Raised by Editing *Sons and Lovers*', in *Editing D.H. Lawrence: New Versions of a Modern Author*, ed. Charles L. Ross and Dennis Jackson, Ann Arbor: University of Michigan Press, 1995, pp. 59–77).

Explanation of the text

An edition produced in the way I have been describing is called a 'critical' edition, which is to say that every word and 'accidental' of the text has been examined critically by the editor, who may have altered certain readings in the copy-text after a considered assessment of all the available evidence. A critical edition will always include a textual introduction (or 'Note on the Text'), which will describe all the texts that have textual authority or significance, indicate the reasons for the choice of copy-text, and point out the nature and scope of the editor's emendation of the copy-text. Also included will be an amount of textual apparatus. This will vary between editions, but usually it will at least record all significant emendations to the copy-text, and it will often list all significant variant readings in texts which carry textual authority. Such apparatus may be presented at the foot of the page, or gathered together at the back of the book, but the purpose of recording it is to provide the information necessary to enable the reader to evaluate and reconsider the textual decisions made by the editor.

In addition to the provision of textual information, the editor will usually provide an introduction to the work being edited and such explanatory annotation as seems appropriate. The introduction should give an account of the historical circumstances of production of the text, including discussion not only of the author who generated it, but of the role of others who may have contributed to its genesis. There should also be an account of the process of publication and subsequent dissemination of the work (who published it; in what form(s); for what kinds of readers, etc.) and of significant aspects of its reception by readers. Explanatory notes are provided to help readers in understanding matters such as the meaning of words that may have become obsolete, and a whole variety of references in the text to historical figures, literary allusions and matters to do with politics, law, religion, social customs, geography, technical terms, etc., etc.

'INTENTIONALIST' AND 'SOCIAL PROCESS' THEORIES OF EDITING

Up to now, what I have presented is the approach to editing that textual scholars have been taking for centuries. The basic premise from which they worked was that an edition of an author's work should fulfil as far as possible his or her intentions, which was usually taken to mean final intentions. Editors might have argued among themselves about what to do when it seemed that authors had substantially changed their intentions over time (as in the case of Richardson), but it was accepted by all that the aim was to establish texts as intended by their authors. Where the surviving versions of the text were faulty or incomplete, it was the duty of editors to attempt to reconstruct what the author might plausibly be assumed to have intended.

The issue of authorial intention has been a vexed and much-disputed one, and indeed the problem of intentionality has been at the heart of much of the recent debate about textual editing. You will find a useful outline of the various opposing points of view in D.C. Greetham, *Textual Scholarship: An Introduction* (New York and London: Garland, 1994, pp. 335–46, 352–7). It is certainly true that the authors of some literary works have changed their 'intentions' so radically over time that these works do not seem to be amenable to an approach aiming at a single text. We have already seen the problems in establishing a single text of *Hamlet*, and this is by no means a lone example from Shakespeare. *King Lear* exists in two printed texts, a quarto of 1608 and the folio of 1623. These are very different from each other. The quarto contains about 300 lines that do not appear in the folio, while the folio has about 100 lines in short passages that are not in the quarto, and in the lines that are common to both there are over 1,000 verbal variants. In the past the two texts were conflated, but, as in the case of *Hamlet*, modern scholars now argue that the folio text represents Shakespeare's later revisions, and constitutes as such a quite different 'version' of *King Lear*. The situation where a literary work exists in multiple versions is not at all uncommon. There are three distinct versions of the fourteenth-century allegorical poem *Piers Plowman*; two of Sir Philip Sidney's prose romance *The Arcadia*; two of Alexander Pope's poem *The Rape of the Lock*; and three of Wordsworth's poem *The Prelude*.

In recent years, a number of textual scholars have begun to question in a more general fashion the emphasis on the intentions of a single author. Two of the scholars most prominently associated with this 'revisionist' school of thought are D.F. McKenzie, especially in his *Bibliography and the Sociology of Texts* (London: British Library, 1986; rep. Cambridge: Cambridge University Press, 1999), and Jerome J. McGann, especially in *A Critique of Modern Textual Criticism* (Chicago: University of Chicago Press, 1983; reprinted Charlottesville: University Press of Virginia, 1992). Literary works, according to McKenzie and McGann and their followers, are not solely the productions of individual 'authors': they are presented to readers as a result of the efforts of a large number of people – copyists, copy-editors, book designers, illustrators, printers, publishers, etc. – all of whom may in various ways make alterations to the text. What they term a 'social' process continues as new and different forms of a work appear, handled by different publishers and read in various forms by successive generations of readers. They emphasise particularly the extent to which the physical format of texts plays a part in the construction of meaning. For McKenzie, 'the book itself is an expressive means' ('Typography and Meaning: the Case of William Congreve', in *Buch und Buchhandel in Europa im achtzehnten Jahrhundert*, ed. Giles Barber and Bernhard Fabian, Hamburg: Hauswedell, 1981, pp. 81–125). In McGann's view, editors need to pay attention not only to the 'linguistic codes' (that is, the words, punctuation, etc.), but also to the 'bibliographical codes', by which he means the format, typography, layout, paper, circumstances of publication, etc. (see *The Textual Condition*, Princeton: Princeton University Press, 1991, p. 77). All this has called into question the 'Greg–Bowers' assumption that the goal of scholarly editing is the production of a single, 'eclectic' edition, in which certain readings are 'privileged' by being incorporated into the 'definitive' reading text, while others are relegated to the textual apparatus as 'variants'.

This attempt to shift the focus of editing away from an emphasis on individual authors, and single 'canonical' works, may also be seen to relate to larger developments in literary theory, for example the idea that texts are fundamentally unstable – that they are processes rather than fixed, single objects. To regard texts in this way must obviously have large consequences for the presentation of scholarly editions. A number of scholars have begun to explore the potential for electronic editions, which would allow a reader interactive access to all the variant states of a given text, and associated materials for its study. Several such 'hypertext' projects are under way, and there is no doubt that they will make an enormous amount of data available to readers. For example, an edition of Chaucer's *Canterbury Tales*, being published as a series of CD-ROMs, will include digitised images and transcriptions of all 84 known manuscripts and the four pre-1500 printed editions of the work – some six million words and 30,000 manuscript pages. As the editor explains, 'the balance of power in editing has shifted from presenting the text as a single editorial artefact, to presenting the text as a series of manuscript objects' (Peter M.C. Robinson, 'Manuscript Politics', in *The Politics of the Electronic Text*, ed. Warren Chernaik, Caroline Davis and Marilyn Deegan, Oxford: Office for Humanities Communication, 1993, pp. 9–15. For further details see www.canterburytalesproject.org/index.html). Such 'editions' open up dizzying vistas of readerly freedom where, apparently, each reader can become a do-it-yourself editor. This, at least, is the argument of one enthusiast, who claims that, because of its interactive nature, hypertext may be said to empower the reader: 'the reader calls forth his or her own text out of the network, and each such text belongs to one reader and one particular act of reading' (Jay David Bolter, *Writing Space: The Computer, Hypertext, and the History of Writing*, Hillsdale: Lawrence Erlbaum Associates, 1991, quoted in *The Politics of the Electronic Text*, p. 6).

The case in favour of what he has termed 'hypermedia archives' has been put strongly by McGann. In an important essay entitled 'The Rationale of Hypertext' (in *Electronic Text*, ed. Kathryn Sutherland, Oxford: Clarendon Press, 1997, pp. 19–46), he argues that the shift now taking place from paper-based text to electronic text will come to be seen as a revolution comparable to the shift from manuscript to print. In his view, the physical constraints of printed scholarly editions have meant that the works of many authors have been represented very inadequately. He discusses the examples of Robert Burns, William Blake, Emily Dickinson and Laetitia Elizabeth Landon as authors who operated in more than one medium, and whose artistic achievements are fundamentally misrepresented in traditional typographical editions. The article also includes illustrations drawn from his own ambitious project, *The Complete Writings and Pictures of Dante Gabriel Rossetti: A Hypermedia Research Archive*. This is designed to bring together digital images of manuscripts, printed texts, sketches, oil paintings and other documents in a decentralised 'hypertext' structure, in which no part is privileged over another, and the reader is encouraged to make order, rather than find order (see www.iath.virginia.edu/rossetti/fullarch.html).

In a useful book discussing the potential gains and losses of a move to electronic editions of literary texts (*From Gutenburg to Google: Electronic Representations of Literary Texts*, Cambridge: Cambridge University Press, 2006), Peter L. Shillingsburg suggests that we should think of these as 'knowledge sites' as opposed to archives or editions. They would be the work of whole teams of scholars, built to outlive their originators and be capable of continuous development and open to many different modes of use. They would be composed of what Shillingsburg terms 'textual foundations' (digitised images and transcriptions of all relevant documents, with full bibliographical and textual analysis of these); 'contexts and progressions' (a whole range of biographical and historical information, explanatory annotation, links to sources, analogues, etc., and detailed linguistic and stylistic analysis); 'interpretive interactions' (the history of reception and adaptation of the work); and 'user enhancements' (allowing readers to mark up, emend, add information, notes, etc.).

It is perhaps easy to be swept away by euphoria when contemplating the arrival of electronic texts. There is no doubt that being able to store and manipulate texts in electronic form means that the laborious task of collating texts can be made easier and quicker. It is also true that electronic editions (or 'hypertext archives' or 'knowledge sites') will make it possible for readers to refer quickly and easily to a mass of information, and, potentially, not just to one edited version of a work, but to a whole series of edited versions attempting to represent authorial intentions at various stages of a work's production. Whether this will change fundamentally the ways in which editions of literary works are published and read is another matter. For all the limitations of the print medium, the great critical editions are some of the most distinguished achievements of literary scholarship. It remains to be seen just how useful (or usable) the new electronic editions will prove to be, and whether they spell the end of the printed codex edition. What they certainly will not do is change fundamentally the work of scholarly editors. As G. Thomas Tanselle has wisely remarked, they will not alter

> the questions we must ask about texts or guarantee a greater amount of intelligent reading and textual study. We will be spared some drudgery and inconvenience, but we still have to confront the same issues that editors have struggled with for twenty-five hundred years.
>
> ('Foreword' to the 'Text Encoding Initiative', at www.tei-c.org/ About/Archive_new/ETE/Preview/tanselle.xml)

QUESTIONS AND EXERCISES

1   Choose one literary work and illustrate with examples what a study of its textual history might tell us.

2   'A correct text is the first object of an editor' (Wordsworth). Using a work (or works) by one author as an example, discuss some of the problems an editor may face in attempting to produce a 'correct' text.

3   Give an account of recent debates among textual scholars about the concept of authorial intentions.

4   Choose one literary work and compare several available editions (if possible including a full-scale scholarly one), discussing how they differ.

5   Take a look at Jerome McGann's editorial work on Dante Gabriel Rossetti at www. iath.virginia.edu/rossetti/fullarch.html. How effective is it in presenting a scholarly edition of Rossetti's works? Are there any drawbacks to such electronic editions as far as the editor or his or her readers are concerned?

SELECTED READING

Fredson Bowers, *Bibliography and Textual Criticism* (Oxford: Clarendon Press, 1964).
Fredson Bowers, *Essays in Bibliography, Text and Editing* (Charlottesville: University Press of Virginia, 1975).
John Bryant, *The Fluid Text: A Theory of Revision and Editing for Book and Screen* (Ann Arbor: University of Michigan Press, 2002).
Philip Cohen (ed.), *Devils and Angels: Textual Editing and Literary Theory* (Charlottesville and London: University Press of Virginia, 1991).
Philip Gaskell, *From Writer to Reader* (Oxford: Clarendon Press, 1978).
D.C. Greetham, *Textual Scholarship: An Introduction* (New York and London: Garland, 1994).
Michael Hunter, *Editing Early Modern Texts: An Introduction to Principles and Practice* (Basingstoke: Palgrave Macmillan, 2007).
Jerome J. McGann, *A Critique of Modern Textual Criticism* (Chicago and London: University of Chicago Press, 1983).
Jerome J. McGann (ed.), *Textual Criticism and Literary Interpretation* (Chicago and London: University of Chicago Press, 1985).
Jerome J. McGann, *The Textual Condition* (Princeton: Princeton University Press, 1991).
D.F. McKenzie, *Bibliography and the Sociology of Texts*, The Panizzi Lectures (London: The British Library, 1986; reprinted Cambridge: Cambridge University Press, 1999).
Peter L. Shillingsburg, *Scholarly Editing in the Computer Age* (Athens and London: University of Georgia Press, 1986).
Peter L. Shillingsburg, *Resisting Texts: Authority and Submission in Construction of Meaning* (Ann Arbor: University of Michigan Press, 1997).
Peter L. Shillingsburg, *From Gutenburg to Google: Electronic Representations of Literary Texts* (Cambridge: Cambridge University Press, 2006).

Ian Small and Marcus Walsh (eds), *The Theory and Practice of Text-Editing* (Cambridge: Cambridge University Press, 1991).

Kathryn Sutherland (ed.), *Electronic Text: Investigations in Method and Theory* (Oxford: Clarendon Press, 1997).

G. Thomas Tanselle, *A Rationale of Textual Criticism* (Philadelphia: Pennsylvania University Press, 1989).

G. Thomas Tanselle, 'Textual Criticism and Literary Sociology', *Studies in Bibliography*, 44 (1991), 83–143. Other essays published by Tanselle in *Studies in Bibliography* have been collected in a series of volumes published by the University Press of Virginia: *Selected Studies in Bibliography* (1979); *Textual Criticism since Greg* (1987); *Textual Criticism and Scholarly Editing* (1990); and *Literature and Artifacts* (1998).

James Thorpe, *Principles of Textual Criticism* (San Marino: The Huntington Library, 1972).

Part 3
Issues and approaches in literary research

Institutional histories of literary disciplines

The place of theory in literary disciplines

Literary research and interdisciplinarity

Literary research and other media

Literary research and translation

6

Institutional histories of literary disciplines

Suman Gupta

To engage with a research project in any discipline in a university is to work in relation to an institutionalised space. Master's or PhD dissertations by graduate students or scholarly publications by academics in the discipline of English Literature or Comparative Literature, despite differences in expectations, have the following institutional considerations in common: first, they are produced in the context of the practices of that discipline; and second, they address an area of knowledge that is pertinent to that discipline. Researchers usually, and necessarily, focus their investigations fairly narrowly in undertaking such research – on specific texts and contexts, particular issues and themes. The research focus is usually delimited in advance by a process of identifying a title, preparing a proposal and chapter plan, getting acquainted with extant research in the area, identifying a suitable methodology. These take up a great deal of time and energy, and consequently the institutional aspects of doing research are usually engaged only tacitly in that process, as operational but not necessarily requiring considered thought or conscious effort. However, researchers are inevitably aware that doing research involves institutional considerations, even if those are not explicitly addressed. The latter extend across various levels, with regard to the programmes and facilities of the specific department/faculty/ university in question; the broad academic set up at national and international levels; the particular practices and expectations that delineate disciplines of knowledge (Literature, History, Geography and so on) at various levels (within universities, in publishing, media, policy-making and resourcing bodies, etc.); and, at the broadest level, the conventions of academic discourse in texts and discursive forums.

Since this Handbook is addressed to those who are, so to speak, entering the business of research and trying to locate themselves and their efforts, this chapter and the next are structured around a historical tracing: the idea is to clarify where the discipline is now in terms of what has happened before.

Accordingly, this chapter picks up the institutional practices (the professions) of English and of Comparative Literature. In a related fashion, the next chapter addresses the institutionally accepted coverage of these disciplinary spaces by tracing a historical account of literary theory (especially Theory with a capital T) – that which is most closely concerned with understanding and testing the scope and relevance of these disciplinary spaces. In both instances the historical trace is a limited one, largely confined to the later twentieth and early twenty-first centuries – to the point where we are now. And in both it will be found that attempting to focus on disciplinary precincts is actually as much an exercise in straying from them.

In moving on to the specific concerns of this chapter – the history of the disciplinary spaces of English and Comparative Literature – a caveat needs to be foregrounded. It is necessary to keep in mind that there is no *one* disciplinary history for English or Comparative Literature. There is, in fact, a multiplicity of histories of the discipline of English Literature in various locations which do not cohere comfortably, and to track all of which would occupy numerous volumes. And Comparative Literature is, by definition, a multicontextual and multicultural and multilingual plethora. A single chronological tracking of institutional disciplinary developments conveys very little of the field in question here. The recourse taken in this chapter, therefore, is to not try and narrate a history of these disciplines. Instead somewhat different strategies are assumed for the two disciplinary spaces respectively: for English Studies existing histories of the discipline in different contexts (UK, USA, postcolonial countries, further afield) are discussed briefly, while for Comparative Literature perceptions of disciplinary crises in the Anglo-American context over a period are noted.

ENGLISH LITERATURE

To designate an institutional space in the academy as distinctively English Literature is to be rather fussily particular. From its philological origins and as a discipline that gradually displaced the classics, English Literature has more often been contained within a broader 'English' (incorporating literature, language, initially history, and more recently cultural studies). The discipline's nomenclature itself has a complex history, and the accruals and indeterminacies of that history are still marked in the names of departments devoted to the discipline. According to Brian Doyle in *English and Englishness* (London: Routledge, 1989), the ideological nuances of naming the discipline were more or less lastingly negotiated between the 1880s and 1920s, when proponents sought to consolidate the value of English studies and their professional status in colleges and universities:

The history of the transition from 'English Language and Literature', 'English and History' and 'English subjects' to the simple and all-embracing generic term 'English' is the history of a complex process of cultural extension and elevation. 'English' came to extend its range of operations beyond any disciplinary boundaries to encompass all mental, imaginative, and spiritual faculties.... English was elevated through being imbued with the kind of cultural authority previously invested in classics, but now with the addition of a powerful national dimension that yet somehow transcended nationality.

(pp. 26–7)

Despite attempts at questioning these political imperatives by renaming the institutional space of the discipline (the university department) since the 1970s, by and large simply 'English' has stuck – and its predominant focus has largely remained literature, with language and increasingly cultural studies and sometimes creative writing alongside.

Even as superficial a matter as the naming of the discipline is redolent with ideological nuances, which a historical perspective of the discipline almost inevitably confronts. In fact, the history of the discipline in all its dimensions is an intensely politicised matter, and this has meant that attempts to historicise it – to understand the discipline through a historical narrative – have themselves been ideologically loaded political interventions whenever they have appeared. It is clear from the quotation above that the historical politics of naming the discipline exists in a tension with Doyle's politics in talking about it as historian of the discipline. Our sense of the discipline is constructed at the conjunction of what we know of the past of the discipline and the manner in which we recall it in the present.

A relatively early post-Second World War attempt to historicise the institutional development of the discipline of English in the UK is D.J. Palmer's *The Rise of English Studies* (London: Oxford University Press, 1965), which came from what was then the liberal-left of the ideological spectrum. This traced the history of English Studies from its Utilitarian and Evangelical inspirations, the establishment of the first departments and chairs at University College (in 1928) and King's College (1931), London, the provision of lectures in English literature at Mechanics' Institutes (beginning with London in 1823) and through extension lecture programmes, and covers the contentious formation of the English School at the University of Oxford in 1894. His exploration of the working-class affiliations of the discipline's origins in the nineteenth century were no doubt directed against the bourgeois establishment within which the discipline seemed to have been ensconced since the Second World War. Looking back on English Studies' institutional history was effectively an act of retrieving an early investment in working-class interests:

However inadequately it was articulated, there was a widespread feeling [in
the nineteenth century] that the spiritual and physical conditions of the
industrial revolution impoverished the cultural lives of a large class of
people, that they had been cut off from their traditional past, and that
therefore they needed to be given new means of establishing connections
with a national cultural heritage. Thus it was the historical attitude to
literature which eventually emerged, and the missionaries of adult education
were particularly concerned with the working classes.

(pp. 39–40)

English Studies' subsequent rise into academia was also presented as a move
away from those marginal origins, ending in the stronghold of the academic
establishment with the founding of the Oxford English School. Palmer's sense
of the marginal origins and subsequent incorporation of the discipline into the
mainstream, gave the enterprise of historicising the institutional space of the
discipline itself a certain contemporary political impetus.

In the UK thereafter the relationship between margin and centre as shadowed
in the history of English has been regularly reiterated, with further marginal
factors being introduced and analytically located. Thus, Chris Baldick's *The
Social Mission of English Criticism, 1848–1932* (Oxford: Clarendon, 1983) noted
the marginal areas that originally brought the discipline of English Studies
into institutional being:

These are first, the specific needs of the British empire expressed in the
regulations for admission to the India Civil Service; second, the various
movements for adult education including Mechanic's Institutes and Working
Men's Colleges, and extension lecturing; third, within this general
movement, the special provisions made for women's education.

(p. 61)

and then proceeded to examine English's institutional embracing of conservative values through such canonised representatives of 'Englishness' as Arnold,
Eliot, Richards and the Leavises. Along the way he touched particularly on
the civilising mission of English in the Indian Civil Services Exam following
the 1853 India Act, made the connection from there to the Oxford School
through the first Merton Professor of English Literature, Walter A. Raleigh
(appointed in 1914), covered the establishment of an English Faculty at the
University of Cambridge in 1919 and discussed the contribution of I.A. Richards and F.R. and Q.D. Leavis to the formation of the discipline thereafter.
Brian Doyle's *English and Englishness* (London: Routledge, 1989) offered a more
up-to-date examination of those marginal origins and particularly the dominant ideology of the prevailing establishment of English. Of particular interest

was his discussion of the manner in which the initial amateur feminine character of the discipline was gradually masculinised and professionalised between the World Wars. Also of interest were his clarification of the role of British state policy (starting from the formation of the English Association in 1907 and the report by its chairman on the state of English, the Newbolt Report, of 1921), and discussion of developments after the Second World War in other (not Oxbridge) British universities till the 1970s. By way of tracing the margin–centre confrontations in the discipline's institutional history, John Dixon's *A Schooling in 'English'* (Buckingham: Open University Press, 1991) focused on three phases: English's emergence through extension lectures and programmes from 1867 to 1892; English at the University of Cambridge between the wars (1919–29); and the incorporation of Cultural Studies in or alongside English, encouraged by the popularity of mass media and international political movements, between 1960 and 1979. Robert Crawford's *Devolving English Literature* (Oxford: Clarendon, 1992) marked a definite step forward in dislocating the historical narrative of the discipline from its English centre – thus both performing and documenting a reorientation of the margin–centre structure in that history. He set out to 'force 'English' to take account of other cultures which are in part responsible for the initial construction of 'English literature' as a subject' (p. 11), and made the case for the Scottish and provincial English invention of English literature and then the Scottish invention of Scottish literature. He traced the former to Adam Smith's teaching of a course of Rhetoric and Belles Lettres at the University of Glasgow in 1751, and charted the development of British literature, interest in American literature, a distinctive Scottish literature and literary modernism itself by Scottish and provincial English littérateurs and scholars.

Behind the intense 1980s and early 1990s period of historicising the discipline in the UK lay the impetus of Theory (with the capital T) on the humanities and literary studies generally, and particularly on English, from, roughly, the 1970s onwards. The institutionalisation of Theory in literary studies is discussed in the next chapter, and a clear relationship between that process and the process of contemplating centres and margins in disciplinary histories traced here will be observed. The impact of Theory was, however, more or less silently in the background in the UK-based histories of the discipline, whereas similar attempts in the USA were more explicitly responsive to Theory. In the USA, attempts at narrating the institutional history of English (not American Studies) took off with the radical argument in Richard Ohmann's *English in America* (New York: Oxford University Press, 1976):

> The humanities are not an agent, but an instrument.... There is no sense in pondering the function of literature without relating it to the actual society

> that uses it, to the centers of power within that society, and to the
> institutions that mediate between literature and the people.

(p. 303)

This involved a critique of the post-Second World War bourgeois culture within which the profession was then described, and which enabled a superficial discourse of freedom to contain the study of English within an elitist and carefully depoliticised professional space. With the establishment-friendly attitude of the academic profession during the anti-Vietnam War protests in mind, Ohmann looked back to the history of English in the USA, and traced the entrenchment of a conservative ideology in the discipline through a range of institutional alignments (the Modern Language Association since its formation in 1883, the Advance Placements and College Board, appointments policy) and through debates underlying the structuring of freshman writing courses in rhetoric (starting from the establishment of the Boylston Professorship in Rhetoric and Oratory at Harvard in 1803).

Taking some of this argument forward, but disinvesting it from radical outcomes, Gerald Graff's *Professing Literature* (Chicago: University of Chicago Press, 1987) looked to the humanistic tradition in the academic discipline of English (and American) literature as a matter of continuities which are more replicated in the present than radically inverted or subverted. He traced the development of institutional spaces for English and American literature in a range of US universities, marking phases and outlining the debates and fissures in each. His account started with the Yale Report of 1828 which resolved to continue focusing on classical education rather than vernaculars, and described how English consisted primarily in the study of rhetoric and oratory till the 1860s, took a more professional turn along the lines of the German philological model from the 1870s, shifted to an emphasis on literature in 1890s, went into a sort of backward-looking limbo in the early decades of the twentieth century, came to be structured around New Humanism in the 1920s, and accommodated the rise and fall of New Criticism from the 1930s to the 1960s. Graff also described the impetus given by 'wartime superpatriotism' after the First World War to the somewhat distinct space for American Literature. With this historical institutional perspective in view, Graff suggested that instead of leading to ever-sharper ideological divides the rise of Theory should encourage the discipline to become more inclusive of different positions – and thereby more professional. Somewhat later, Robert Scholes's *The Rise and Fall of English* (New Haven: Yale University Press, 1998) juxtaposed a quickly sketched out history of the discipline in the USA, focusing particularly on Yale from the eighteenth century, and his personal encounters with contemporary theory (and Theory) since the mid twentieth century. This was by way of demonstrating that English had 'risen' from oratory to a somewhat sacralised inculcation of liberal values through literature in the course of the nineteenth century, and in that sense the discipline has been 'falling' in the late twentieth century since that sense of values has been undermined by Theory. Scholes's remedy for English was to propose a return 'to the roots of our liberal arts tradition, and reinstate grammar, dialectics and rhetoric at the core of college education' (p. 120).

It would appear that, while the path of historicisation tracked from Palmer to Crawford in the UK moved increasingly towards a need to decentre the discipline, that from Ohmann to Scholes moved towards recentring it. This is, however, somewhat misleading. In the USA the tide of Theory and its political aspirations were considerably more powerfully felt and vociferously debated than in the UK (which might explain the responsive difference) and, besides, much of the drive towards decentring and change in the USA was attached to the more immediately relevant American Studies and American Literature – by this stage, at least in the USA, an established disciplinary field that is quite separate from English.

The tendencies marked in the disciplinary histories of English above naturally extended further afield. As observed already, such histories had been structured carefully around negotiations between margins and centres, and with implicit political impetuses throughout – a desire to make the discipline politically efficacious. These histories were also political interventions in the current state of the discipline, made either by appealing to or descrying past institutional aspirations. Debates about Theory in the course of the 1980s both actuated and complicated these interventions. In particular, the growing popularity and institutional inculcation of postcolonial literature and theory (also discussed in the next chapter) brought about a heightened sensitivity to the geopolitics of the discipline, and gave the matter of margins and centres a clearly articulated geopolitical nuance. This was available to some extent in Crawford's decentering of the history of English, and unsurprisingly other decentred histories of the disciplines in postcolonial contexts were already being explored. The Indian connection in the development of the discipline had been picked up by Palmer and explored briefly by Baldick. Gauri Viswanathan's *Masks of Conquest* (London: Faber and Faber, 1989) went back to the nineteenth-century debate between Orientalist and Anglicist educationalists in India to present the institutional placement of English as caught between the contrary logics of colonial assimilation and imperial cultural hegemony. Viswanathan traced the antecedents of the debate in 1835 when the Anglicists got the upper hand – the year of both Thomas Macaulay's famous 'Minute on Indian Education' and Governor-General William Bentinck's English Education Act – and the aftermath. She outlined how the Evangelical and

Utilitarian arguments that Palmer had discerned in England played out in India, and discussed the changing rationale of English as it entered the Indian university system when it came to be instituted in 1857. Viswanathan's work was a self-conscious intervention in the institutional present of the discipline:

> When, in our times, students and faculty clamour for a broadening of curriculum to include submerged texts of minority and third world cultures, the knowledge that the discipline of English developed in colonial times would appear likely to strengthen their claims and force their opponents to reconsider the premises of the traditional Eurocentric curriculum.
>
> (pp. 166–7)

Another example of a tracing of the history of the discipline in a postcolonial context is available in David Johnson's *Shakespeare and South Africa* (Oxford: Clarendon, 1996). This charted the development of English in South Africa from 1800 to the 1990s, by focusing not merely on the institutional space of the discipline in the tertiary-education sector but also in scholarship and schooling. Johnson traced the threads of these interlinked aspects of the discipline by following the manner in which Shakespeare has been received and instrumentalised for ideological ends – imperialist and racist – in different phases of South African history. In the course of narrating what is effectively a history of the discipline of English in South Africa, a case was made for embracing the radical turn of Theory with regard to that context.

There have been a host of books which chart in different ways the histories and institutional politics of English: Patrick Hogan's *The Politics of Interpretation* (New York: Oxford University Press, 1990); Carl Woodring's *Literature* (New York: Columbia University Press, 1990); Harold Fromm's *Academic Capitalism and Literary Value* (Athens: University of Georgia Press, 1991); Sandra Gubar and Jonathan Kamholtz's edited volume *English Inside and Out* (New York: Routledge, 1993); Josephine Guy and Ian Small's *Politics and Value in English Studies* (Cambridge: Cambridge University Press, 1993); Robert Heilman's *The Professor and the Profession* (Columbia: University of Mississippi Press, 1999); Donald Hall's edited volume *Professions* (Urbana: University of Illinois Press, 2001); Jeffrey Williams's edited volume *The Institution of Literature* (Albany: State University of New York Press, 2002); and Philip W. Martin's edited *English* (Basingstoke: Palgrave, 2006), come to mind. Arguably, however, these and the other works referred to above still enable but a limited sense of the histories of English as an academic discipline. These historical accounts of the discipline are overwhelmingly Anglocentric – they are premised on the assumption that the discipline is centred in contexts which are ordinarily Anglophone, either in the sense of having English as a native language (particularly UK, Ireland, USA) or as a language of everyday use among others (postcolonial contexts such as India, South Africa, Nigeria, Kenya). It is now widely recognised that the English language is well on its way to becoming a global lingua franca. An unprecedented quarter of the world's population, widely dispersed, use the English language, and useful models for understanding this spread in sociolinguistic terms are in place. There are obvious geopolitical reasons for this spread – as David Crystal puts it:

> British political imperialism had sent English around the globe, during the nineteenth century, so that it was a language 'on which the sun never sets'. During the twentieth century, this world presence was maintained and promoted almost single-handedly through the economic supremacy of the new American superpower.
>
> (*English as a Global Language*, Cambridge: Cambridge University Press, 2003, p. 10)

And there is no doubt that if a conventional productive view of literature and culture (i.e. a view that is focused on authors and cultural producers) is eschewed in favour of a more open receptive and circulatory view (i.e. tracing ways in which texts and cultural products are received and circulated in different linguistic and cultural contexts), the global spread of English would be seen to encompass not just currents within the language but also in literature and culture – not least in how the discipline of English is constituted at an institutional level. It seems likely that the discipline should increasingly be thought of and reoriented not as centred in Anglophoneness, but as emanant from an interlingual field, where receptions and translations and cultural cross-fertilisations are more the norm than otherwise.

The fact is that English Studies, in the broad sense of attending to the English language and Anglophone literature and culture, has been ensconced as an academic discipline in ordinarily non-Anglophone contexts for a while and is increasingly becoming more so. In some non-Anglophone contexts – as, for example, Germany, the Netherlands, France, Norway – it has been pursued in higher education and scholarship for almost as long as in the UK or USA. In others it has been introduced relatively recently and has grown enormously in a relatively short time. In Arabophone-Francophone Morocco, for instance, though introduced only in the 1960s English is now one of the highest recruiting subjects in the Humanities in most universities. A historical perspective on the institutional discipline of English needs to extend beyond the Anglocentrism it still maintains – certainly within the dominant (in this context) Anglophone academy – and take account of the disciplinary spaces in ordinarily non-Anglophone contexts. In doing so systematically it is likely to be found that the dominant narrative of the institutional history of English outlined above needs to be comprehensively reconsidered. This is, as yet, a sadly neglected area in English scholarly works. A useful contribution, focusing on the development of English Studies in a range of continental European countries, is Balz Engler and Renate Haas's edited volume *European English Studies* (Leicester: The English Association, 2000). This has contributions by historians of the discipline from Portugal, Spain, Italy, France, Netherlands, Norway, Denmark, Austria, Poland, Czech Republic, Slovakia, Slovenia, Serbia, Romania, Bulgaria and Germany. German 'Anglistics', in particular, had a noteworthy role in defining the discipline in its initial phases not just in continental Europe but in the USA too. The many fascinating insights to be found in this volume cannot be usefully summarised in a short space, but in terms of the preceding observations, it is striking that these histories seldom subscribe to the structuring devices noted above. The development of the discipline in these countries is not along the lines of margins and centres in terms of class/gender/race or urbanity/provinciality or coloniality/postcoloniality in the ways charted above. Nor are these as concerned immediately with the impact of Theory (and they have always had theory). In each of these countries the history of English Studies has a powerful autonomous internal dynamic, reflexive of the political and cultural environments therein, negotiating with and amid the study of other languages and literatures and cultures. Such histories can be written for contexts outside Europe too. A sort of mutual awareness and cultural affinity is only to be expected among European countries, but the fact is that English Studies has substantial histories well beyond. There are occasional indications that such histories are beginning to be researched and tracked. Bob Adamson's *China's English* (Hong Kong: Hong Kong University Press, 2004) makes a fascinating survey of the political impetuses underlying the curriculum and teaching of English at the junior secondary level in Chinese schools since 1949. The equivalent for English in China's higher education cannot be far behind, especially given the immense investment that the Chinese government has made in this area. Numerous other histories of English are waiting to be written, and when they are our view of the discipline will probably become quite different from what it is today.

COMPARATIVE LITERATURE

As noted in the introduction to this chapter, whereas the disciplinary history for English can be economically considered in terms of existing historical narratives, the disciplinary history of Comparative Literature needs a different strategy. Though as a designation for an area that can be institutionally structured the phrase is relatively recent – and is usually referred to H.M. Posnett's *Comparative Literature* (London: Kegan Paul,

Trench and Co., 1886) – the methods and practices circumscribed by it can be traced back to antiquity. Even in institutional terms, over the twentieth century the field has been dispersed across too wide a range of contexts to be historicised meaningfully in the space available here. In the context of this Handbook, concerned as it is with institutional disciplinary locations that inform scholarship in the present, a more delimited exercise makes sense: a brief charting of the manner in which proponents of the discipline have understood it and its institutional practices, primarily in the Anglo-American academy, since the 1960s.

Pedagogy or research in Comparative Literature in the Anglo-American academy at the turn of the 1950s would have been defined as the comparison of literary works from two or more national or linguistic traditions read in their original (almost exclusively European) languages. In relation to that view of the discipline, the thread here can be usefully picked up from René Wellek's well-known 1958 presentation at the Second Congress of the International Comparative Literature Association (ICLA): 'The Crisis of Comparative Literature' (published in *Comparative Literature 2*, ed. Warner P. Friedrich, Chapel Hill: University of North Carolina Press, 1959). This pondered the double-bind of the discipline at the time: on the one hand, in the post-Second World War context Comparative Literature was regarded 'as a reaction against narrow nationalism' (p. 153); but, on the other hand, Wellek felt its basis was and should remain comparison of 'national literatures'. The problem – and this is why he perceived a crisis – was that the basis of comparison in national terms allowed narrow nationalisms to reinsert themselves in insidious ways. The remedy Wellek recommended was to not dispense with the national basis of comparison, but to cultivate a distinctive understanding of literature as a medium which enables a humanistic apprehension of 'ideal universality', so that 'Man, Universal man, man everywhere and at any time, in all his variety, emerges and literary scholarship ceases to be an antiquarian pastime, a calculus of national credits and debts and even a mapping of networks of relationships' (p. 159). In brief, he recommended sticking with the national basis in the *comparative* of 'Comparative Literature', and asserting an approach to the literature of 'Comparative *Literature*' that is predeterminedly universalist. He enlarged on this position in responses to criticisms of the paper in the American Comparative Literature Association (ACLA) Meeting of 1965, and in his essay 'The Name and Nature of Comparative Literature' (in Wellek, *Discriminations*, New Haven: Yale University Press, 1970). He didn't feel that the national basis should be meddled with by such distracting notions as World Literature, or that his distinctive universalist vision should be questioned.

Wellek's understanding of literature was akin both to humanist liberal convictions and New Critical close reading that were popular in Anglo-American circles then. The most significant shift in the understanding of literature that took place from the 1970s was, as observed above and discussed in the next chapter, due to the advent of Theory. The impact of Theory in Comparative Literature wasn't particularly profound in the 1970s. Robert Clements's survey of the academic field of Comparative Literature in 1978 essentially stuck with national literatures as the basis of comparison, but registered Wellek's warning and the emergence of Theory in the five substantive approaches it identified for the discipline:

> the study of (1) themes/myths, (2) genre/forms, (3) movements/eras, (4) interrelations of literature with other arts and disciplines, and (5) the involvement of literature as illustrative of evolving literary theory and criticism. The reading of literature must be in the original language.
>
> (*Comparative Literature as Academic Discipline*, New York: Modern Languages Association of America, 1978, p. 36)

Not insignificantly, points (1) to (3) diverted attention away from territorial imperatives without undermining them, in line with Wellek's recommendation; and (5), and perhaps to some extent (4), seemed to recognise that literary theory and criticism are now separate from critical engagement with literature in the conventional fashion. This was pretty much in line with the ACLA Greene report on the state of the discipline of 1975 (published in *Comparative Literature in the Age of Multiculturalism*, ed. Charles Bernheimer, Baltimore: Johns Hopkins University Press, 1995, pp. 28–38).

In the course of the 1980s several important developments took place. Theory became institutionalised in literary studies, and disposed literature as a field of political awareness and agency – especially along the lines of identity politics and cultural materialism. The consequent reconfiguration of literary studies naturally had its effect on Comparative Literature, which had to move away from Wellek-like assumptions, and away from the national basis of comparison with a universalist vision of literature. One kind of response was to emphasise the formalist/thematic basis of comparison in a more provisional and open fashion than theretofore, and without making it conditional on national or cultural bases. This was exemplified in Earl Miner's *Comparative Poetics* (Princeton: Princeton University Press, 1990), which assumed a suitably tentative 'practical principle' of comparison, as follows:

> The practical principle holds that comparison is feasible when presumptively or formally identical topics, conditions, or elements are identified. Of course what is presumptively but not actually identical soon betrays difference. With tact and luck, however, we may find the difference just great enough

to provide interest, and the presumed identity just strong enough to keep
the comparison just.

(p. 22)

The 'practical principle' formed the basis of a study of certain Western and
Eastern texts. This East–West comparison was implicitly presented as a
particularly revealing exercise because of the perceived extent of cultural difference. An East–West comparison had sometimes been seen as a sticky
patch since the early twentieth century; with 1980s literary and political preoccupations in mind it was ploughed as fertile ground in Anglo-American
Comparative Literature – but the harvest was limited. This was because the
kind of linguistic competence required limited the field, especially given the
disciplinary insistence on working with original languages. Nevertheless the
possibilities of East–West comparison were attractive, not least because this
seemed a suitable field in view of Theory-informed aspirations and related
growth of interest in identity politics and postcolonialism. One of the consequences was reconsideration of the status of translations in the discipline.
A. Owen Aldrige, for instance, put up a spirited defence for the use of
translations in East–West Comparative Literature in *The Reemergence of
World Literature* (Newark: University of Delaware Press, 1986). Susan
Bassnett's *Comparative Literature* (Oxford: Blackwell, 1993) concluded a
survey of the field by recommending a move for the discipline towards Translation Studies. For Bassnett this recommendation was bolstered by a sense
that the discipline was in decline, due, among other factors, to the rise of
Theory.

The need to respond to the political impetus of Theory was keenly felt in the
early 1990s, and comparatists were particularly anxious about the implications.
Wlad Godzich's essay 'Emergent Literature and Comparative Literature' put in
a call to align the discipline with larger political trends of the time:

> I would like to put forward the following claim: the 'field' of Comparative
> Literature is field. In other words, I take it that, within the prevalent
> organisation of knowledge, it is incumbent upon comparatists to inquire into
> the relationship of culture to givenness, to its other.
>
> (*The Culture of Literacy*, Cambridge, MA: Harvard University
> Press, 1994, p. 284)

For Godzich this meant greater attention to what he called 'emergent literature', defined fairly neutrally as 'literatures that cannot be readily compre-
hended within the hegemonic view of literature that has been dominant
within the discipline' (p. 291). More circumspectly, but with not dissimilar

intentions, came Charles Bernheimer's 1993 report to the ACLA, with recommendations to expand Comparative Literature curricula to include 'ideological, cultural and institutional contexts as well as close analysis of rhetorical, prosodic and other formal features'; to mitigate 'old hostilities to translation' while accepting that 'knowledge of foreign languages remains fundamental'; and to play an 'active role in multicultural recontextualization of Anglo-American and European perspectives' (in *Comparative Literature in the Age of Multiculturalism*, ed. Bernheimer, pp. 42–6). Bernheimer's misgivings about this direction are documented in the discussion of this report that he edited shortly afterwards, as was the general anxiety about remaining institutionally valid and discrete as a discipline.

The anxiety about institutional validity came with good reason. The political thrust of Theory led to the emergence of subdisciplinary spaces akin to but departing from literary studies, and absorbing its energies, which took over some of the key markers of Comparative Literature. In the course of the 1980s and 1990s Cultural Studies began working across ethnic, linguistic and geopolitical boundaries not only with sociological methodologies, but also with close attention to texts (particularly mass media and new media texts) and with a particular awareness of the impact of Theory on literary studies. One of the responses to the Bernheimer report was Rey Chow's paper, 'In the Name of Comparative Literature', which found little to distinguish the ambitions of Comparative Literature as set out in the report from Cultural Studies as it was already being conducted, and suggested that 'instead of simply resisting or discrediting cultural studies ... comparative literature could borrow from cultural studies by way of opening itself to the study of media other than word-based literature' (in *Comparative Literature in the Age of Multiculturalism*, ed. Bernheimer, p. 115). Steven Tötösy de Zepetnek's edited volume, *Comparative Literature and Comparative Cultural Studies* (West Lafayette: Purdue University Press, 2003) presented several papers trying to give content to a rapprochement between Cultural Studies and Comparative Literature, notably in the editor's own contribution, which recommended a merged field of 'comparative cultural studies' (pp. 259–62). Perhaps more than Cultural Studies however, the prerogatives of Comparative Literature began slipping into subdisciplinary spaces *within* the literary studies that were previously devoted to canonical literatures, particularly English and American Literature. These were, in keeping with the politics of Theory, now primarily identity-centred spaces, aligned with Postcolonial Studies, Black Studies, Women's Studies, Gay Studies and so on. It was difficult to see how accepting Bernheimer's recommendations could alleviate the anxieties of disciplinary distinctiveness for Comparative Literature. It was rightly observed that the political possibilities of comparing literatures had shifted from nation-bases (the need to interrogate national politics while at some level accepting national boundaries) to identity-bases (the need to interrogate identity politics while at some level accepting identity-based differences), and that somehow this shift has taken place outside the disciplinary ken of Comparative Literature. Bernheimer himself expressed this anxiety most succinctly:

> Identity politics are particularly anxiogenic for the comparatist who ventures beyond the European arena or gets involved with ethnic cultures at home. No matter how many years you may have given to the study of a culture, if it is not yours 'in the blood', it will always be possible for you to be found lacking in some quality of authenticity. The more literatures you try to compare, the more like a colonizing imperialist you may seem.
>
> (*Comparative Literature in the Age of Multiculturalism*, p. 9)

A response to these anxieties began emerging from within Comparative Literature in the late 1990s. This consisted primarily in rethinking and reworking the idea of World Literature, drawing upon and away from Goethe's *Weltliteratur* (a term he used in a letter to Johann Peter Eckermann in January 1827). Aldrige, in *The Reemergence of World Literature* (1986), already referred to above, had revived the idea in the context of East–West Comparative Literature. However, Aldrige's reiteration of World Literature or rather 'universal literature', defined as 'the sum total of all texts and works throughout the world', was given as separate from Comparative Literature, which was understood as 'the study of any literary phenomenon from the perspective of more than one national literature or in conjunction with another intellectual discipline or even several' (p. 56). Up until this point World Literature had been regarded as more an idealistic than a functional concept, useful for considering literature in an abstract way rather than for the institutional practice of literary studies. Since the late 1990s the concept of World Literature began to be pushed towards a more pragmatic institutional function.

The impetus of a universalist position akin to World Literature has been considered cautiously, but without eschewing its idealistic nuances, in Gayatri Spivak's stock-taking of Comparative Literature in *Death of a Discipline* (New York: Columbia University Press, 2003). This tried to mediate the 'radical' political agenda of Theory in Comparative Literature both by asserting the importance of taking 'the languages of the Southern Hemisphere as active cultural media rather than as objects of study by the sanctioned ignorance of the metropolitan migrant' against the hegemony of 'global English' (p. 9), and by maintaining a presumptive conceptual horizon that recognises collectivity: 'the collectivity that is presumed to be the condition and effect of humanism is the human family itself' (p. 27). However, Spivak's cautious gesture towards the universal horizon of the 'human family' was left as the idealistic anterior of the discipline, an idea that is always *before* the critic, a question rather than an answer that makes the comparative enterprise provisional itself, a formulation that always 'begs the question'. Spivak's idea for a new Comparative Literature therefore didn't have much to do with World Literature apropos institutional practice, and recommended instead alignment with social-science-oriented 'area studies' (popular in the US academy since the 1950s).

Rather less abstract and more institutionally friendly thought, in the sense of making it amenable to curriculum building and pedagogy and scholarship, has been given to the idea of World Literature by Pascale Casanova in *The World Republic of Letters* (1999; trans. M.B. DeBevoise, Cambridge, MA: Harvard University Press, 2004), in essays by Franco Moretti in the early 2000s ('Conjectures on World Literature', *New Left Review* 1 (January–February 2000), 54–68; 'More Conjectures', *New Left Review* 20 (March–April 2003), 73–82), and by David Damrosch in *What is World Literature?* (Princeton: Princeton University Press, 2003). Casanova produced a theory of international literature based on competition between different national literatures, with each fighting for control over 'literary time'. This involved a curious double-take. On the one hand, this suggestively outlined a theory of World Literature as a sort of autonomous 'republic' in itself, following a literary logic and sense of time and space irrespective of geopolitical boundaries and conflicts:

> What is apt to seem most foreign to a work of literature, to its construction, its form, and its aesthetic singularity, is in reality what generates the text itself, what permits its individual character to stand out. It is the global configuration, or composition, of the carpet – that is, the domain of letters, the totality of what I call world literary space – that alone is capable of giving meaning and coherence to the very form of individual texts.... In this broader perspective, then, literary frontiers come into view that are independent of political boundaries, dividing up a world that is secret and yet perceptible by all (especially its most dispossessed members); territories whose sole value and sole source is literature, ordered by power relations that nevertheless govern the form of the texts that are written in and that circulate throughout these lands; a world that has its own capital, its own provinces and borders, in which languages become instruments of power.
>
> (p. 3)

On the other hand, however, it later turned out that this space is mapped according to the emergence of nation-states in Europe after the sixteenth century, through the medium of national languages. This move defeated the suggestive assertion quoted above, and moreover took the whole concept in a peculiarly Eurocentric direction in practice. Nevertheless, the conceptual suggestiveness of Casanova's global Republic of Letters, of World Literature in those terms, does lead into more methodologically plausible and institutionally realisable ideas of World Literature. Franco Moretti's provocative essay 'Conjectures on World Literature' made several proposals of a practical sort that are of interest here. Assuming a world-systems perspective of literature, Moretti contemplated the scholarly pursuit of World Literature as occurring at a metatheoretical level of 'distant reading' – where the conventions of close reading are dispensed with in favour of registering patterns discerned in scholarship that has already engaged literary texts in different languages and traditions. According to Moretti, to understand literary history in terms of a world-system rather than a national or linguistic tradition means that:

> it will become 'second hand': a patchwork of other people's research, *without a single direct textual reading.* Still ambitious, and actually even more so than before (world literature!); but the ambition is now directly proportional *to the distance from the text*: the more ambitious the project, the greater must the distance be
>
> (p. 57)

After pondering the somewhat sanctified status that close reading has held and continues to hold in literary studies, Moretti went on to clarify what the relation of literary texts to such distanced reading in World Literature might be:

> Distant reading: where distance, let me repeat it, *is the condition of knowledge*: it allows you to focus on units that are much smaller or much larger than the text: devices, themes, tropes – or genres and systems. And if, between the very small and the very large, the text itself disappears, well, it is one of those cases when one can justifiably say, Less is more. If we want to understand the system in its entirety, we must accept to lose something.
>
> (p. 57)

This was an eminently practical suggestion, even if somewhat shocking given the conventions of a literary education that prevail. It is possible to envisage its adoption within the institutional practice of a World Literature course, perhaps at postgraduate level, where students will already have experience of both analytical literary reading and engagement with literary scholarship. Similarly practical suggestions, but from a quite different direction, appeared in David Damrosch's *What*

Is World Literature? (2003). Here, instead of, like Moretti, proposing an adjustment to modes of critically engaging a given concept of World Literature (as the totality of all literature), Damrosch begins by defining the concept so as to delimit it and render it manageable (but without losing its global scope):

> I take world literature to encompass all literary works that circulate beyond their culture of origin, either in translation or in their original language ... a work only has an *effective* life as world literature whenever, and wherever, it is actively present within a literary system beyond that of the original culture.
>
> (p. 4)

Or, as he puts it otherwise: 'My claim is that world literature is not an infinite, ungraspable canon of works but rather a mode of circulation and of reading' (p. 5). The implications of this mode of defining World Literature for institutional practice are inferable from Damrosch's three-fold clarification of its scope in his conclusion:

1   World literature is an elliptical refraction of national literatures.
2   World literature is writing that gains in translation.
3   World literature is not a set canon of texts but a mode of reading: a form of detached engagements with worlds beyond our own time and place.

> (p. 281)

The pragmatic edge of Damrosch's approach, and its possible usefulness for institutional purposes, is self-evident. Damrosch has himself made moves towards the institutional entrenchment of his version of World Literature by taking the first necessary steps – setting the parameters of a course by putting together an anthology, and delineating pedagogic practices for the field. He edited the *Longman Anthology of World Literature* (New York: Longman, 2002/3) and wrote a companion volume for it, *Teaching World Literature* (New York: Pearson Education, 2005).

These moves towards harnessing World Literature within institutional practice, as an offshoot from or reorientation of the institutional space of Comparative Literature, are not without their problems. The contradictions within Casanova's views are noted already. It remains unclear whether Moretti's World Literature through distanced reading is, in practice, realisable in a meaningful way given the unevenness of available primary scholarship for different national/linguistic traditions. Or, whether such distanced reading wouldn't be at such a remove from literary texts and their specific contexts that debilitating distortions will be introduced in scholarship. Damrosch's 'culture of origin', which texts of World Literature cross out of or from, is open to doubt. Where and how a text originates may be thought of as neither determinate nor attributable. Nevertheless, what seems to be emerging here is an idea of the institutional practice of literary studies which is increasingly not described by linguistic or national norms, but in terms of an extensive field of literature which is, at least conceptually, all-encompassing. The point is to not try to contain and pigeon-hole everything that such a field might consist in, but to engage with literature and criticism and theory in such a way that the normativeness of linguistic and national traditions is undermined, and the horizons of an extensive and fluid and in-flux field of literature in the world comes within view. At any rate, in the 2004 ACLA 'Report on the State of the Discipline' (edited by Haun Saussy as *Comparative Literature in an Age of Globalization*, Baltimore: Johns Hopkins University Press, 2006), Saussy's leading paper, 'Exquisite Cadavers Stitched from French Nightmares', expressed satisfaction that now 'Comparative literature is not only legitimate: now, as often as not, ours is the first violin that sets the tone for the rest of the orchestra' (p. 3).

QUESTIONS AND EXERCISES

English literature

1   Summarise the ways in which the institutional practice of English can be understood now: (a) insofar as it has been reckoned with in histories of the discipline; and (b) insofar as attempts to historicise the discipline have themselves sought to intervene in that institutional practice.

2   In your view, in what ways may attempts at locating the history of English on a global scale – taking account of the discipline in both ordinarily Anglophone and ordinarily non-Anglophone contexts – modify or change our predominantly Anglo-centric view of the discipline?

3   In what ways, if any, do accounts of the history of English impinge upon your particular area of research?

4   What bearing, if any, might an awareness of the history of English as a discipline have on your practical experience of engaging with a research project in an institutional setting?

Comparative literature

1   Summarise: (a) the different sorts of crises that have been perceived in the discipline of Comparative Literature since the 1960s; and (b) the ways of addressing those crises that have been contemplated.

2   What do you feel are the pros and cons of trying to realise an institutional practice for World Literature? In what ways, if at all, would that be different from the institutional practice of Comparative Literature so far?

3   In what ways, if any, do developments in Comparative and World Literature impinge upon your particular area of research?

4   What bearing, if any, might developments in Comparative and World Literature have on your practical experience of engaging with a research project in an institutional setting?

7

The place of theory in literary disciplines

Suman Gupta

In the last chapter, it was observed that the advent of 'Theory' (with a capital T) has played a significant role in recent histories of literary disciplines. By 'Theory' I mean that aspect of conceptualising literature and criticism in general terms (i.e. not just in relation to specific texts and contexts) which has become *a distinct institutionally recognised component of disciplines of literary studies*, so that it is now ensconced in pedagogy and academic discourse. Attempts at conceptualising literature and criticism without such institutional impetus – or 'theory' (with a small t) – have a considerably longer history. We would probably need to go back to Aristotle's *Poetics* or Horace's *Ars Poetica* or Bharatamuni's *Natya Shastra* or Cao Pi's *Lun Wen* or other such from classical antiquity to begin a historical trace. However, the term 'theory' itself, and in the latter sense, was particularly in the air by the 1970s as something distinctive and new in literature and criticism. In this chapter we are concerned with the relatively recent, 1970s onwards, institutional appropriation of Theory from theory.

Current approaches to Theory actually seldom engage with its close connection to recent institutional histories of literary disciplines. That Theory now exerts an institutional pressure is, however, something that most students of literature – particularly those embarking on research – will readily acknowledge. Postgraduate students are given to understand that their projects and dissertations must demonstrate an awareness of Theory, even if not directly addressed to theoretical questions. In some quarters this causes anxiety, as a wide-ranging knowledge of various 'schools' of Theory seems to be called for. This anxiety actually arises because of the misconceived manner in which Theory is now presented in dominant academic discourse: as a body of knowledge that is out there, distinct from and yet somehow inevitably relevant to literature and criticism, which has to be acquired and applied. Though Theory often enjoins historicisation and contextualisation, it itself appears as a peculiarly ahistorical and acontextual formation. It is seemingly categorised into 'schools' such as Liberal Humanism, Formalism, Structuralism, Marxism, New Criticism, Poststructuralism and Deconstruction, New Historicism, Postmodernism, Postcolonialism, Feminism, Queer Theory and so on, all of which could be relevant in different ways anywhere in literature (any text, any period, any place). In a contrary spirit, I argue here that Theory is not a given field of knowledge with many 'schools' which has to be sampled and picked from and applied, but is an institutional extrapolation from an ongoing process of debating and thinking about literature and criticism. This process entails questioning and debating disciplinary prerogatives (and often flows out of disciplinary boundaries), and it is moreover a process which is itself contextualised and historicised. Theory is the institutional extrapolation from a dynamic and contingent process of thinking about literature and criticism – an extrapolation from theory.

In fact, regarding Theory as a given field of knowledge is itself an institutional ploy: a strategy for taming its dynamic and in-process character, and making it amenable to curricula and textbooks (key markers of academic institutionalisation). The role of Theory textbooks in particular – which all students of literature are now required to study and use at some stage – in promoting that view is itself worth exploring. Theory textbooks are useful, of course, in offering surveys and overviews and pat formulations to depart from, and literary students and researchers should take recourse to them as points of departure whenever it suits them. But these should not simply be accepted and used as transparent reference books but also located in terms of the institutional processes and significances of Theory. This chapter attempts to provide such an awareness to supplement existing Theory textbooks, and can be regarded as material supplementary to a standard Theory textbook. It is divided into three sections. The first traces the process through which theory came to be institutionally appropriated as Theory from the 1970s, and led thereafter to the Theory Wars (including 'against Theory' and 'after Theory' debates). The second section offers brief notes on three currently in-vogue terms in Theory ('literary text', 'culture' and 'identity'), by way of demonstrating how these incorporate contextually nuanced debates and negotiate disciplinary boundaries – in ways which are often neglected in Theory textbooks. The third section presents a brief critical appraisal of Theory textbooks themselves.

THE TRAVELS OF THEORY

Two influential directions of thinking about literature and criticism – of theory – merged into the institutional construction of Theory towards the end of the 1970s. It is difficult to say when theory became Theory in any exact sense, but the two directions are usefully expressed at around the same time in Paul de

Man's essay 'The Resistance to Theory' (1980–1; published in his *The Resistance to Theory*, Manchester: Manchester University Press, 1986) and Edward Said's *The World, the Text and the Critic* (London: Vintage, 1983, including essays written between 1969 and 1981). Both are reckonings with something that is already thought of as 'theory', and both are on the cusp of the institutional adoption of Theory.

De Man's 'The Resistance to Theory' presented its own sense of the emergence of theory in literary studies in the following words:

> Literary theory can be said to come into being when the approach to literary texts is no longer based on non-linguistic, that is to say historical and aesthetic, considerations, or, to put it somewhat less crudely, when the object of discussion is no longer the meaning or the value but the modalities of production and of reception of meaning and of value prior to their establishment – the implication being that the establishment is problematic enough to consider its possibility and its status.
>
> (p. 7)

Or, as de Man summarised it, Theory 'occurs with the introduction of linguistic terminology in the metalanguage about literature' (p. 8).

This effectively aligned the term 'theory' with two extant ways of thinking about literature and criticism. On the one hand, it located theory in relation to a developing strain of criticism that attends closely to language (is inspired by developments in linguistics and the philosophy of language). This strain can be traced back to the linguistic formulations of Ferdinand de Saussure, which encouraged critics like Roman Jakobson, Gérard Genette, Michael Riffaterre and the early Roland Barthes to analyse texts as careful manipulations of the basic structures of language. More importantly for de Man, theory incorporated the development along that strain of the poststructuralist work of the later Barthes and Julia Kristeva (which focused on the limitations of linguistic structures) and, particularly, the deconstructionist philosophy of Jacques Derrida (which focused not on the stability of linguistic structures but on the contradictions and fissures and slipperiness of language).

On the other hand, there was also a gesture towards formalist approaches to literature (largely a matter of locating literary texts within a scheme of categories and types according to their generic forms and stylistic devices) and the conventions of close reading (usually conducted to get to the bottom of what the author meant and why texts give pleasure to or have beneficial effects on readers). A host of influential British and American critics were contained in this gesture – almost the entire range of critics who had defined the institutional function of English from the nineteenth century onwards, especially those now thought of as liberal humanists and New Critics. But the gesture was as much one that accepted something of formalism and close reading as one that rejected the manner in which it had been practised earlier by explicitly disavowing 'historical and aesthetical considerations'. The latter meant that de Man dislocated close reading and formalism from such matters as what texts were intended for or why readers enjoy or benefit from them. Actually, in uniting these strains within the undertaking of theory de Man comprehensively removed both from 'historical and aesthetical considerations'. De Man thereby presented theory as a somewhat new (and rather precious) enterprise of excavating the philological and rhetorical devices of literature, in a manner that is informed by linguistic theory and philosophy, and in a manner which has echoes of conventional close reading and formalist methodologies, but without any normative (trying to evaluate) or social (trying to discern contextually specific ideological implications) investments. It was an influential approach, and allowed proponents to both carve out an institutional location and to enact a quite disturbing (at the time) departure from familiar institutional practices in literature departments.

Said's take on theory in *The World, the Text, and the Critic* took issue with the political and social disinvestment of the de Man version of theory.

> From being a bold interventionary movement across the lines of specialization, American literary theory of the late seventies has retreated into the labyrinth of 'textuality,' dragging along with it the most recent apostles of European revolutionary textuality – Derrida and Foucault – whose trans-Atlantic canonization and domestication they themselves seemed sadly enough to be encouraging. It is not too much to say that American or even European literary theory now explicitly accepts the principle of non-interference, and that its peculiar mode of appropriating its subject matter (to use Althusser's formula) is *not* to appropriate anything that is worldly, circumstantial, or socially contaminated. 'Textuality' is the somewhat mystical and disinfected subject matter of literary theory.
>
> (p. 3)

That this attack on the de Man version of theory was sieved through religious metaphors – 'apostles' and 'canonization' and 'mystical' – was not merely to pack a stylistic punch; Said suspected serious complicity in such theory with neoconservative and 'overtotalising' tendencies. Said proposed instead attention to what he called 'travelling theory' – a historically and contextually nuanced tracing of engagements with literature and criticism that are also already thought of as theory, with an explicit focus on ideological and 'worldly' concerns. This recalled strains of thinking and debate which de Man had deliberately ignored: drawing inspiration from Marxist class analysis and materialist history, as in the work of Georg Lukács, Raymond Williams and Lucien Goldmann. Said reminded readers of the social value of criticism that drew upon philosophical formulations by Louis Althusser (especially in relation to ideological state apparatuses) and Michel Foucault (particularly in his accounts of the operations of power in discourse formations). Said's pioneering work on Orientalism derived from these formulations. Effectively, Said's version of theory was in the same breath a rejection of the de Man version and an updating of politically effective, socially aware, contextually located, historically informed, intellectually responsible engagement with literature and criticism.

Both the de Man and the Said versions of theory, though contrary in bent, were united in their desire to break away from dominant disciplinary practices in the Anglo-American academy of the time – which was powerfully centred in liberal humanist evaluation and New Critical close reading. As it happened, Said's call for political responsibility and de Man's depoliticised focus on language in literature through theory somehow got transposed onto each other. An institutional construction of Theory emerged from this uneasy transposition, drawing on both versions and despite their differences. This process was aided by their shared sense of opposition to the prevailing disciplinary formation, which in turn allowed for a curious mixture of terminology in other contemporary and consequent engagements with theory. Thus, Geoffrey Hartmann's celebration of the de Man version of theory in *Criticism in the Wilderness* (New Haven: Yale University Press, 1980) was couched in terms which often resonated with Said's left-wing politics:

> The relation of creative and critical must always be reenvisioned; and while the revisionists may overturn this or that orthodoxy, this or that fixed ideal, and while they specifically expose the falsification, even repression, of Romantic origins in Arnoldian and much New Critical thought, their reversal does not fix, once again, the relation of creative and critical. The variety and indeterminacy of that relation are disclosed in a radical way.
>
> (p. 9)

Terms like 'reenvisioning', 'revisionists', 'overturning orthodoxy' and 'ideals', 'radical way' – all redolent with Marxist associations – gave the ahistorical unaesthetical project of de Man-like theory a political force. Thus too, Frank Lentricchia's *Criticism and Social Change* (Chicago: University of Chicago Press, 1983) managed to see theory both as 'a type of rhetoric' in de Man fashion and as opening up political intervention in Said fashion:

> I conceive of theory as a type of rhetoric whose persuasive force will not be augmented in our time by metaphysical appeals to the laws of history, ... and the kind of Marxist theory that I am urging is itself a kind of rhetoric

whose value may be measured by its persuasive means and by its ultimate goal: the formation of genuine community.

(p. 13)

Lentricchia also positioned this mixed-up reading of theory as of institutional moment: 'our potentially most powerful political work as university humanists must be carried out in what we do, what we are trained for' (p. 7). In that transposition of two directions of theory and bringing of this hybrid within institutional precincts, within professional practice, Theory had already, in some sense, become manifest.

The notion that theory, as a new sort of analytical mode that is attentive to language and philosophy apropos literature and that contains an emancipative political desire, should reorient and revitalise the institutional practice of literary studies led to the concretisation of Theory in the course of the 1980s and early 1990s. How theory should be fitted into the profession of literature led to a heated debate (often called the Theory Wars) and certain institutional responses. In the course of these, Theory in the institutionally recognised sense settled and assumed its current shape. Within literary studies Theory was concretised through curricula and canons and pedagogy, given form in department memberships and recognition of academic status, transmitted in categorisations of booklists and libraries, reiterated in funding practices, ensconced in academic discourse at large.

Since theory came to be perceived as a radical oppositional force to the institutional ideology of literary studies in place, the contemplation of its incorporation in literary studies was necessarily a political step. This was complicated by the larger political aspirations of theory, or by the transposition of worldly responsibilities (à la Said) on the deconstructionist project. This was also complicated by the fact that it wasn't immediately evident in what fashion the alteration of the institutional space of literary studies by theory would relate to (perhaps serve) the larger political aspirations of theory in the world. It was questions along these lines which actuated the Theory Wars, through which Theory became ensconced in literary disciplines.

At one level this was a debate about the political ambitions of Theory as part of the literary professions. Debaters pondered qualms about these ambitions. Gerald Graff wondered whether theory's effect on the humanities wasn't actually 'mirroring the very society they seek to oppose' (*Literature Against Itself*, Chicago: University of Chicago Press, 1979, p. 26); Eugene Goodheart saw in it an 'inability to deal with the question of values and, in particular, of its own values' (*The Skeptic Disposition in Contemporary Criticism*, Princeton: Princeton University Press, 1984, p. 175); William Cain worried that 'The political debates in contemporary theory are intense, even frenzied, but not very productive or precise' (*The Crisis in Criticism*, Baltimore: Johns Hopkins University Press, 1984, p. xiv); Howard Felperin was doubtful about 'whose politics it serves or advances' (*Beyond Deconstruction*, Oxford: Clarendon, 1985, p. 214); Art Berman pondered 'the social powerlessness of the literary critic' (*From the New Criticism to Deconstruction*, Urbana: University of Illinois Press, 1988, p. 302); Ralph Cohen observed that the institutional inculcation of theory by its proponents 'delimits both their vocabulary and their contribution to the larger non-academic audience they wish to change' (*The Future of Literary Theory*, ed. Ralph Cohen, New York: Routledge, 1989, p. x), and so on.

At another level, and particularly from the early 1990s onwards, the Theory Wars were addressed to vociferous arguments 'against Theory' (by now Theory was seen as institutionalised) – which marked a conservative response ranging from cautious liberalism to downright right-wing assertion. This was particularly addressed to the perception that the political desire of theory had turned into the institutionalisation of identity politics (along the lines of race, gender and sexuality particularly) in Theory. In the cautious liberal mould, Denis Donoghue was anxious to clarify that 'I hope you understand that I am not, in the vulgar phrase, "against theory".... What I am against is the confusion of theory with principles – or rather, the confusion of theories with principles and ideologies' (*The Pure Good of Theory*, Oxford: Blackwell, 1992, pp. 47–8). He later pointed to identity-based 'schools' of Theory as the place where this happens (*The Practice of Reading*, New Haven: Yale University Press, 1998, p. 100). Similarly, Stanley Fish expressed doubts about identity-based political aspirations being realised through the profession of literary studies:

> feminism, gay rights activism, and the civil rights movement did not originate in the academy, and academic versions of them acquire whatever extra academic influence they may have by virtue of something already in place in public life; academic feminism, academic gay rights studies, and academic black studies do not cause something but piggy-back on its prior existence.
>
> (*Professional Correctness*, Oxford: Clarendon, 1995, p. 86)

Along crude right-wing 'against Theory' lines there appeared John Ellis's attack on the 'race-gender-class orthodoxy' of Theory, with a desire to reinstate Western society's superiority against the reprobate record of Asian and African countries (*Literature Lost*, New Haven: Yale University Press, 1997). Not dissimilarly, but somewhat more temperately, Valentine Cunningham was ironic about Theory because, he felt, it was leading to the neglect of 'the Judeo-Christian tradition [that] dwells constantly on the sweetness of the Word of God' (*Reading After Theory*, Oxford: Blackwell, 2002, p. 148).

As the Theory Wars unfolded, in themselves giving weight to the institutional status of Theory, three kinds of institutional response were firmly giving shape to Theory's space in academia. First, Theory was systematically introduced in courses and programmes of literary disciplines – in English, for instance. All the apparatus for this became quickly available, especially as a plethora of Theory textbooks and readers appeared in the market. And, indeed, in the course of the 1980s these programmes assimilated the political desire of theory by arranging Theory predominantly along the lines of identity-based aspirations. This was naturally because emancipative political aspirations had been powerfully conceptualised already and over an extensive period by Feminist, Black, Gay/Queer/Lesbian, Postcolonial intellectuals with reference to texts, and fitted the worldly concerns of the period in question. I go into the political background and the nuances of 'identity' in Theory below.

Second, there were occasional attempts to take Theory away from implicitly elitist institutional spaces of literary studies and find alternative spaces for cultural studies, which address a broader range of texts (including mass-market texts and texts in other media). In the course of the 1980s and 1990s numerous literary studies departments in the USA and UK developed cultural studies sections within their fold; in some instances cultural studies, so to speak, 'broke away' from literary studies and were constituted as new programmes or departments.

Third, another kind of institutional response to Theory sought an interdisciplinary dimension within the disciplinary space of literary studies. This was variously and consistently contemplated and sometimes acted upon through the 1980s. As an institutional response to Theory, in *The Pursuit of Signs* (London: Routledge and Kegan Paul, 1981) Jonathan Culler recommended collaborative arrangements between literary studies departments and departments such as philosophy, linguistics, anthropology, sociology, psychology and history for the benefit of literature students. Towards the end of the 1980s, Gerald Gruff applauded the promise of 'numerous programs now being planned and implemented which integrate literary theory and history in an interdisciplinary framework, often under such rubrics as "cultural studies" and "cultural history"' ('The Future of Theory in the Teaching of Literature', in *The Future of Literary Theory*, ed. Ralph Cohen, p. 266).

In the course of the 1980s and 1990s, through the vicissitudes of the Theory Wars and such institutional responses, Theory became firmly entrenched and assumed its institutional character in the academy. In the late 1980s and particularly 1990s 'against Theory' arguments were particularly strongly pressed, and it seemed for a while as if academic politics might stifle Theory in its institutional infancy. Those who felt called upon to defend Theory adopted the interesting strategy of doing so by, in some sense, going beyond Theory. The defence of Theory had to look forward to 'after Theory', when its political effect would be realised not just in the academy but in the world at large. Primarily this involved registering how the institutional practice of Theory has fallen short and should be reconsidered to lead to a more egalitarian world – especially in terms of marginalised identities – 'after Theory'. In that spirit appeared Thomas Docherty's *After Theory* (London: Routledge, 1990) and Paul Bové's *In the Wake of Theory* (Hanover: Wesleyan University Press, 1992). Docherty's 'after Theory' hoped to release the revolutionary potential of theory after the institutionalisation of Theory: 'successful institutionalisation of theory, modernism and marxism, has stymied the radical pretensions of their movements and philosophies; and, what is worse, theory and marxism have become complicit with the institutional imposition of limits upon their revolutionary potential' (p. 1). Bové's 'after Theory' arose from a similar perception:

> Even though we live in an age that increasingly exercises both hegemony and domination in and through sign-based structures, the literary academy not only failed to reorganize itself to address the new social and intellectual problems created by these structures, but it has returned to 'core curricula' and tried to minimize the influence of 'radicals' within the academy.
>
> (p. 26)

Despite their doubts about institutionalised Theory, both were hopeful about what is to come 'after Theory': both sought to keep the political desire to resist hegemony and champion subaltern and marginal voices alive from and beyond Theory.

As 'after Theory' studies proliferated in the course of the 1990s and early 2000s, somewhere the optimistic turn of the phrase changed. From the forward-looking optimism of Docherty and Bové, 'after Theory' gradually became an expression of disappointment in Theory. The argument gradually shifted to decrying the loss of the political desire of theory through its institutional appropriation as Theory. This shift can be traced through the appearance of 'after Theory' studies such as Martin McQuillan, *Post-Theory* (Edinburgh: Edinburgh University Press, 1999); *What's Left of Theory?*, ed. Judith Butler, John Guillory and Kendall Thomas (New York: Routledge, 2000); Eduard Strauch, *Beyond Literary Theory* (Lanham: University Press of America, 2001); *Life After Theory*, ed. Michael Payne and John Schad (London: Continuum, 2003); Ivan Callus and Stefan Herbrechter, *Post-Theory, Culture, Criticism* (Amsterdam: Rodopi, 2004); *After Criticism*, ed. Gavin Butt (Oxford: Blackwell, 2004); Vincent Leitch and Jeffrey Williams, *After Theory* (London: Routledge, 2005). Terry Eagleton's *After Theory* (London: Allen Lane, 2003) is particularly worth noting here: it argued that the institutionalisation of Theory, and structuring thereof along the lines of identity politics, had effectively depoliticised Theory. Eagleton's doubts about identity politics were not widely shared, but the disappointment he expressed resonated with many.

It is clear in the above that accounts of theory, Theory, 'against Theory' and 'after Theory' often overlapped and coexisted within a dynamic process of debates and arguments. They certainly all continue to coexist – and that's pretty much where the matter rests now.

TRACING TERMS IN THEORY

In this section I present some notes on three key terms in Theory – the 'literary text', 'culture' and 'identity' – which cut across the various 'schools' it has been divided into. The following is not by way of presenting a comprehensive discussion of these, but to serve two purposes. First, I have argued so far that it is necessary to understand Theory not as a given field but as a dynamic process of debates and arguments. That, of course, attaches not only to Theory in general but also to some of its focal terms. The following notes highlight ways in which key terms accrue and shift meanings and connotations, and move across disciplinary and contextual boundaries. Second, I have suggested above that this chapter should be read as supplemental to standard Theory textbooks. The following notes are precisely in directions which seem to me to be neglected in most standard Theory textbooks.

The literary text

The notion of the literary text – and therefore of authors and readers – is obviously one of the constitutive elements of literature and criticism, and central to Theory. The connotations of 'text' have a particularly long and complex history which I will not go into here – anyone undertaking literary research undoubtedly already has a sufficient sense of this. What follows are some quickly sketched points on relatively recent turns that the term has gone through under the aegis of Theory.

Understanding the connotations of 'text' has been considerably less problematic than grasping what makes a text *literary*. One sort of conventional recourse has been to find some formal description general enough to contain the myriad variety that is recognised as literary, encapsulating all the fluid generic and subgeneric categories and rhetorical/linguistic possibilities that can be plausibly registered as such. This has been attempted from a vast range of theoretical positions: in terms of Theory's division of the field, by Russian Formalists (like Yuri Tynyanov and Mikhail Bakhtin), by Structuralists (like Roman Jakobson, Roland Barthes, Gérard Genette, Tzvetan Todorov), by Phenomenologists (like Roman Ingarden), by the uncategorisable Northrop Frye, among numerous others. The *raison d'être* of such attempts has been questioned so insistently – as being ahistorical, insensitive to sociopolitical contexts and ideological leanings, indifferent to readerly or interpretive constructions, simply philosophically untenable, etc. – that such characterisations of the literary text have largely been abandoned. A relatively rare and recent attempt at presenting a formal-linguistic theory of literary texts by Antonio García-Berrio in A *Theory of the Literary Text* (Berlin: Walter de Gruyter, 1992) can be cited to briefly convey the ambition of such an enterprise. The following is the simplistic initial statement which is thereafter complicated at considerable length:

> The literary or poetic text establishes, effectively, certain more precise and even conventional fixed limits for the creator of literary or poetic types of expression, which are unknown in the elaboration of the standard communication text. From the very start, the author of a sonnet works under the pressure of a closed textual space. He accepts a pre-set dimension for his discourse, which artistically specializes each of his operators and decisions regarding thematic invention, structural arrangement and elocution at every level.... Without knowing such stringent limits, the constructor of a theoretical piece or novel is similarly aware of the existence of relatively conventional boundaries, experienced, adopted and patterned for the communicative-aesthetic efficacy of said discourses.
>
> (p. 64)

This sounds like a rather restrictive description of literariness, but could be adjusted to allow for considerable flexibility. The generic closure of textual space that authors work with reference to could include, for instance, testing and even subverting the limits of that closure.

The usual objections to such formalist text-centred approaches dwell on the productive and receptive dimensions. The literariness of the text arguably cannot be grasped by looking at the text in itself. It seems natural that the author's life and times may provide a useful frame here, but in fact that too is now regarded as misguided. Processes of the production of a text include considerably more agents (influences, publishers, reviewers, translators, etc.) and factors (existing presumptions about what is literary, what is acceptable, how texts circulate, etc.) than an individual author can determine. The literariness of a text is therefore now considered to be an emanation from existing discourse formations, a sociopolitical ethos, a historical period, modes of book production and circulation, and so on. The 'death of the author' that Roland Barthes so influentially announced was because of such an understanding of texts and literariness (see his 'The Death of the Author', in *Image, Music, Text*, selected and trans. Stephen Heath, London: Fontana, 1977); and yet the idea of an author is so powerful a convention of literary studies that its 'return' (as Seán Burke, in his *Death and Return of the Author*, Edinburgh: Edinburgh University Press, 1992, was to phrase it) seems to be always at hand. Consideration of the receptive aspects of literature also produces substantial challenges to the formalistic text-centred approach. Reception could be constructed within the text at one level, as Wolfgang Iser's formulation of the 'implied reader' suggested. For Iser, the text manipulates readers to obtain a range of possible readings by bringing their sense of relevant associations and selections. '[The implied reader] embodies all those predispositions necessary for a literary work to exercise its effect – predispositions laid down, not by empirical outside reality, but by the text itself' (*The Act of Reading*, Baltimore: Johns Hopkins University Press, 1978, p. 34). However, this is still too text-centred for some reception critics. In a series of influential formulations starting with the 'informed reader' and moving towards a concept of 'interpretive community', Stanley Fish first 'challenged the self-sufficiency of the text by pointing out that its (apparently) spatial form belied the temporal dimension in which its meanings were actualized', and, second, argued that literary texts are actually constructed even before they are read, in terms of pre-agreed strategies of reading that exist in 'interpretive communities' (*Is There A Text In This Class?*, Cambridge, MA: Harvard University Press, 1980, pp. 2, 171). If literary meaning has to be brought to the text, then the text, of course, does not contain literariness in itself.

Troublesome as these now familiar reflections on the literary text continue to be, further dimensions of complication are introduced by recent developments, especially innovations like digitisation of texts and growing familiarity with hypertexts (as in the Internet). These have distinct implications for literature and criticism which are worth noting.

Early studies of modifications in concepts of reading and writing in relation to hypertexts foretold promising developments for literature and criticism. For instance, Jay David Bolter anticipated that electronic texts opened up the possibility of 'interactive fiction': 'a nonlinear fiction, which invites the reader to construct a dialogue with the text' (*Writing Space*, Hillsdale: Erlbaum, 1991, p. 121). In this writers would be called upon to think of their work not as 'a closed and unitary structure' but 'as a structure of possible structures', and readers would cultivate the ability to become a 'second author, who can then hand the same text to other readers for the same treatment' (p. 144). Subsequent attempts to come to terms with the development of hypertext within literary studies have followed broadly two directions. First, it has been suggested that hypertext reveals practices and proclivities that are already implicit in literature and criticism but as yet insufficiently understood. Jerome McGann's notion of 'deformative' rather than 'interpretive' reading (in his *Radiant Textuality*, Basingstoke: Palgrave, 2001) is relevant here. Briefly, the idea is that though readers are accustomed to read texts 'deformatively' at various levels (often cross-referring or going back and forth), in 'interpreting' texts there is a strong convention to impose linearity (going from beginning to end). Hypertexts, however, encourage explicitly deformative reading and therefore reveal aspects of reading which are suppressed by the linear conventions of interpretation. Second, digitisation and hypertexts open up new possibilities which can comprehensively change current practices of text editing and textual criticism. These enable processes of textual juxtaposing and cross-referencing, for instance, which potentially render the need to identity definitive or original texts redundant. John Bryant (*The Fluid Text*, Ann Arbor: University of Michigan Press, 2002) and Jerome McGann have considered the theoretical implications, and foreseen radical changes in the shaping and maintenance of literary archives hereafter.

Culture

As observed above, the invocation of 'culture' has had a significant role to play in the institutional turns of Theory, and indeed it presents a kind of institutional battleground itself. 'Culture' has distinct connotations in disciplinary traditions rooted in anthropology/sociology and in the humanities, including literature, and its evocations in Theory within literary disciplines negotiate these distinct connotations uneasily. In fact, its emergence in Theory is itself in the context of a confrontation between sociology/anthropology and the humanities.

The confrontation can be briefly conveyed by recalling an exchange at a 1989 symposium in the State University of New York, Binghampton. Here sociologists Stuart Hall and Roland Robertson, and anthropologist Ulf Hannerz, presented their account of recent developments in the field of culture under conditions of globalisation. These assumed a perspective of culture which sociologist Immanuel Wallerstein usefully summarised in his contribution to the proceedings:

> On the one hand, culture is *by definition* particularistic. Culture is the set of values or practices of some part smaller than some whole. This is true whether one is using culture in the anthropological sense to mean the values and/or practices of one group as opposed to any other group at the same level of discourse (French vs. Italian culture, proletarian vs. bourgeois culture, Christian vs. Islamic culture, etc.), or whether one is using culture in the belles-lettres sense to mean the 'higher' rather than the 'baser' values and/or practices within any group, a meaning which generally encompasses culture as representation, culture as the production of art-forms. In either

usage, culture (or a culture) is what some persons feel or do, unlike others
who do not feel or do the same things.

But, on the other hand, there can be no justification of cultural values
and/or practices other than by reference to some presumably universal or
universalist criteria.

('The National and the Universal: Can There Be Such a Thing as
World Culture?', in *Culture, Globalization and the World System*,
ed. Anthony King, Basingstoke: Macmillan, 1991, p. 91)

Such sociological/anthropological reckonings with contemporary culture were
followed by responses which revealed some unexpected differences. Among
the respondents was art historian Janet Wolff, who objected that:

[The preceding] papers are 'pre-theoretical' with regard to developments in
cultural theory. None of them is able to recognize the nature of culture as
representation, nor its constitutive role with regard to ideology and social
relations. They operate with the notion of 'culture' as an identifiable realm
or set of beliefs, objects or practices, more or less determined by social and
economic relations, with more or less independence from and effectivity on
the social process. Cultural theory, however, has stressed the 'materiality' of
culture, by which is meant the 'determinacy and effectivity of signifying
practices themselves'. Codes and conventions, narrative structures, and
systems of representations in texts (literary, visual, filmic) produce meaning
and inscribe ideological positions.

('The Global and the Specific: Reconciling Conflicting Theories of
Culture', in *Culture, Globalization and the World System*, ed.
Anthony King, 1991, pp. 170–1)

Wolff's was recognisably a contemporary (as opposed to Wallerstein's 'belles-
lettres sense') Theory-informed humanities perspective on culture. According
to this, culture, i.e. cultural discourses and representations and texts, *constitutes* ideology and social relations rather than appears as by-products or expressions of ideology and social relations. This is a matter of emphasis: from the
sociological/anthropological perspective culture arises as a result of prevailing
ideologies and social relations, whereas from the humanistic perspective
culture makes possible and moulds ideologies and social relations.

The distinct emphases placed on culture from the two disciplinary perspectives have an important bearing on subsequent debates about culture in
Theory. On the one hand, the humanistic assertion that cultural texts and
discourses constitute ideology and social processes occasionally impressed sociologists and anthropologists, who then sought to incorporate that emphasis
within their disciplinary pursuits. On the other hand, confidence in that con-

stitutiveness of cultural texts and discourses has led literary studies to open up – some would say, encroach upon – areas conventionally addressed in sociology, anthropology, political studies, etc. It has even encouraged literary studies to move away from a definitive commitment to literary texts, and encompass a broader field of cultural texts (mass-market texts and 'texts' in different media).

The incorporation of a literary emphasis on culture into the sociological/anthropological field is evidenced in Arjun Appadurai's work. In a 1990 essay he proposed the relationship of culture and globalisation through a juxtaposition of the metaphor of landscape on several discursive areas, denoted in a self-explanatory fashion as ethnoscapes, technoscapes, financescapes, mediascapes and ideoscapes. These were meant to convey fields of overlapping cultural flows, and indicate that 'these are not objectively given relations which look the same from every angle of vision, but rather they are deeply perspectival constructs, inflected very much by the historical, linguistic and political situatedness of different sorts of actors' ('Disjuncture and Difference in the Global Cultural Economy', in *Global Culture: Nationalism, Globalization and Modernity*, ed. Mike Featherstone, London: Sage, 1990, p. 296). It is possible to think of Appadurai's '-scapes' as being close in spirit to 'texts' from a literary perspective. From the later 1990s, sociologist Jeffrey Alexander also sought to develop a Theory-inspired method of 'cultural sociology' at the expense of the existing methodology of the 'sociology of culture'. His reflections in this direction are collected in *The Meanings of Social Life* (New York: Oxford University Press, 2003).

It may be recalled from the previous section that one of the institutional responses to Theory was to propose a Theory-centred cultural studies as a departure from literary studies. Such a move was most lucidly conceptualised in Anthony Easthope's *Literary into Cultural Studies* (London: Routledge, 1991). Easthope felt Theory had initiated a paradigm shift in literary studies which undermined the hegemonic ideology that is at the heart of literature itself, and recommended a separation of cultural studies, within which the political direction of Theory could be more meaningfully realised:

> Cultural studies should situate its pedagogic subject not primarily in relation to truth but rather to the textual structures within which he or she is actually constituted ... Confronting textuality not just cognitively – as generalisable meaning – but experiencing the work/play of the signifier and to move secondarily to criticism and analysis may disclose for the subject something of his or her own actual determinacy and situatedness.
>
> (p. 180)

In this Theory-informed breakaway Easthope called for attention to texts of mass and popular culture broadly understood (written and in other media). It has been a popular subdiscipline within literary disciplines, and occasionally a separate humanistic discipline alongside literary disciplines, since. This process of taking possession of culture within Theory in the 1990s and onwards has a close association, also as observed in the previous section, with identity politics.

Identity

The period of the moves from theory to Theory to 'after Theory' in literary studies coincided with a period of sociopolitical transitions of international significance. In the 1950s and 1960s a large number of African and Asian countries became independent from their colonial rulers, and began a process of decolonisation and postcolonial national consolidation. In Western Europe and North America, the 1960s and to some extent 1970s were marked by anti-Vietnam War protests and a widespread left-wing student movement which found common ground with a surge of identity-based movements. Particularly noteworthy among the latter were the Afro-American civil liberties movement, second-wave feminism, and the gay and lesbian movement. The 1980s in the USA (Ronald Reagan took office as President in January 1981) and UK (Margaret Thatcher became Prime Minster in May 1979) brought to power governments which systematically instituted government deregulation and privatisation measures. There was also a perceivable hardening of conservative attitudes towards minorities in these countries. Privatisation and deregulation were adopted as international economic strategies in the 1980s and 1990s, mainly through the operations of the International Monetary Fund and World Bank. These often undermined or limited state-led poverty alleviation and economic stabilisation measures, which in turn gave rise to a range of social movements, often identity-based, against such policy changes around the world. In the course of the 1980s a series of communist governments, following single-party and strongly centralised systems, collapsed after mass demonstrations. This process was attended by growing disenchantment with the concept of class as the locus of the Left movement, or with the international working-class movement as the structure on which Left politics was centred. The attention of both Left and liberal political alignments shifted gradually from class to identity as the fulcrum of political mobilisation and social movements.

As it happened, identity-based political positions, such as feminist, gay, ethnic and racial movements, had considerable traditions of being expressed through literature and criticism. Understandably, the travels of worldly (in Said's sense) theory towards institutionally ensconced Theory through this period became the ground upon which identity-based political aspirations could be constructed and discussed. In specific terms the politics of gender, sexuality, race and ethnicity, and in general terms the politics of difference, multiculturalism, pluralism, marginality and postcolonialism, were all hotly debated in Theory. As literary disciplines provided, through Theory, a field in which the politics of identity could be performed and clarified, so too Theory aspired both to rejuvenate and modify the undertaking of identity-based political activism and thinking. As Theory gradually became institutionalised in the course of the 1980s and 1990s, it also substantially came to be structured around identity-based positions. Theory textbooks broke the dynamic travels of theory into 'schools', which now multiplied along identity lines: Feminist Theory, Gay/ Queer Theory, African American Studies, Postcolonial Theory, etc. Literary anthologies along these identity-based lines marked the introduction of concordant courses or curricular reform. Appointments and research projects concretised the institutional inculcation of identity in the literary academy. In fact, as observed above, the Theory Wars were largely centred on the politics of identity. As with the Theory Wars, so with the related Canon Wars: Paul Lauter (*Canons and Contexts*, New York: Oxford University Press, 1991), John Guillory (*Cultural Capital*, Chicago: University of Chicago Press, 1993) and Gregory S. Jay (*Taking Multiculturalism Seriously*, New York: Cornell University Press, 1997) called for an opening up of the Anglo-American canon to the literature of marginalised identities, while Harold Bloom (*The Western Canon*, New York: Harcourt Brace, 1994) asserted the need to maintain the integrity of the Western canon.

If literary disciplines ended up institutionalising identity politics in the process of institutionalising Theory, sociology and anthropology and political theory had been devoted to unravelling the social processes underlying identity from a considerably earlier stage. In fact, the sociopolitical developments briefly outlined above were naturally immediately the *objects* and *field* of sociological, anthropological and political analysis. The focus on identity in Theory was cognisant of sociological debates, and – as with culture – both drew upon and departed from sociological frames of discussion, and eventually seemed at some level to converge. Sociologists in particular had a long-drawn interest in identity as something that is mediated between individuals and collectives and society in general. Early sociological engagements with identity came from several directions: Norbert Elias's attempts to structure the processes between 'I-identity' and 'we-identity' since the 1930s (*The Society of Individuals*, Oxford: Blackwell, 1991); George Herbert Mead's consideration of social processes that regulate understanding of selves and assuming of roles (*Mind, Self and Society*, Chicago: University of Chicago Press, 1934); Marcel Mauss's attempts to delineate the social construction of the self in various cultural contexts (*Sociology and Psychology*, London: Routledge and Kegan Paul, 1979 [1950]); Erving Goffman's studies of how individuals perform themselves in everyday life (*The Presentation of Self in Everyday Life*, Harmondsworth: Penguin, 1959) and of how social identity is constructed and what role stigmatisation plays in it (*Stigma*, Harmondsworth: Penguin, 1964); Erik Erikson's formulations of identity (*Identity*, New York: Norton, 1968). The problems of accommodating marginal group identities within liberal societies picked up in sociological study in the 1970s in response to some of the above-mentioned occurrences of the period. Henri Tajfel's social psychological work based on intergroup discrimination experiments conducted in the 1970s (*The Social Psychology of Minorities*, London: Minority Rights Group, 1978), and John J. Gumperz's sociolinguistic research of collective-identity construction (edited, *Language and Social Identity*, Cambridge: Cambridge University Press, 1982) were significant interventions in this direction. Since then almost every influential political theorist and sociologist and anthropologist has engaged with the question of collective and marginal identities in contemporary liberal democracies and in the contemporary international/global social order. That from the 1980s literary disciplines, with the institutional inculcation of Theory, appeared to become primarily a field wherein the ambitions and ambiguities of identity-based political positions are performed was something that sociologists could scarcely overlook. Some – such as Arjun Appadurai (*Modernity at Large*, Minneapolis: University of Minnesota Press, 1996) and Jeffrey Alexander (*The Meanings of Social Life*, New York: Oxford University Press, 2003) – approached this in a constructive spirit and incorporated aspects of Theory into sociological analysis.

On the whole, sociologists have tended to be sympathetic to and incorporate where possible the perspectives of Theory. The proponents of Theory in literary disciplines have generally been less aware of these developments in sociology, and Theory textbooks and curricula in the literary academy still give very little attention to the sociology of identity.

THEORY TEXTBOOKS

In a discussion between Gerald Graff and Jeffrey R. Di Leo on the manner in which Theory textbooks are used in literary studies, Di Leo talks of

> what I call the 'cookie cutter approach' to theory ... [which] works something like this: apply literary theory 'A' to literary text 'B'. Result: a valid interpretation of literary text 'B' (and a successful use of literary theory 'A'). On this strategy, students think that criticism and theory are some kind of game wherein points are scored for the production of valid

interpretations. Textbooks ... that have primary texts along with selections
like 'What is Deconstruction?' and 'What is Feminism?' promote this type
of trivial use of theory, albeit I think unwittingly.

('Anthologies, Literary Theory, and the Teaching of Literature',
Symploke, 8, 1–2 (2000), 113)

In this chapter I have attempted to present a view of Theory which is designed
to discourage such a 'cookie cutter approach'. The idea has been to engage
with Theory as the institutionally adopted aspect of an ongoing process of
theory, which develops through debates and arguments that are conditional
on geopolitical and historical contexts. This view of Theory is, as I observed
in the introduction, at odds with the widely accepted 'cookie cutter approach'
– constantly reified in the academy, in pedagogy and even scholarship, by the
structure of Theory textbooks. To end this chapter it is appropriate to turn a
critical gaze on Theory textbooks themselves; that is something that Theory
textbooks also do not usually do.

The development of the 'cookie cutter approach' can be traced fairly clearly
after the earliest instances of Theory textbooks, such as Catherine Belsey's
Critical Practice (London: Methuen, 1980) and Terry Eagleton's *Literary Theory*
(Oxford: Blackwell, 1983). Unlike later textbooks, these presented a continuous argument of their own while summarising and synthesising a range of
approaches. Catherine Belsey clarified as an overarching theme in her book
the recent emergence of a 'new critical practice' (p. 55), arising from scepticism
about New Critical and formalist approaches, and drawing upon the ambiguities of language and the drives of ideology. Terry Eagleton delineated different
formulations of literary theory as conditional to their historical and political
contexts, and framed these within an overarching argument: 'I have tried to
popularize, rather than vulgarize, the subject. Since there is in my opinion no
"neutral", value-free way of presenting it, I have argued throughout a particular
case, which I hope adds to the book's interest' (p. vii). The case made had to do
with an understanding of what literary value and institutional literary history
consist in, and what sort of political agendas for literary theory can be inferred.
Both Belsey and Eagleton gave summaries and exegeses of each of the theoretical approaches they covered. But these were ancillary to the overarching
design of their books: broadly, the advocacy of literary theory as a coherent
enterprise, following a direction (the connecting argument of their narratives),
which conveyed a sense of theory's ongoing travels, and some underlying interest in the rejuvenated prospects for institutional literary studies. Necessarily,
such an arrangement of the narrative meant that the different approaches were
constantly understood with regard to each other, as deriving from and questioning and needing to be weighed in terms of each other.

From about the mid-1980s and into the 1990s, Theory textbooks appeared in quick succession – indicative of the need to address the rapid institutional inculcation of Theory – and in these the 'cookie cutter approach' became the structuring device. Raman Selden's A Reader's Guide to Contemporary Literary Theory (Brighton: Harvester, 1985) exemplifies this direction. It presented a sequence of 'schools' of literary-theoretical approaches which seemed to be more or less discrete conceptual wholes, accessible with reference to select representative texts and theorists. Selden did – and others who follow his structure do – mark out the overlaps and cross-references that operate across the field at large; but the disposition of literary theory into a sequence of conceptual wholes and *without* an overarching argument presented the field as a divided house, with every room containing its own realised and potential extensions. Russian Formalism, Marxist theories, Structuralist theories, Poststructuralist theories, Reader-oriented theories, Feminist criticism occupied here their own chapters and reading lists, and shouldered each other with a few grudging acknowledgements of their mutually regarding progressions. Subsequent editions of Selden's guide upped the emphasis on 'cookie-cutting' endeavours. The 1989 edition included a chapter on New Historicism; the 1993 edition was co-authored with Peter Widdowson and included sections on Postcolonial criticism and a substantial section on 'Black, Women-of-Colour, and Lesbian Literary Theories'; the 1997 edition added Peter Brooker to the co-authors and had now a separate chapter on Postcolonial theory (with a section on race and ethnicity) and one on 'Gay, Lesbian and Queer Theories'. The direction of expanded 'cookie cutting' was clearly to embrace a proliferation along the lines of identity politics.

By a fallacious leap, this direction of textbook structuring led to the *reductio ad absurdum* that the maximum validity of each approach could be demonstrated if each could be shown as producing valid interpretations for *one* literary text (or, at least, a small number of works of fiction or poetry). Thus Steven Lynn's *Texts and Contexts* (New York: Harper Collins, 1994) started off, in the first chapter, by demonstrating how each of the theories he was going to expand on thereafter could be applied to a single text. With the demands of given institutional needs in mind, Michael Ryan's *Literary Theory* (Oxford: Blackwell, 1999) was the first to announce its organising principle precisely in this fashion:

> I felt that students would be aided by seeing theory at work in the practical reading of texts. And I felt the important differences between theories – the way each illuminated a different aspect of a work of literature – would be clearer if they were comparatively applied to the same literary work. But it turned out to be difficult to find readings of varying critical perspectives of the same work. Each school seemed to favor certain kinds of texts, with, for

example, the deconstructionists favoring symbolic poetry and the Marxists realist novels. I decided at that point – around the mid-1980s – to write my own readings of the same text, each of which would assume a different critical stance or theoretical perspective.

(p. viii)

An additional twist in the development of the 'cookie cutter approach' in Theory textbooks involved getting rid of the dynamism and differences *within* each so-called 'school'. This evolved gradually through most of the above-mentioned (and other such) textbooks, Selden-onwards. The idea here was that each approach can be reduced to a set of summary and characteristic practices. The possibility of generalising a 'school' thus both facilitated its functional use in pedagogy and hardened each cut-and-dried 'school' to the point of passivity. A ruthless application of this is found in Peter Barry's *Beginning Theory* (Manchester: Manchester University Press, 1995).

Theory textbooks such as those mentioned here are, of course, useful tools – but only if they are placed within a broad perspective of theory and Theory themselves. They offer a useful initial introduction to a process which is valuable if it can be complicated further, and they themselves trace something of the history of Theory. To make the best of them they need to be approached critically themselves. For those engaging in research it is imperative to have something more than a 'cookie cutter approach' to Theory.

QUESTIONS AND EXERCISES

1   In what ways is the above account of Theory relevant, if at all, insofar as: (a) it has a bearing on your specific area of research or research topic?; and (b) you are engaging with the practicalities of research in literary studies? Make a point-wise list for each.

2   Are issues of the 'literary text', 'culture' and/or 'identity' relevant to your specific area of research or research topic? If so, in what ways?

3   Do the issues raised in this chapter have any bearing on the ways in which you have thought about these terms in the context of your research so far?

SELECTED READING

The following are not 'recommended' in the sense of presenting the field of literary theory in an authoritative fashion, and should be approached with the above discussion in view.

Peter Barry, *Beginning Theory: An Introduction to Literary and Cultural Theory* (Manchester: Manchester University Press, 1995; second edn 2002).
Catherine Belsey, *Critical Practice* (London: Methuen, 1980; second edn 2002).
Terry Eagleton, *Literary Theory: An Introduction* (Oxford: Blackwell, 1983; second edn 1996).
M.A.R. Habib, *Modern Literary Criticism and Theory* (Oxford: Blackwell, 2007).
Steven Lynn, *Texts and Contexts: Writing about Literature with Critical Theory* (New York: Harper Collins, 1994; second edn 1998; third edn 2001).
Michael Ryan, *Literary Theory: A Practical Introduction* (Oxford: Blackwell, 1999).
Raman Selden, *A Reader's Guide to Contemporary Literary Theory* (Brighton: Harvester, 1985; second edn 1989; third edn with Peter Widdowson 1993; fourth edn with Peter Widdowson and Peter Brooker 1997).

8

Literary research and interdisciplinarity

David Johnson

In the 1972 collection *Counter Course: A Handbook for Course Criticism*, edited by Trevor Pateman (Harmondsworth: Penguin), each of the major academic disciplines is subjected in turn to radical critique. In the chapter on English Literary Studies, Joe Spriggs complains that the discipline is doing little more than 'wittering away to itself in bored, irrelevant little formulae' (p. 238). In arguing for a radical overhaul of 'Eng. Lit.', Spriggs insists that the first priority must be an engagement with other disciplines: 'Criticism if it is to be conducted ... needs to find its explanatory feet. This needs history, anthropology, psychology and philosophy more than what has got by as lit. crit. in the past' (p. 240). The conviction that bringing different academic disciplines into dialogue with each other would rejuvenate not only the study of literature but all disciplines was widely shared in the late 1960s and 1970s. In the decades since, the study of English Literature has been changed dramatically by exchanges with the disciplines of history, psychology, anthropology and philosophy, to name but a few. Before considering these more recent interdisciplinary encounters, however, a brief history is required of how the discipline of literary studies emerged and constituted itself in relation to other disciplines.

THE CONFLICT OF THE FACULTIES

The grouping together of poetry, music and the visual arts into a system of fine arts for contemplation and study occurred for the first time in the eighteenth century. Treatises written in England, France and Germany sought common principles for the comparative analysis of the fine arts, culminating in the constitution of a separate subdiscipline within the discipline of philosophy. Charles Batteux's *The Fine Arts Reduced to a Common Principle* (1746), for example, grouped together music, poetry, painting, sculpture and dance as 'fine arts', arguing that their shared end is pleasure. Moses Mendelssohn in *Reflections on the Sources and Relations of the Fine Arts and Letters* (1757) translated Batteux's categorisation into a German idiom, agreeing that the unity of the fine arts is grounded in their capacity to move their audiences: 'Poetry, eloquence, beauty in shapes and in sounds penetrate through the various senses to our souls and rule over our dispositions. They can make us happy or depressed at will' (quoted in Martha Woodmansee, *The Author, Art, and the Market: Rereading the History of Aesthetics*, New York: Columbia University Press, 1994, p. 14). In the specific case of literature, this instrumentalist theory tying the fine arts directly to pleasure came under pressure in the second half of the century as the number of readers increased and the appetite for sensationalist books grew. With serious authors like Goethe failing to compete in the marketplace with more popular writers, an alternative theory of the fine arts and poetry/literature was outlined by Karl Philipp Moritz in *Toward a Unification of All the Fine Arts and Letters under the Concept of Self-sufficiency* (1785). Rejecting Mendelssohn's theory that the value of the work of art derives from its capacity to give pleasure to the public, Moritz argued that works of art (including works of literature) should be self-sufficient totalities to be contemplated exclusively for their own sakes, independent of external relationships or effects. According to Moritz, 'men of taste' would value such superior works, whereas 'the rabble' would continue to seek 'diversion' and 'pleasant sensations' in popular works (quoted in Woodmansee, *The Author, Art, and the Market*, p. 20). Cultural historian Martha Woodmansee summarises the shift:

> As literature became subject to the laws of the market economy [Mendelssohn's] instrumentalist theory ... was found to justify the wrong works [namely] the products of the purveyors of strong effects, with whom more demanding writers could not effectively compete.
>
> (Woodmansee, *The Author, Art, and the Market*, p. 32)

Moritz's theory – reinforced and cemented as the German theoretical defence of high culture or *Kultur* – soon became the dominant theory of art/literature in the nineteenth century, and was a necessary condition for the study of literature as a discrete discipline.

Roughly contemporaneous with the categorisation of literature as one of the 'fine arts' within the subdiscipline of philosophy, there were energetic debates in Germany more generally about (1) how the different disciplines related to each other, and (2) how the different disciplines related to the state. The most influential formulation of how the disciplines should be configured was Immanuel Kant's *Conflict of the Faculties* (also translated as *Contest of the Faculties*), which appeared initially as three different essays in the 1790s. Kant distinguishes between the three higher faculties of Theology, Law and Medicine on the one hand, and the lower faculty of Philosophy on the other. The three higher faculties have a vocational function – to train priests, lawyers and doctors – and it is the duty of the state to police how such vocational training should proceed. The lower faculty of Philosophy, however, has no such responsibility for vocational instruction; independent of state interference, it judges on the basis of Reason the teaching of the other faculties. Functioning correctly, the relationship between the higher and the lower faculties produces a universally grounded rationality – the state must protect the university in order to guarantee the rule of reason in public life, but at the same time, Philosophy must ensure the university does not become an unmediated instrument of state power. The effect is that the lower faculty of Philosophy ultimately turns out to be the higher. The 'conflict of the faculties' arises when the boundaries distinguishing the higher and lower faculties blur, either when the state or the higher faculties enter the field of Philosophy to challenge the free exercise of Reason, or when the faculty of Philosophy exceeds its jurisdiction and directly criticises the state or the higher faculties. These distinctions are not always clear cut; in 1794 Kant himself precipitated a conflict of the faculties when he stood accused by the State Censor of misusing Philosophy '"to distort and disparage many of the cardinal and basic teachings of the Holy Scriptures and Christianity" and of leading youth astray' (Howard Caygill, *A Kant Dictionary*, Oxford: Blackwell, 1995, p. 123). Kant's *Conflict of the Faculties* continues to be read as 'a consistent case for academic freedom as well as a still timely assessment of the forces within and without the university which threaten it' (Caygill, *A Kant Dictionary*, p. 124).

Kant's division of the faculties, with Philosophy (including the study of literature) functioning as an independent check on the state and on the teaching of the vocational higher faculties, fundamentally influenced the conceptualisation of the modern university in early-nineteenth-century Germany. Wilhelm von Humboldt and Johan Gottlieb Fichte adapted Kant's formulation in constituting the University of Berlin, and although they argued over details, the resultant organisation preserved the division between vocational and philosophical faculties, with the latter retaining their autonomy. Whereas Kant installed Reason as the ultimate arbiter, however, for Humboldt and Fichte the key term was Culture, or more specifically, a national culture. What this meant was that the university was simultaneously responsible for vocational training (as before) and for both constituting a national culture and then inculcating that culture in students. This formulation has proved immensely influential: cultural theorist Bill Readings argues that '[s]uch an idea of the University with culture as its animating principle has defined both the University's shape as a modern institution and its relationship to the nation-state' (*The University in Ruins*, Cambridge, MA: Harvard University Press, 1996, p. 69). And he continues that what was crucial in this shift from Reason (Kant) to Culture

(Humboldt and Fichte) as the independent antimony to vocational training in the modern university has been the notion of a national literature. For Readings, 'the national literature department gradually comes to replace the philosophy department as the center of the humanities, and a fortiori, as the spiritual center of the University' (p. 69). The development of universities in the major Western nations in the nineteenth century broadly follows Read-ings's schematic intellectual history, as national literatures were institution-alised in Germany, France, Spain and Britain. In Victorian Britain, Cardinal John Henry Newman repeated these German idealist precepts – first that there 'are two ends of education; the end of the one is to be philosophical, of the other to be mechanical'; and second, that 'by great authors the many are drawn into a unity [and] national culture is fixed' (*The Idea of the University: Defined and Illustrated*, London: Longmans, Green and Co., 1925, pp. 112, 193).

Newman's (borrowed) arguments on the division of disciplines in the univer-sity and on the central place of great authors in drawing 'the many' into a national culture, contributed to the entrenchment of English Literature as the centralising discipline in Britain up until the crisis in studying 'Eng. Lit.' in the 1960s. Before moving on to the break up of 'Eng. Lit.', it is necessary to summarise more precisely what the discipline of studying English literature involved. In the first place, it involved the analysis of a limited corpus of liter-ary works. In analysing how the meaning of 'literature' has mutated, Raymond Williams summarised how the focus of the discipline had narrowed since the eighteenth century:

> So, you have in sequence, first, a restriction to printed texts, then a narrowing to what are called 'imaginative works', and then finally a circumscription to a critically established minority of 'canonical' texts. But also growing alongside this there is another and often more potent specialization: not just Literature, but English Literature.... [T]he actually very diverse works of writers in English are composed into a national identity – the more potent because it is largely from the past – in which a mood, a temper, a style, or a set of immediate 'principles' ... are being celebrated, taught, and – where possible – administratively imposed.
> (*Writing in Society*, London: Verso, 1983, pp. 194–5)

Second, the methodology for studying the selected major works of English literature had evolved into the rigorous close analysis of the language of the literary text in isolation. Designated 'practical criticism' in Britain (following I.A. Richards) and 'new criticism' (following *inter alia* Cleanth Brooks) in the USA, literary studies eschewed theoretical introspection or dialogue with other disciplines in analysing and evaluating literary works. Indeed, by the

1950s indifference towards disciplines outside English Literature shaded into hostility in the pronouncements of influential figures like F.R. Leavis. In 'Components of the National Culture' (1968), an ambitious comparative essay on the state of the major disciplines in Britain, Perry Anderson attributed the self-enclosed methodology of literary studies to the discipline's assumption that students of literature shared a 'stable system of beliefs and values … [and were] a morally and culturally unified audience' (in *English Questions*, London: Verso, 1992, p. 98). As this assumption came under heavy assault in the 1960s and 1970s, the study of English literature was forced to renegotiate its relationship with other disciplines.

FROM LITERARY TO CULTURAL STUDIES

The first major challenges to the inherited assumptions and procedures of English literary studies were expressed in the work of Raymond Williams, Richard Hoggart and Stuart Hall. In *Culture and Society 1780–1950* (1958) and *The Long Revolution* (1961), Williams insisted that the understanding of 'culture' should be extended beyond its association with elite literary and artistic achievements to include its anthropological or social meaning: 'culture is a description of a particular way of life, which expresses certain meanings and values not only in art and learning but also in institutions and ordinary behaviour' (*The Long Revolution*, Harmondsworth: Penguin, 1965 [1961], p. 57). In *The Uses of Literacy* (1958), Hoggart applied the techniques of literary analysis sympathetically to the working-class cultural products and practices of 1930s Britain – newspapers, magazines, music and popular fiction – and contrasted them with the US-influenced mass culture of the post-war years. In *The Popular Arts* (1964), Hall and co-author Paddy Whannel rejected Hoggart's nostalgia for bygone working-class cultures, and sought to analyse popular cultural forms (including popular literary works) in their own terms. Although individual critics had written with sympathy and insight about popular culture (see, for example, George Orwell's 1940 essay 'Boys' Weeklies'), and there had been studies on the corrupting effects of mass culture (see for example, Denys Thompson's 1939 book *Between the Lines; or, How to read a newspaper*), these publications by Williams, Hoggart and Hall presaged a fundamental shift in attitude towards how cultural texts beyond the received literary tradition should be studied.

Accompanying the expansion of *what* texts might be included in literary studies was an equally fundamental shift in understanding *how* such texts might be studied. In this latter respect, the rapprochement with other disciplines was vital. In Chapter 7 Suman Gupta describes the place of Theory in Literary Studies, and it is difficult to separate the rise of Theory from the rise of interdisciplinary studies, since it was to the adjacent disciplines that literary critics turned in order to develop a theoretical vocabulary and methodology appropriate to the new texts analysed and fresh questions posed in literary studies. The title of Anthony Easthope's retrospective study *Literary into Cultural Studies* (London: Routledge, 1991) expresses these developments of the 1970s and 1980s, as he contrasts how literary studies constitutes itself as 'a coherent, unified and *separated* discipline [as opposed to] cultural studies, which draws on a range of knowledges conventionally discriminated into disciplines: semiotics, structuralism, narratology, art history, sociology, historical materialism, conventional historiography, poststructuralism, psychoanalysis, deconstruction' (pp. 171–2). Easthope's list of 'conventionally discriminated' disciplines might be disputed (is 'art history' a discipline in quite the same way as 'historical materialism'?), but what his survey captures is the excitement promised by transgressing the disciplinary boundaries of literary studies. In *British Cultural Studies* (1990), Graeme Turner expresses a similar optimism to Easthope, as he records the contributions to interdisciplinary cultural studies made by institutions – the Birmingham Centre for Contemporary Cultural Studies (from 1964), the Centre for Television Research at Leeds University (from 1966), the Centre for Mass Communication Research at Leicester University (from 1966), The Open University Mass Society and Communication courses (from 1977), the Glasgow Media Group (1974–82) – as well as by new journals like *Screen and Cultural Studies*; by feminist journalist-academics like Angela McRobbie, Ros Coward and Judith Williamson; and by certain publishers, most notably Methuen's New Accents series under the general editorship of Terence Hawkes. In his Conclusion, Turner consciously echoes Marx's famous injunction that 'philosophers have only interpreted the world, in various ways; the point is to change it' (Marx and Engels, *The German Ideology*, London: Lawrence and Wishart, 1970, p. 123), as he argues that cultural studies is uniquely equipped to take up Marx's challenge:

> Cultural studies does present a radical challenge to the orthodoxies within the humanities and social sciences. It has enabled the crossing of disciplinary borders and the reframing of our ways of knowing so that we might acknowledge the complexity and importance of the idea of culture. Cultural studies' commitment to understanding the construction of everyday life has the admirable objective of doing so in order to change our lives for the better. Not all academic pursuits have such a practical political objective.
> (Turner, *British Cultural Studies: An Introduction*, Boston: Unwin Hyman, 1990, p. 227)

It is worth marking and emphasising the distance from Newman's desire in the nineteenth century to use the great authors of English literature to unify 'the many' into a national culture to Turner's ambition 100 years later to mobilise *all* authors *and* other disciplines in order to 'change our lives for the better'.

The transition from the single-discipline study of great works of English literature to the interdisciplinary study of all varieties of cultural texts did not occur in isolation. It was part of a much wider change in how societies were studied and how knowledge was organised, as the US anthropologist Clifford Geertz explains via a number of vivid examples:

> [This blurring of genres] is philosophical inquiries looking like literary criticism (think of Stanley Cavell on Beckett or Thoreau, Sartre on Flaubert), scientific discussions looking like belles lettre *morceaux* (Lewis Thomas, Loren Eiseley), baroque fantasies presented as deadpan empirical observations (Borges, Barthelme), histories that consist of equations and tables or law court testimony (Gogel and Engerman, Le Roi Ladurie), documentaries that read like true confessions (Mailer), parables posing as ethnographies (Castenada), theoretical treatises set out as travelogues (Lévi-Strauss), ideological arguments cast as historiographical inquiries (Edward Said), epistemological studies constructed like political tracts (Paul Feyerabend), methodological polemics got up as personal memoirs (James Watson). Nabakov's *Pale Fire*, that impossible object made of poetry and fiction, footnotes and images from the clinic, seems very much of the time; one waits only for quantum theory in verse or biography in algebra.... The present jumbling of varieties of discourse has grown to the point where it is becoming difficult either to label authors (What *is* Foucault – historian, philosopher, political theorist? What Thomas Kuhn – historian, philosopher of knowledge?) or to classify works (What is George Steiner's *After Babel* – linguistics, criticism, culture, history? What William Gass's *On Being Blue* – treatise, causerie, apologetic?)... It is a phenomenon general enough and distinctive enough to suggest that what we are seeing is not just another redrawing of the cultural map – the moving of a few disputed borders, the marking of some more picturesque mountain lakes – but an alteration of the principles of mapping. Something is happening to the way we think about the way we think.
>
> (*Local Knowledge*, London: Fontana, 1993 [1983], pp. 19–20)

By ranging across so many disciplines, Geertz not only conveys the scale of how the disciplines were reconfigured in the period 1960–80, but also makes it clear that the whole phenomenon was not driven exclusively by the kinds of radical agendas pursued by Easthope and Turner. In contrast to proponents of Literary-to-Cultural Studies, the exemplary cross-disciplinary intellectuals and writers Geertz cites above represent a much wider mix of political positions.

As the dust has settled on this dramatic reshaping of the disciplines in Western universities, relationships between disciplines have had to be renegotiated. How are we to understand these relationships in the new dispensation? There are at least two interesting answers. The educational anthropologist Tony Becher, who explored the state of interdisciplinary studies by interviewing 220 academics spanning 12 disciplines and 18 institutions in the UK and USA, writes in Darwinian terms about 'the traumas of the birth of new disciplinary groupings, the death of old ones, the occasionally dramatic metamorphosis of those in middle life, [and] the process of steady evolution [of others]' (*Academic Tribes and Territories. Intellectual Enquiry and the Cultures of the Disciplines*, Milton Keynes: Open University Press, 1989, p. 21). Extending the survival-of-the-fittest metaphor, Becher characterises university academics as 'tribes of academe', who 'define their own identities and defend their own patches of intellectual ground by employing a variety of devices geared to the exclusion of illegal immigrants' (p. 24). Comparing disciplinary boundaries to the political borders separating nations, he argues that they are alike in that they denote 'possessions that can be encroached upon, colonized, or reallocated. Some are so strongly guarded as to be virtually impregnable; others are weakly guarded and open to incoming and outgoing traffic' (p. 36). Continuing in this vein, Becher argues that academic disciplines ruthlessly police their own boundaries:

> Any systematic questioning of the accepted disciplinary ideology will be seen as heresy and may be punished by expulsion; any infiltration of alien values and practices will be ... dealt with ... by direct resistance or by incorporation into the prevailing framework.
>
> (p. 37)

These grim generalisations are moderated when Becher concedes that when

> adjoining disciplinary groups lay claim to the same pieces of intellectual territory ... this does not necessarily entail a conflict between them. In some cases, depending on the nature of the claimants and the disposition of the no-man's land, it may involve a straightforward division of interest; in others it may mark a growing unification of ideas and approaches.
>
> (p. 38)

In the two decades since Becher's study was published, this latter, more cooperative version of interdisciplinary study has become more common.

A second reading of how the disciplines now relate to each other is offered by the literary critic Marjorie Garber. In a witty and wide-ranging essay, Garber argues that conflicts between academic disciplines are governed not only by rules analogous to those of turf battles and boundary disputes (as Becher argues), but also by what she calls 'discipline envy'. Following Freud, Garber argues that

> Boundary marking by disciplines, demarcating what does and doesn't count as history or philosophy or literary studies, is about training and certification

and belonging to a guild, but it is also, sometime, about the 'narcissism of small differences' – a sibling rivalry among the disciplines.

(*Academic Instincts*, Princeton: Princeton University Press, 2001, p. 54)

Garber's argument proceeds by extending Freud's insight about relationships within families and groups to disciplines:

> Freud's argument about the narcissism of small differences appears in his discussion of group psychology, where he extrapolates from a perception about groups: 'almost every intimate emotional relation between two people which lasts for some time – marriage, friendship, the relations between parents and children – contains a sediment of feelings of aversion and hostility.' The same thing happens with groups, he says, and there the hostility is less cloaked by repression: 'of two neighbouring towns each is the other's most jealous rival; every little canton looks down upon the others with contempt. Closely related races keep each other at arms length; the South German cannot endure the North German, the Englishman casts every kind of aspersion upon the Scot, the Spaniard despises the Portuguese.' Similarity and contiguity, says Freud, breed distrust, rivalry, comparison, even, perhaps, self-hatred or self-doubt projected upon the nearby other. Each group is saying to itself, in effect, 'I am not like that. If you look closely, you can see.' What appears to be a family resemblance needs to be disavowed as part of the project of constituting the self. Disciplines have, historically, often founded themselves on such 'minor differences'.

(pp. 54–5)

The first example Garber suggests is the discipline of philosophy, which was defined by Plato on the basis of its 'minor differences' from sophistics or sophistry. Whereas Plato-the-philosopher was determined to expel the falsehoods perpetrated by the sophists, Garber reads the competition between proximate disciplines in a more nuanced light, defining 'envy' in general as the 'desire to equal another in achievement or excellence; emulation and (a sense derived from the French *envie*) a wish, desire, longing, enthusiasm' (p. 57), and 'discipline envy' specifically as 'the wish, on the part of an academic discipline, to model itself on, or borrow from, or appropriate terms and vocabulary and authority figures of another discipline' (p. 62). Garber observes that literary studies has 'yearned to be, or model itself on: linguistics, anthropology and ethnography; social science, natural science, psychoanalysis, sociology, history, and various strands of philosophy, from aesthetics to ethics' (pp. 65–6). But at the same time, literary studies has itself on occasion been the object of 'discipline envy' from disciplines like history and cultural anthropology. Garber concludes that although the hierarchy of disciplines fluctuates, the structure of 'discipline envy' endures:

> New disciplines develop; others fade away. Envy, or desire, or emulation, the fantasy of becoming that more complete other thing, is what repeats, [namely] this tendency in academic and intellectual life to imagine that the truth, or the most revealing methods, or the paradigm with the answer, is … in your neighbour's yard or department or academic journals other than your own.
>
> (p. 67)

Notwithstanding the extensive borrowings across disciplinary boundaries at the level of research, what both Belcher's 'turf battle' model and Garber's 'discipline envy' model underestimate is quite how resistant established disciplines like English Literary Studies have been to the encroachments of new disciplines at the level of institutional practice. In the case of interdisciplinary Cultural Studies, the ambitions of Easthope and Turner have been frustrated in at least two respects. First, the British state in its overall audit of UK higher education courses *still* does not allocate an independent disciplinary identity to Cultural Studies. The Higher Education Statistics Agency (HESA) records that in the academic year 2006/7 there were 60,310 students pursuing degrees in English at institutions of higher education, whereas no figures are recorded for Cultural Studies. However, in the same year there were 27,225 students of Media Studies, which has increasingly become the 'home' of Cultural Studies (see www.HESA.ac.uk, accessed 20 October 2008). The continuing hegemony of English is confirmed by the student advice website http://hotcourses.co.uk, which for 2007/8 identifies 329 undergraduate and 163 postgraduate courses in English at British institutions of higher education, and 77 undergraduate and 67 postgraduate courses in Cultural Studies (www.hotcourses.co.uk, accessed 20 October 2008). These statistics indicate that there are many degrees and courses in English, but that there are no single-discipline degrees and only a number of courses in Cultural Studies. This does not necessarily mean that the post-1960s tendency towards interdisciplinary study has been entirely reversed, but it does suggest that the well-established disciplines like English have continued to dominate the curriculum. English might have appropriated insights, critical vocabularies and methods from adjacent disciplines, but as an institutional practice it has at no stage conceded its independent disciplinary identity.

Second, the radical claims made for interdisciplinary cultural studies too have foundered. Julie Thompson Klein argues that the ideal of interdisciplinary teaching and scholarship in fact appeals to both the Left and the Right, since 'all interdisciplinary activities are rooted in the ideas of unity and synthesis, evoking a common epistemology of convergence' (*Interdisciplinarity*, Detroit:

Wayne State University, 1990, p. 11). In other words, everyone now agrees that interdisciplinary study is a 'good thing'; political disagreements centre on quite how it is to be constituted. Looking at the role of universities in a wider context, Masao Myoshi argues that the traditional function of Western universities in both generating and preserving a national culture and in training a professional elite to administer that culture has been fundamentally changed by the rise since the 1960s of transnational corporations (TNCs). As TNCs have superseded the nation state, they have required a transnational professional workforce to manage a globalised economy, and Myoshi argues that universities have been obliged to provide that workforce: 'Those in economics, political science, sociology, and anthropology, as well as business administration and international relations, are not expected to be harsh critics of the TNC practice, being compliant enough to be its explicators and apologists' ('A Borderless World? From Colonialism to Transnationalism and the Decline of the Nation State', *Critical Inquiry*, 19 (1993), 748–9). If we refer back 200 years to Kant's division of the faculties, this is what is to be expected from the vocational 'higher faculties', but what of the contemporary equivalent of the 'lower faculties'? Myoshi concludes that (interdisciplinary) cultural studies and multiculturalism – the direct disciplinary descendants of Kant's faculty of Philosophy – fall well short of providing the necessary critical judgements of both the vocational faculties and the political and economic world beyond the university:

> In the recent rise in cultural studies and multiculturalism among cultural traders and academic administrators, inquiry stops as soon as it begins. What we need is a rigorous political and economic scrutiny rather than a gesture of pedagogic expediency.... To the extent that cultural studies and multiculturalism provide students and scholars with an alibi for their complicity in the TNC version of neo-colonialism, they are serving, once again, just as one more device to conceal liberal self-deception.
>
> (p. 751)

Myoshi's criticisms of the limits of interdisciplinary cultural studies might appear unrealistic, but they are consistent with Kant's ideals for the university, and provide a necessary point of reference in considering the examples of literary research and interdisciplinarity discussed below.

INTERDISCIPLINARY APPROACHES TO LITERARY TEXTS

Although departments of interdisciplinary study might not have replaced the single-discipline model of university organisation, even the most cursory glance at recent monographs, essay collections and journal articles published in Literary Studies reveals that the study of literary texts (defined in the broadest possible sense) has been fundamentally redefined by extensive traffic from other disciplines. This is not to suggest that the kinds of turf battles described by Belcher or the structure of discipline envy described by Garber have disappeared; rather it indicates that crossing disciplinary boundaries in order to draw on extra-literary-critical insights and methods has overcome anxieties about maintaining discipline 'purity'. In practice, Literary Studies has engaged with certain disciplines more than others, and I now consider briefly three of its most productive encounters – with Philosophy, with History and with Psychoanalysis.

Philosophy itself is of course a discipline with a long and complex history, and it is necessary to specify at the outset *which* branch of Philosophy has influenced Literary Studies. The most geographically proximate version of Philosophy – the British tradition of analytical philosophy – has exerted a relatively modest influence, whereas the work of Continental philosophers like Roland Barthes, Michel Foucault, Jacques Derrida, Pierre Bourdieu and Umberto Eco has contributed profoundly to the redefinition of English Literary Studies. In particular, their constant interrogation of disciplinary vocabularies, boundaries, protocols and institutional consequences has lent impetus and credibility to similar efforts by Anglo-American academics. In essays and articles subsequently translated and collected as *Mythologies* (1973), *The Pleasure of the Text* (1975) and *Image-Music-Text* (1977), Barthes developed and applied semiotic analysis to a wide variety of literary, philosophical and visual texts. Foucault did not provide critical readings of multifarious cultural texts in the same way as Barthes, but in *The Order of Things: An Archaeology of the Human Sciences* (1966) he provided an influential account of how the intellectual disciplines mutated from the Renaissance to the modern era – how general grammar became philology, how the analysis of wealth became political economy, how natural history became biology, and how psychology, sociology and criminology emerged in the nineteenth century with the historically constituted category of 'man' as their object of study. In two important essays, 'Mochlos; or The Conflict of the Faculties' (in *Logomachia: The Conflict of the Faculties*, ed. Richard Rand, Lincoln: University of Nebraska Press, 1992) and 'The Principle of Reason: The University in the Eyes of its Pupils' (*Diacritics* (Fall 1983), 3–20), Derrida returned to Kant's 1790s essays on the conflict of the faculties, and considered how Philosophy in particular and the academic disciplines more generally in contemporary Western universities are configured first in relation to each other, and second, in relation to the state. From a sociological rather than a philosophical point of view, Bourdieu in *Homo Academicus* (1984) undertook exhaustive fieldwork in order to compare the disciplinary values internalised by students and professors in the arts and sciences (the contemporary equivalents of Kant's 'lower' and 'higher' faculties).

Two quite different examples convey the variety of these encounters between Literature and Philosophy. Eco's *Travels in Hyper-reality* (1986) is an entertaining collection of essays which range in focus across several disciplines, from film (a semiotic analysis of *Casablanca*), to sport (the political function of the football World Cup) and philosophy (Aquinas's reconciliation of Aristotle and Catholic doctrine). Eco's willingness to flout traditional disciplinary codes takes place both from essay to essay and within individual essays – in 'Sports Chatter', for example, he combines anecdotes from his youth with long quotations from Heidegger's *Being and Time* and political analysis of anti-government protests during the Mexico Olympics. Derrida's *Glas* (1974) is a work of a quite different order. Up to four passages of writing in different fonts are juxtaposed per page, ranging in content from quotations from the philosophy of G.W.F. Hegel and (in less detail) Immanuel Kant; the literary works of Jean Genet; letters received by Hegel and Genet; diary entries and letters written by Hegel and Genet; exegeses of Hegel and Genet's writings; and exegeses of writers and works discussed by Hegel and Genet (like *Antigone*). There are no footnotes, endnotes, references or index, and much like a formally adventurous postmodern novel, *Glas* makes particular demands upon the reader, as meaning must be constructed by reflecting actively upon the connections (or absences of connection) between Hegel's public political philosophy of the state and Genet's private worlds of sex and the family. One reviewer describes *Glas* as offering 'philosophical readings of literary authors and literary analyses of the heroes of philosophy' (Alexander Nehamas, quoted on the back cover of *Glas*, trans. John P. Leavey and Richard Rand, Lincoln and London: University of Nebraska Press, 1986).

As in the case of the encounter between Literary Studies and Philosophy, the first step in assessing the encounter of Literary Studies and History is to acknowledge the complex disciplinary history of History itself. John Burrow introduces his ambitious survey *The History of Histories* (New York: Random House, 2007) by noting that 'History ... has been republican, Christian, constitutionalist, sociological, Romantic, liberal, Marxist and nationalist. All of these have left residues in subsequent historical writing; none at the moment dominates it' (p. xviii). There were attempts before the 1960s to historicise literary criticism, notably by English Marxists like Christopher Caudwell and Alick West in the 1930s, who explored how literary texts had been determined by their socioeconomic contexts, and thus anticipated the more theorised encounters between Literary Studies and History of recent decades. Dominated by 'new historicism' in the USA and 'cultural materialism' in the UK, literary critics have gone well beyond reading secondary histories in order to provide 'background' to their chosen literary texts and authors, and have engaged in detail with historiography (Hayden White's *Metahistory* (1973) and

Tropics of Discourse (1978) have been standard points of reference) and critical theory (Foucault's genealogical model of history-writing has exerted a defining influence, especially on the new historicists). In addition, in order to construct ever-more persuasive arguments, literary critics have turned to the kinds of archival work previously undertaken exclusively by historians. What this has meant in the first instance is that a more sophisticated critical/theoretical vocabulary has developed for describing the relationship between the 'literary text' and the 'historical context', including questioning whether the opposition between 'text' and 'context' might itself not be reframed in terms of 'orders of discourse'. In the search for a theoretical vocabulary for articulating the relation between Literature and History, a tradition derived from Marx (including Walter Benjamin, Theodor Adorno, Georg Lukács, Terry Eagleton) competes with and at times complements a tradition derived from post-war French philosophy (Barthes, Foucault, Derrida, Jean-François Lyotard).

In addition to registering the different historical *approaches*, the literary critic reading History is compelled to distinguish competing historical *interpretations* of the relevant historical moment. In other words, critics might well agree that the literary text must be read in its historical context, but will disagree over the meaning and significance of that context. An example from Shakespeare criticism will clarify the point. In the early history play *2 Henry VI* (c.1591), the rebel leader Jack Cade gives expression to popular grievances, violently challenging the authority of the monarch until he is beheaded in Act IV scene 9. Cade has proved a difficult character for critics, as Jean Howard explains: 'Does Shakespeare create this character simply to discredit popular rebellion, or does he use Cade to articulate the legitimate grievances of the common people and employ Cade's brutality as a disquieting mirror of the brutality of the ruling classes?' (*The Norton Shakespeare*, ed. Stephen Greenblatt and others, New York: W.W. Norton, 1997, p. 206). The new historicist critic Annabel Patterson analyses the text and context of *2 Henry VI*, and warmly approves Shakespeare's achievement in creating Cade as a character who 'fails every test for the proper popular spokesman ... [and exemplifies] the specious mediation of popular goals and grievances' (*Shakespeare and the Popular Voice*, Oxford: Blackwell, 1989, pp. 48, 50). The cultural materialist critic Richard Wilson examines the same text and context in a different light, arguing that the negative figure of Cade in *2 Henry VI* is rooted in Shakespeare's own economic investment in suppressing the London cloth-workers' protests in the 1590s. He concludes contra Patterson that Shakespeare's depiction of Cade is character assassination:

> Shakespeare's Cade is a projection of the sexual and cannibalistic terrors of the Renaissance rich. The scenes in which he figures should be interpreted

as a self-interested intervention by the management of The Rose [Theatre] in London's crisis, and a cynical exploitation of atavistic fears.

(' "A Mingled Yarn": Shakespeare and the Cloth Workers', *Literature and History*, 12 (1986), 176)

This bald summary does not do justice to what are complicated arguments, but the wide gulf between Patterson and Wilson's reading of the play and its historical context demonstrates that Literary Studies' recourse to History frequently raises as many questions as critical possibilities.

The relationship between Literature and Psychoanalysis is complicated in different ways, not least because one of the founding texts of Psychoanalysis is a work of literature – the Greek tragedy *Oedipus Rex*. Sigmund Freud referred extensively to literary examples in developing his psychoanalytic categories and procedures, but perhaps the most famous psychoanalytic reading of a literary work before the 1960s was Ernest Jones's study of 'Oedipus and Hamlet', which was the first chapter of his *Essays in Applied Psychoanalysis* (1923). Jones sees Hamlet as a version of Oedipus: Hamlet cannot kill Claudius because by having killed his father (Hamlet senior) and marrying his mother (Gertrude), Claudius stands in the way of his own desire; as a result, Hamlet's desire is repressed into the unconscious, causing his crippling incapacity to act. Whereas Freud's ideas dominated encounters between Literature and Psychoanalysis in the first half of the twentieth century, in the post-1960s period Jacques Lacan's reinterpretations of Freud were the principal points of reference in interdisciplinary dialogues (see Maud Ellman's collection of essays *Psychoanalytic Literary Criticism* (1994)). As questions were raised about the Eurocentric orientation of Psychoanalysis, psychoanalytic literary critics have responded by reframing their analyses of literary texts to question the universality of Western definitions of mental illness. A good example of this more historically nuanced mediation of literary and psychoanalytic analysis is Jacqueline Rose's essay 'On the "Universality" of Madness: Bessie Head's *A Question of Power*' (*Critical Inquiry*, 20 (1994), 401–18). Rose focuses on the South African writer Bessie Head's autobiographical novel *A Question of Power* (1974), and argues that terms like '*hallucination* and *paranoia* in themselves overlook a fundamental cultural difference. To put it another way, the boundaries between reality *and* hallucination are culturally specific *and* historically (as well as psychically) mobile' (p. 407). Rose's essay is exemplary in another respect. All critics today are eclectic in their use of terms, methods and insights from different critical theories and different disciplines, and Rose's essay – which I have highlighted for its dialogue between Literature and Psychoanalysis – might as fruitfully be read for its application of feminist literary theory, or postcolonial theory, or even (with its many footnotes referencing histories of Southern Africa) of cultural materialist/new historicist theory.

CONCLUSION

Literary research today requires at the very least an openness to other disciplines, but there remain both dangers and opportunities in undertaking interdisciplinary study. Of the dangers, the failure to appreciate the distinctive histories and methodologies of contending disciplines is potentially the most damaging. But at the same time, interdisciplinary study allows unprecedented scope for posing new questions and it enables the pursuit of individual research interests in ways that were inconceivable 30 years ago.

QUESTIONS AND EXERCISES

1   Do any of the following ideas still have any influence or relevance?

   • Moritz's distinction between literature favoured by 'men of taste' and 'the rabble';

   • Kant's desire that Philosophy (including Literature) should exercise Reason in judging vocational instruction in particular and the state and society in general; and

   • Newman's ambition to unify great authors into a national culture.

2   What were the distinctive methodological practices of the discipline of English Literature before 1960? Do any of these practices survive?

3   Why was the study of English Literature in the 1960s and 1970s in crisis?

4   How did Cultural Studies differentiate itself from the study of English Literature?

5   Summarise Belcher and Garber's explanations of how academic disciplines relate to each other. Which of the two explanations is the more persuasive?

6   Summarise how the discipline of Literary Studies has negotiated its encounter with the disciplines of Philosophy, History and Psychoanalysis.

SELECTED READING

Perry Anderson, *English Questions* (London: Verso, 1992).
Tony Becher, *Academic Tribes and Territories. Intellectual Enquiry and the Cultures of the Disciplines* (Milton Keynes: Open University Press, 1989).
Anthony Easthope, *Literary into Cultural Studies* (London: Routledge, 1991).
Marjorie Garber, *Academic Instincts* (Princeton: Princeton University Press, 2001).
Joe Moran, *Interdisciplinarity* (London: Routledge, 2002).
Julie Thompson Klein, *Interdisciplinarity* (Detroit: Wayne University Press, 1990).

Bill Readings, *The University in Ruins* (Cambridge, MA: Harvard University Press, 1996).

Graeme Turner, *British Cultural Studies. An Introduction* (Boston: Unwin Hyman, 1990).

Raymond Williams, *Writing in Society* (London: Verso, 1983).

Martha Woodmansee, *The Author, Art, and the Market. Rereading the History of Aesthetics* (New York: Columbia University Press, 1994).

9

Literary research and other media

Delia da Sousa Correa, with contributions by

Sara Haslam and Derek Neale

What happens when a book becomes an opera or a film? What is going on when writers invoke the visual arts or music? How shall we discuss Benjamin Britten's *A Midsummer Night's Dream*, or the portrait described in Robert Browning's 'My Last Duchess'? This chapter considers how literary research might deal – at theoretical and practical levels – with connections between literary texts and works in other media. It offers a brief introduction to some of the ways such relationships can become relevant to a diversity of research interests. Multimedia works or adaptations of literary texts into other media are obviously important here, and this chapter ends with an account by Derek Neale of a film adaptation of a text by the twentieth-century writer Janet Frame. But the title 'literary research and other media' also covers research that investigates references to other media within literary texts. Such research can be undertaken for a variety of reasons and work on literature and other media has become an important facet of the growing interdisciplinarity of literary research. (This is apparent in conference and seminar programmes at interdisciplinary research centres, including the Centre for Research in the Arts, Social Sciences and Humanities in Cambridge, whose acronym, CRASSH, conveys some of the excitements and perils of throwing different disciplines up against each other.)

The discussion of literary research and other media in this chapter is intended to inform your own current or potential research interests. It begins with a discussion of interdisciplinarity with an emphasis on what connections with other media might afford their writers and readers. It goes on to reflect on how different media have, variously, offered particular affinities with literature and concludes with three case studies illustrating some of the work that can be generated by a research interest in literature and other media (respectively music, painting and film).

For literary researchers, the study of other media affords new insights into literary texts and the cultures that produce them. Inevitably, allusions to other media within literary texts also tend to provide explicit or implicit commentary on the writer's own art. Whether invoking another art form or object, as characteristic in Victorian literature, or drawing attention to the writer's own technique, as in much Modernist writing, arresting 'intermedial' moments within literary texts occupy a special place in our experience as readers. As Mary Ann Caws puts it, they

> enable the intrusion of another genre into the narrative text ... Passages heavy in repeats, delays and temporal markings, as in an incantatory or impassioned lyric tone, may be seen as penetrated by musical structure. Static arrests and heavy outlining, as well as the description of, or reference to, actual or imagined art objects insist on visual and spatial perception; highly posed scenes, with vivid dialogue and gesture, are felt as calling upon dramatic form ... in each case ... a density usually absent from the single genre creates a privileged space and a remarkable moment, brief or prolonged, which remains in the mind thereafter.
>
> (*Reading Frames in Modern Fiction*, Princeton: Princeton University Press, 1985, p. xi)

Caws begins with a sonic example, but her main concern is relationships between literature and the visual arts. This is an area that has received considerable attention, exemplified by the combined literary and art-historical analysis employed over the past few decades to provide new vantage points from which to understand the literature and painting of the Victorian or Modernist periods (e.g. Kate Flint, *The Victorians and the Visual Imagination*, Cambridge: Cambridge University Press, 2000). The case study of Ford Madox Ford by Sara Haslam near the end of this chapter is an example of how a literary scholar might set about investigating relationships between literature and the visual arts. My own case study discusses an operatic adaptation. The relatively new but expanding field of literature and music has also explored ways of reading allusions to music and sound within literary texts. Work in this area ranges widely from, for example, analysis of the ways in which Modernist writers, such as Mansfield, Woolf or Joyce, undertook structural and stylistic analogies with music, to investigation of how literary dramatisations of musical performance illuminate the social and ideological contexts for music-making during the Victorian period, or a more wide-ranging interest in 'soundscape'. In the case of a writer like George Eliot, whose use of auditory allusion is especially rich, attention to her use of music simultaneously enhances readings of the formal aspects of her work – of those moments that stand out from the surrounding text as described by Caws in the quotation above – and of the social, ideological and aesthetic contexts for her writing (da Sousa Correa, *George Eliot, Music and Victorian Culture*, Basingstoke: Palgrave Macmillan, 2003). For researchers interested in relationships between literature and other media, music itself provides a powerful metaphor for the kind of scrutiny that emphasises the vertical, or 'homophonic' relationships between different art forms, rather than viewing them horizontally, or 'polyphonically', with only intermittent attention to moments of harmonious coincidence (Daniel Albright, *Untwisting the Serpent: Modernism in Music, Literature, and Other Arts*, Chicago: University of Chicago Press, 2000, p. 5).

Enthusiasm flourishes for an ever-growing array of work on literature and other media, despite moments of self-scrutiny as to the value or possibility of 'interdisciplinarity'. The term itself has come in for much criticism, but without any alternative finding general favour. Criticism that simply borrows terms or methodology from another field has been described as having only a tenuous claim to interdisciplinarity; a truly interdisciplinary analysis of literature and music, for example, should make a claim to be regarded simultaneously as literary criticism and as musical analysis. Such rigorously comparative studies as this are rare, and, as Lawrence Kramer has quipped, good ones rarer still ('Dangerous Liaisons: The Literary Text in Musical Criticism', 1989; reprinted in *Critical Musicology and the Responsibility of Response: Selected Essays*, Aldershot: Ashgate, 2006, p. 35). If we do not subscribe to an exclusive notion of interdisciplinarity, it becomes possible for those who are primarily literary critics, or art historians, or musicologists, to engage with sister disciplines. Methodological borrowings can generate a shared revision of critical practice, which in turn influences the way in which relationships between the disciplines develop – a very literal form, therefore, of interdisciplinarity.

However, while opening up welcome opportunities, research across different media raises practical as well as theoretical issues that suggest that there are reasons to respect as well as to challenge divisions between disciplines. The discipline-specific skills required for work in music or the visual arts, for example, bring the practical issues of interdisciplinarity into sharp focus. Nevertheless, while some level of knowledge is clearly required for productive engagement with another discipline, this chapter is particularly aimed at researchers who, having their feet planted within the already varied terrain of literature, are considering what might be the rewards and hazards of extending their interests into other media. For some, an existing interest in another discipline and its relationship with literature will be the chief motivation; others will find that they are led into interdisciplinary work by the nature of the texts that they are researching.

Research across different media is clearly valuable when dealing with periods or authors that do not fit comfortably with current discipline boundaries. For example, many of the best-known artists and intellectuals from the medieval period practised equally in several media. Hildegard von Bingen (1098–1179) was an innovator in science, medicine, philosophy and music; Guillaume de Machaut (c.1300–77) was a scholar, poet and composer; while the anonymous manuscript the *Roman de Fauvel* (1316/17) is a multimedia work combining poetry, chronicle, music and image. This multimediality has subsequently been appropriated, piecemeal, into different disciplinary fields. In consequence, researchers in one field are often unaware of the full range of work undertaken by some of the most famous figures from these centuries.

The way in which the discipline of 'English' has expanded to include research on popular art forms or in electronic and multimedia production in our own day also requires us to look beyond disciplinary horizons. Theoretical interrogations of whether literary texts have a status distinct from 'texts' in other media and the growth of Cultural Studies have fostered, and been fostered by, interdisciplinarity. Research combining work in literature with an awareness of other media prompts engagement with issues currently debated within 'English', as within other disciplines. Such work has both partaken of the extended opportunities offered by Cultural Studies and shared in a recent critical scrutiny of the 'cultural turn', endorsing the importance of the defining conditions in which art, literature and music are consumed, yet lamenting our neglect of issues of aesthetic value: those intransigent questions about what the defining qualities of visual, literary and musical arts might be, and why what is viewed, read or heard matters to us. For some, a research interest in literature and other media involves a choice between opposing critical paths (Peter Dayan, *Music Writing Literature, from Sand via Debussy to Derrida*, Aldershot: Ashgate, 2006), while for others it potentially offers an opportunity to have one's cake and eat it – to combine the reading of culture with a mode of reading that concerns itself with how and whether we can discuss the formation of a specifically 'literary' language. Such questions tend particularly to come to the fore when we assess adaptations of literary texts into other media. Adaptations, and metaphorical parallels with other arts, imply the possibility of some form of 'translation' between literary and other forms; yet, at the same time, they draw attention to what is unique about each particular medium. Our meditations on what a film director, opera composer or painter have made of a literary text frequently prompt judgements about the adaptation's 'authenticity': as a version of the source text and/or as a work in its own right. In thinking about this, we implicitly reflect on what is particular to the experience of 'literature' as opposed to works in other media. Thus contemplation of literature's relationship with other media can usefully prompt reflections upon what we mean by 'literature' itself; it is paradoxically the case that we sometimes seem to come closest to saying what literature is, or how it matters, when drawing analogies with other arts.

Ut pictura poesis (poetry is as painting).

(Horace, *Ars Poetica* (c.19–18 BCE))

All art constantly aspires towards the condition of music.

(Walter Pater (1877))

As illustrated by the two quotations above, different arts/media have at different times found favour as the most potent parallels for literature. Horace and Pater illustrate different conceptions and a historical shift. Horace's alliance of painting and poetry emphasises their joint powers of representation. For Pater, however, it was music's lack of capacity for representation, its transcendent ineffability that placed it at the head of the aesthetic hierarchy and made its condition that to which all other arts aspired (see his 'The School of Giorgione', in *The Renaissance: Studies in Art and Poetry*, second edn, rev., London: Macmillan, 1877, p. 140). Music embodied Pater's ideal of an entirely abstract art, and indeed another context within which such opposing analogies for literature can be discussed is in relation to contending drives towards abstraction and representation in all the arts (see Daniel Albright, *Untwisting the Serpent*).

Music and poetry had, of course, long been considered 'sister arts' in relation to their formal structures and affective power. However, for Pater, a valorisation of the non-representational nature of music was part of his celebration, in the infamous 'Conclusion' to *The Renaissance* in 1873, of 'the love of art for art's sake' (p. 213). His older contemporary, John Ruskin provides a contrasting example of how the relationship between literature and the other arts might be perceived. Ruskin himself was a superlatively intermedial and interdisciplinary figure who drew and painted as well as writing prolifically on an immense array of subjects including art, architecture, economics, geology, mythology and society. His early writings emphasised connections between literature and painting – Horace's *ut pictura* – with the two arts linked by their expressive as well as representational powers. However, Ruskin subsequently found an elaborate analogy for literature in music, or rather in two competing types of music, represented by the ancient contest between Apollo and Marsyas. On one side was the ordered music of Apollo's lyre, whose strings emblematised a balanced and proportionate framework for artistic expression. For Ruskin, Apollonian music had to be combined with words, whose representational force helped to contain music's affective power. Opposed to this was the sensual, wordless music of Marsyas's pipes, which Ruskin heard echoed in the industrial steam whistles of his day and which stood for licentiousness in life and art (see Delia da Sousa Correa, 'Goddesses of Instruction and Desire: Ruskin and Music', in *Ruskin and the Dawn of the Modern*, ed. Dinah Birch, Oxford: Oxford University Press, 1999). Despite its apparently purposeful agenda, readers of Ruskin's prose might conclude that it is his rhetorical command of the seductive powers of Marsyas, rather than Apollonian principles of order, that makes it persuasive to them.

Both Ruskin and Pater show how ideological and aesthetic preoccupations inevitably influence an understanding of the relationship between literature and other media. Among the reasons that music still appeals as an analogy for literature in our own day, is the extent to which the abstract uncertainties of musical meaning have increasingly seemed to mirror the uncertainties of linguistic signification, as analysed in much twentieth-century philosophical and critical theory. Once, the representational power of language and the visual arts made these natural companions; now language is valued for the referential uncertainty that was previously music's preserve, and music offers a fund of analogy for literature and new modes of understanding language itself. This last is exemplified in Wittgenstein's insight that 'understanding a sentence is much more akin to understanding a theme in music than one may think' and the insistent, if troubling, relevance of music within the theories of Jacques Derrida (Peter Dayan, 'The Force of Music in Derrida's writing', and Daniel Albright, 'Stances towards Music as a Language', in *Phrase and Subject: Studies in Literature and Music*, ed. Delia da Sousa Correa, Oxford: Legenda and MHRA/Maney Publishing, 2006, pp. 45–58, 18). For literary researchers, this interest in analogies between music and language offers a revivification of the longstanding association of music and poetry as sister arts (see Lawrence Kramer, *Music and Poetry: The Nineteenth Century and After*, Berkeley: University of California Press, 1984). We live in a culture which, while saturated with music and noise, is most consciously attuned to the visual. Victorian writers paid close attention both to visual detail and to qualities of voice. Modernist writers engaged synaesthetically with the arts, aspiring to the non-discursive qualities of music in their conspicuous displays of literary technique, but drawing too on the colours and visual rhythms of post-impressionist art, and the jump-cut, long-shot, close-up techniques of the new (and scarcely respectable) art of cinema. Today, the established media of film and other visual arts have been joined by a hydra-headed proliferation of electronic and virtual multimedia with the potential to unite sound and sight (Steven Connor, 'The Modern Auditory I', in *Rewriting the Self: Histories from the Renaissance to the Present*, ed. Roy Porter, London: Routledge, 1997, p. 221).

For writers and readers of literature, the possibilities for interdisciplinary engagement are dizzying. The three case studies that follow are a very selective sample of work that might be undertaken by literary researchers. They nevertheless usefully represent many of the practical and theoretical issues that will confront researchers on any number of interdisciplinary projects.

1   *Literature and Music:* This examines the collaboration between Michael Berkeley and David Malouf in the creation of their opera based on *Jane Eyre*. It explores how librettist and composer function as 'readers' and 'translators' of the novel.

2   *Literature and Painting:* A case study of Ford Madox Ford explores what his engagement with painting offered Ford as a writer and how a scholarly investigation of connections between his literary output and the visual arts impacts on readings of his novels.

3   *Literature and Film:* This approaches film adaptation from both a practical and a critical standpoint. It also includes discussion of ways in which writing can be described as having 'filmic' qualities.

The first case study discusses an operatic version of one of the most-adapted texts from English literature, Charlotte Brontë's *Jane Eyre* (1847). The emphasis here is on ways in which a literary researcher might start to think about adaptations of literary texts into other media. It offers an opportunity to consider both a specific adaptation of a literary text and what role the activity of adaptation might play in creative production more generally. Recent work such as Linda Hutcheon's *A Theory of Adaptation* (London: Routledge, 2006) emphasises that adaptation has always been fundamental to the way that stories are told. Thus adaptation is a concept that applies to translations between a host of different media and also to the intertextual relations between literary texts. Influenced by Cultural Studies, the academic study of the varied afterlives of literary texts has been encouraged by broadened categories of cultural value. These have prompted research on popular as well as more conventionally studied media, and analysis of their cultural significance. Much work on adaptation takes place within Film Studies, but there has also been a significant shift towards the study of adaptation across a host of other disciplines, which have become interested not only in the work of screenwriters and film directors but also of 'performers, cinematographers, editors, and composers – not to mention parodists, comic-book artists, video game designers, and opera composers and librettists' (Thomas Leitch, review of Hutcheon, *A Theory of Adaptation*, in *Literature/Film Quarterly*, 35, 3 (2007), 250). Thus Classicists working on the reception history of Greek tragedy are now likely to investigate the political contexts for its representation over recent centuries

and are as interested in *Medea* on film, or the significance of cross-dressed bur-
lesque versions of *Medea* in nineteenth-century London, as in its original performance (see *Medea in Performance 1500–2000*, ed. Edith Hall, Fiona
Macintosh and Oliver Taplin, Oxford: Legenda, 2000; Edith Hall and Fiona
Macintosh, *Greek Tragedy and the British Theatre, 1660–1914*, Oxford: Oxford
University Press, 2005). There is of course much to be said about drama as a
medium in its own right, and as a genre constantly invoked within non-
dramatic literary forms. Limitations of space mean that we discuss drama here
only as a crucial element within opera and film adaptations.

CASE STUDY 1: LITERATURE AND MUSIC

Michael Berkeley and David Malouf, Jane Eyre: An Opera in Two Acts (2000)

The rich adaptation history of *Jane Eyre* has been explored in detail in
Patsy Stoneman's pioneering study *Brontë Transformations: The Cultural
Dissemination of Jane Eyre and Wuthering Heights* (London: Prentice-Hall,
1996), and more recently in *A Breath of Fresh Eyre: Intertextual and Intermedial
Reworkings of Jane Eyre*, ed. Margarete Rubik and Elke Mettinger-Schartmann
(Amsterdam: Rodopi, 2008). *The Brontës in the World of the Arts*, ed. Sandra
Hagen and Juliette Wells (Aldershot: Ashgate, 2008) also includes discussion
of illustrations and literary, dramatic, film versions and musical adaptations and
settings of their work. *Jane Eyre* was frequently adapted for the stage from the
year of its first publication, but although music played an integral part in a
number of nineteenth-century melodrama versions, it was not adapted as an
opera until the 1960s. Berkeley and Malouf's collaboration allows us to explore
how librettist and composer function as 'readers' and 'translators': in Malouf's
view, 'no libretto can reproduce the novel from which it is drawn … The best a
libretto can do is to reproduce the experience of the book in a new and *radically
different form*' (quoted in Stephen Benson, *Literary Music: Writing Music in
Contemporary Fiction*, Aldershot: Ashgate, 2006, p. 48).

Malouf and Berkeley compressed the novel's action into a potent 90 minutes.
Their opera is set entirely at Thornfield, omitting the narrative of Jane's earlier
life and her flight from Rochester. The musical dramatisation is achieved by
five contrasting voices, soprano (Jane), baritone (Rochester), girl soprano
(Adèle), mezzo (Mrs Fairfax) and contralto (Mrs Rochester), frequently augmented by specific instrumental colour (oboe for Jane, flute for Adèle, or bass
clarinet to suggest Mrs Rochester's laughter).

Malouf wanted 'an equivalent' for the compelling 'intimacy' and 'enchantment' of Jane's narrative voice. His starting point was to identify a pre-existing
element in the novel that '*demands*' music (see his libretto for *Jane Eyre: An*

Opera in Two Acts, London: Vintage, 2000, p. ix). Chief in offering 'an essentially musical possibility' was the uncanny moment when Jane hears Rochester's disembodied voice calling her. The opera is structured as Jane's interiorised recollection at this moment: the cry of 'Jane, Jane' resounds at the outset as it enacts Jane's arrival at Thornfield. Thus its germ is the realisation of a vocal image that arises at a key moment in the source text.

Malouf describes this moment as the 'strangest' and 'the most romantic' memory for readers of the novel and its uncanny and romantic elements are intensified in the opera's dramatisation of Jane's memories. He suggests that the vocal medium facilitates a concentrated dramatic realisation:

> Music makes its own space. Voices meet and join there, whatever the real distance between them. Jane can be, at one moment, inside the house ... and in the next, with just a few bars of musical transition, outside on the ice, with Mr Rochester's horse rearing above her.
>
> (Malouf, *Jane Eyre: An Opera in Two Acts*, p. ix)

'The great thing that music can do', Malouf believes, 'is point up an inner turmoil of frustrated desires' (Tom Service, 'Michael Berkeley: *Jane Eyre*', Booklet for Chandos Recording, Music Theatre Wales, 2002 CHAN 9983, p. 7). Berkeley's orchestration enables the music to comment on the action and dramatise psychological undercurrents running through the novel. Maintaining 'a dark glissando-y turbulence', it conveys 'suppressed eroticism' and sense of threat even at times of ostensible happiness: with a 'constant worried music going on in the bass' when Mrs Fairfax and Adèle inspect the wedding veil (Service, 'Michael Berkeley: *Jane Eyre*', p. 7).

The familiarity of *Jane Eyre* as a literary text and as the subject of numerous adaptations into film, presents challenge and advantages. It discouraged a 'Hollywood'-style representation of its narrative scope (Service, 'Michael Berkeley: *Jane Eyre*', p. 6), and meant that audiences could be expected to recognise some of the mythic, fairy-tale and gothic elements highlighted by the opera. Berkeley and Malouf's mode of dramatisation meets the practical demands of opera and its need, as perceived by Malouf, to establish a romantic (albeit here disturbing) world of mythic enchantment. It highlights not only romantic and uncanny aspects of which readers are already aware, but extends music's role as an agent of the uncanny to illuminate 'previously hidden corners of the story' (Service, 'Michael Berkeley: *Jane Eyre*', p. 7). One such hidden corner, I would suggest, is indeed the importance within Brontë's novel of voices and of auditory allusion, not always something to which twenty-first-century readers are especially attuned. In the novel, Rochester's disembodied voice harks back to the image of the physical 'cord' that he previously claimed joined him to Jane, a visual image that hovers on the auditory in its suggestion of a musical string even before it is translated into Rochester's cry (Charlotte Brontë, *Jane Eyre*, 1847; ed. Margaret Smith, Oxford: Oxford University Press, 2000, p. 252; see also Delia da Sousa Correa, '*Jane Eyre* and Genre', in *The Nineteenth-Century Novel: Realisms*, ed. da Sousa Correa, London: Routledge, 2000, p. 111). Berkeley describes Brontë's novel as 'essentially operatic … because it's predicated on the idea of voices – voices that are heard through a kind of telepathy, voices that come out of the ether' (Patsy Stoneman, 'Operatic and Musical Versions', in *The Oxford Companion to the Brontës*, ed. Christine Alexander and Margaret Smith, Oxford: Oxford University Press, 2003, p. 356).

Berkeley's opera conveys some of the intense interiority of Jane's narrative voice. At the same time, the centrality of that voice is modified as the opera provides musical and dramatic space for other voices. Like Rochester's, Mrs Rochester's voice is heard from early on, realising the preoccupation of recent rewritings of Jane Eyre with giving Bertha her own voice and a constant haunting presence. It parallels the technique employed in another *Jane Eyre*-related work, Polly Teale's play *After Mrs Rochester*, throughout which Bertha remains physically on stage. The play is based on the life of Jean Rhys, whose 1966 novel narrating Antoinette/Bertha's life in the Caribbean prompted the shift of interest onto the character of Bertha evident in critical and artistic accounts of Brontë's novel over the past 50 years. Berkeley records that he and Malouf devised their opera 'with Jean Rhys's *Wide Sargasso Sea* firmly having been read by both of us' (Benson, *Literary Music*, p. 49). They show Mrs Rochester as possessed of a sensual sexuality, but sad rather than mad, bewailing the captivity that makes her a 'living ghost' (Malouf, *Jane Eyre: An Opera in Two Acts*, p. 20). Their character is firmly 'Mrs Rochester' rather than 'Bertha', and her vocal and physical presence alongside Jane implies Jane's usurpation in a way not featured in Brontë's novel. Their opera also exposes some of the racial undertones of Brontë's text. Rochester bewails the 'taint' following his marriage, while Mrs Rochester's voice is constantly described as 'dark as molasses' and she dances to 'Caribbean' music before attempting to set Rochester alight (Malouf, *Jane Eyre: An Opera in Two Acts*, pp. 7, 12, 14, 24).

Rhys's novel is only one of a wide range of highly conscious intertextual references to different literary and operatic traditions within the opera. Its opening orchestral glissandi are reminiscent of Benjamin Britten's *A Midsummer Night's Dream* and it also harks back strongly to Britten's operatic version of another *Jane Eyre*-related text, Henry James's *The Turn of the Screw*. Into this predominantly Modernist idiom is woven an eclectic postmodern mixture of references to dance-hall melodies and earlier operatic styles. When Adèle appears, she chooses the mad scene from Donizetti's *Lucia di Lammermoor* to demonstrate her skill in dancing and singing and her account of the opera's famous love-duet melody is doubled by Mrs Rochester's voice offstage (Malouf, *Jane Eyre:*

An Opera in Two Acts, p. 7). The obvious relevance of this opera to Mrs Rochester is later augmented by allusion to *The Bride of Lammermoor*, the novel by Walter Scott (a favourite author of Brontë's), which inspired Donizetti's opera. Jane becomes 'The bride of Thornfield' in Adèle and Mrs Fairfax's enraptured commentary on the wedding veil shortly to be destroyed by the existing 'Mrs Edward Rochester, the ghost of Thornfield' (Malouf, *Jane Eyre: An Opera in Two* Acts, p. 20).

Opera involves dramatic and visual effects as well as words and music. In the original staging, curved mirrors suggested the doubling relationships between characters and enabled Mrs Rochester's final 'abandoned' dance to culminate in a reflected conflagration that engulfed her (Stoneman, *Brontë Transformations*, p. 357). The opera ends very rapidly after this, with the blinded Rochester all but stumbling out of the flames into Jane's embrace. This conclusion has been criticised as unconvincing, or as undermining claims to have portrayed Mrs Rochester sympathetically, sacrificing her all too readily in the interests of the romantic resolution that the opera privileges beyond its original place in the novel (see Walter Bernhart, 'Myth-making Opera: David Malouf and Michael Berkeley's Jane Eyre', in Rubik and Mettinger-Schartmann, *A Breath of Fresh Eyre*, pp. 325 n. 11, 327). A final love duet between Jane and Rochester recalls both grand romantic opera and the twentieth-century musical. Given the opera's self-conscious play on operatic and literary conventions, it arguably lays bare rather than simply elides the price of romantic fulfilment within the colonial discourse of the source text(s). Berkeley not only claims that Mrs Rochester is sympathetic, but defines her as 'a tragic figure' (Service, 'Michael Berkeley: *Jane Eyre*', p. 6). Perhaps this work also exposes the brutality of tragic opera, whose plots, feminist critics have argued, constantly enact the destruction of women whose sexuality transgresses conventional bounds (Catherine Clément, *Opera: Or, The Undoing of Women*, trans. Betsy Wing, London: Virago, 1989).

For literary researchers, this operatic adaptation invites reflection on how translation into another medium (in opera, a multimedia form) enriches interpretation of Brontë's novel and its constant reinvention in criticism and art. Research spanning literature and other disciplines challenges us to think about the requirements of different media in their own right and inspires fresh insights on the work of literary criticism (prompting investigation, for instance, of relationships between the creation of a 'voice' in writing and the tangible voices of music (Benson, *Literary Music*, pp. 59–60)). The Berkeley/Malouf opera also shows us that reading *Jane Eyre* has simultaneously become a process of reading the 160 years of cultural history that separate us from the novel's first publication.

CASE STUDY 2: LITERATURE AND PAINTING

Ford Madox Ford in Colour, by Sara Haslam

Ever since I read Thomas Hardy's *Tess of the D'Urbervilles* (1891) as an undergraduate I have been interested in the ways in which writers make use of visual material in their writing. (Think of the early descriptions of Tess's 'peony mouth', distinctive red ribbon, and first blush.) When, later, I came to work on Ford Madox Ford, it was clear his debt to painterly techniques was stronger still. This was partly to be explained by Ford's brand of Modernism. His apprenticeship as a novelist was served with Joseph Conrad, and they developed together a theory of impressionism in novel writing, dedicated to making the reader 'see' (Ford called the third part of his memoir of Conrad (1924) 'It Is Above All to Make You See'). Ford wanted the novel to replicate in some way the mind's experience of 'various unordered pictures' – similar to what Virginia Woolf would famously term 'myriad impressions' in her essay 'Modern Fiction' in 1919. But long before Ford met Conrad, or the term 'Modernism' was common currency, he was particularly dedicated to investigating and expressing the links between literature and painting in his art.

Ford's early fairy tales were visual in appeal, colourful in the extreme (all 'blue hills' and 'red-gold sunsets', for example, in *The Brown Owl*, London: T. Fisher Unwin, 1981, p. 7), and were either illustrated, or inspired, by artists he was related to or knew: Ford Madox Brown, Edward Burne-Jones, Dante Gabriel Rossetti. His second published book of poetry was titled in full *Poems for Pictures and for Notes of Music* (1900), and contains a 'Song Drama in One Act' which owed a debt to Burne-Jones. A poem from the same collection, 'Beginnings', takes as its subject Rossetti's first painting, *The Girlhood of Mary Virgin*. Earlier still, Ford had also shown an abstract interest in the inter-referentiality of the Arts. In *Ford Madox Brown*, a biography of his grandfather, he wrote of Dumas being 'the Master' of the young painter and Chaucer the inspiration (London: Longmans, Green and Co, 1896, p. 47). This model was developed to a high degree by the textually obsessed Pre-Raphaelites, the group of painters to which Ford owed most. In the late nineteenth century, then, Ford was busy refining his writing in significant ways in relation to the visual arts generally and the work of the Pre-Raphaelites in particular.

These painters taught him about setting scenes, creating drama and exploiting visual effects in his writing. Readers who recognise the signs of homage being paid infer a deeper vein of meaning in Ford's writing, but those who don't still benefit from the shadow play, the formal tricks and plot excitements that might be related to the paintings he knew well. The climactic scene of *Privy Seal* (1907), when Katherine Howard finally succumbs to King Henry, owes something both to Rossetti's *Beata Beatrix* – and its emphasis on love and death – and the earlier wood engraving, *Saint Cecilia*. Rossetti's *La Donna della Finestra* also performs a catalytic function in the disastrous breakfast party at the start of *Parade's End* (1924–8). There are many less-specific instances of painterly influence too. Some appear in *The Portrait* (London: Methuen, 1910), a romance set in the eighteenth century. Throughout the novel characters are contrasted against a white backdrop for effect (e.g., pp. 25, 28). In one scene Ford uses candles and 'cockling windowglass' – and see a version of *La Donna della Finestra* (1879) for a painted example – to explain the 'confusing undulations of light' framed against a 'translucent and liquid bar of light in the sky' (p. 134).

Primarily, however, the painters that Ford knew, taught him about colour. His early books are in a real way dedicated to explorations of colour, colour technique and all related effects. He often exhibits an intellectual understanding of the value of colour. In his criticism of *The Girlhood of Mary Virgin*, for example, he knows that the different books are colour-coded to signify the theological Virtues (*Rossetti: A Critical Essay on his Art*, 1902; London: Duckworth, 1914, p. 22). The predominance of the colour blue in *The Good Soldier* (1915) – what Bill Hutchings calls 'all those blue eyes' and the way in which they are both 'immensely attractive and strangely inscrutable' (in 'Ford and Maupassant', *Ford Madox Ford's Modernity*, ed. Max Saunders and Robert Hampson, Amsterdam and New York: Rodopi, 2003, p. 267) – might well also suggest a familiarity with Goethe's theory of colour, in which blue is a 'stimulating negation', 'a kind of contradiction between excitement and repose' (*Goethe's Theory of Colours*, London: John Murray, 1840, p. 311). (Goethe's theorising of the colour blue is well-known, and the Pre-Raphaelites placed him on their 'List of the Immortals', as reproduced in Ford's book about them, *The Pre-Raphaelite Brotherhood*, London: Duckworth, 1908, p. 105.)

Goethe's premise that 'people experience a great delight in colour' (p. 304), developed notably by Kandinsky a century later, is explained partly by physics, partly by emotion and partly by nature. If Ford had no direct experience of Goethe's theory, the natural argument had a proponent who was unquestionably, and influentially, much closer to home: John Ruskin. For Ruskin, as well as for Goethe, colour was to show nature and life (though Ruskin also possessed strong views as to the moral limits of colour). Lindsay Smith reads Ruskin, and his privileging of colourists like Turner, in the context of the contemporary rise in photography, and the 'medium's reduction to monochrome of the rainbow's spectrum' (in 'Thinking Blues', *Transactions and Encounters: Science and Culture in the Nineteenth Century*, ed. Roger Luckhurst and Josephine McDonagh, Manchester: Manchester University Press, 2002, p. 55). Ford was in favour of the rainbow. He uses the phrase 'the joy of colour' in his book on Madox

Brown (p. 404), and colour often signifies abundant life and nature in his own work. In *The Panel* (1912), the bedroom of the seductive Flossie Delamare is a riot of enticing pink, and Mrs Kerr Howe, a widow with designs on protagonist Teddy Foster, becomes especially dangerous once she has put off her black. In ways like this, the work colour does in a text is linked to its emotional connotations and effects, its sheer physicality. Ford's tendency to place strong, positive colours against black shows he knows how to extract the most use from a colour in the reader's mind's eye – making it as easy and as satisfying as possible to, as I pointed out in my introduction, *see*.

Finally, however, and perhaps most importantly, there are links to be made between this use of colour and Ford's Modernism. Ford became the Modernist exemplar he did, to a large degree because of his visual technique. Towards the end of *The Pre-Raphaelite Brotherhood* comes the following important section:

> It is indeed pleasant to think of these London painters emerging from their gloomy surroundings. They chased ... all the year round, over the bright valleys of the earth, their ideals of luminosity; from the backcloths of bright earth and bright sky they cut out, as if with sharp knives, square panels of eternal paint. They gave to material phases of Nature a relative permanency, a comparative immortal life.
> ... these Pre-Raphaelites succeeded very miraculously in rendering a very charming, a very tranquil, and a very secure England
> They never convey to us, as do the Impressionists, or as did the earlier English landscape painters, the sense of fleeting light and shadow.
>
> (pp. 164–5)

Admiring though it is, this quotation also provides evidence of Ford's sense of the limitations of these painters. He outgrew them, after all. Yes, there is a satisfactory, life-affirming permanence and stability in their work, but this quotation displays restlessness also, a need for forward movement, for questioning variance and lightness, for a moment of transition.

Theories of colour treat of its movement, or of its creation of a sense of movement. Maurice Denis, among other critics, has written about the movement in Cézanne's colour ('Cézanne', 1907) and in an interview in 1979, artist Janice Biala, Ford's partner for the last ten years of his life, linked Ford's aesthetic to that of the great painter (*The Presence of Ford Madox Ford*, ed. Sondra Stang, Pennsylvania: The University of Pennsylvania Press, 1982, p. 223). Fittingly, Ford relies on colour to achieve the Modernist picture that is the *Parade's End* breakfast party; it helps him to realise the sense of rival perspectives, tension, but most particularly movement. It's not about the colour itself, but where it is going, and what it is mutating into – a force to make the provocative Mrs Duchemin swoon in front of the object of her affections, for example. (A good contemporary comparison is Miss Pym's flower shop at the outset of Woolf's *Mrs Dalloway* (1925) in which colour accelerates sensation.) In *Provence*, Ford reveals that he can write with full knowledge of the greys of the Nordic character and landscape because the colour will come again, moving him on, such that he can edit his London prose, bring it to life and simultaneously write the 'little crisp sentences like silver fish jumping out of streams' (Philadephia: J.B. Lippincott, 1935, p. 139). Blues and greens are no longer simply static or everlasting; they are answered and given depth by the blacks and greys of mutating shadow and Modernist uncertainty.

CASE STUDY 3: LITERATURE AND FILM

Reading film: **An Angel at My Table** *by Derek Neale*

This last case study looks at Jane Campion's 1990 film *An Angel at My Table*, the adaptation of Janet Frame's autobiography of the same title (London: The Women's Press, 1990). Films are often remediated stories which originate from a variety of sources, sometimes obscure, sometimes eminent, as with Frame's three-volume memoir. Since the 1970s and the influence of structuralism, film criticism has tended to perceive film performance as 'text', with the growing assertion of its own theoretical framework and vocabulary, distinct from the literary sphere. As in literary theory there are various schools and approaches but, as the image is film's predominant *modus operandi*, much film study tends to be preoccupied with optical modes of representation and visual narrative methods; it analyses the use and content of shots, narrative segmentation, scene-linking techniques, and is largely if not exclusively concerned with non-verbal signification. This case study can only touch briefly on possible avenues of approach to film studies, but it is interesting to note that such approaches are made more complex when both film adaptations and the original texts on which they are based are scrutinised. Adaptation studies, which evolved in parallel with film studies, has developed its own agenda, one which has gradually grown away from its original orthodoxy of gauging a film's proximity to its adapted text (what became known as 'fidelity criticism'). More recently studies of adaptation have come to focus on the intertextuality at work with a more free-ranging approach to the analysis and comparison of the respective narrative contents and methods, and in ways which avoid perceptions of the originating text as primary.

The narrative in Jane Campion's film operates by using series of juxtaposed images – shots which if viewed in isolation might not make any narrative sense. This shot and scene montage narrative appears as a wordless poem that often requires the film's reader to imagine what might lie between the partial, uninflected images. This is most apparent in a key early scene: the young Frame's first, dangerous encounter with lying, where she is caught out by her teacher, Miss Botting. Sergei Eisenstein, the founding theorist of montage, traces the method of partial images to nineteenth-century literature and visual arts. For instance, he evokes Zola and two paintings by Manet, *Bar at the Moulin Rouge and Bar at the Folies-Bergère* ('Lessons from Literature', trans. Jay Leyda, in *Film Essays with a Lecture*, London: Dobson, 1968, pp. 81–2) where characters are obscured by other elements within the scene; yet, Eisenstein claims, it would never appear that these characters were, 'anatomically, half-people'. He suggests these 'clots of real detail', however partial, produce detailed characterisations. Elsewhere Eisenstein traces montage back to the early Hollywood film maker D.W. Griffith ('Dickens, Griffith and the Film Today', trans. Jay Leyda, in *Film Form*, New York: Meridian, 1957, pp. 195–255), who in turn acknowledges Dickens as his role model. Griffith took from Dickens the prevalent spliced-strand method used by many other nineteenth-century novelists – Thackeray, George Eliot, Trollope, Meredith, Hardy – which is billed by Eisenstein as the 'montage of parallel action': one narrative is left pulsing as another begins, so delaying reader gratification. This montage method is often referred to as the 'cut' in modern discussion and should not be confused with 'montage sequence', another modern usage, which is related to Eisenstein's versions of montage but which is an accelerated and exaggerated version of the method, one which is widely deployed but often disparaged by screenwriting orthodoxies.

When talking of Dickens's influence on Griffith, Eisenstein identifies other narrative techniques and optical qualities that cross over between genres and media – frame composition, close-up, shifting emphasis using special lenses, and even 'dissolve' (in the opening of the last chapter of *A Tale of Two Cities*). He also elaborates upon the type of montage that we can recognise in *An Angel at My Table* – the type which doesn't cut between characters or narrative strands, but instead cuts between partial, inconclusive images of the same character, as with the figures in the Manet paintings. Dickens does this using syntax and the insertion of brief, revealing clauses. Eisenstein illustrates using a passage involving Mr Dombey from *Dombey and Son*, suggesting that this method in effect engages the performative imagination of the reader. Something of the characterisation is partial but, when surrounded by the other elements, a detailed and dramatised characterisation with interiority arises.

The same is true of the characterisation in Campion's film, specifically in the scenes leading up to Janet's confrontation with Miss Botting. Its effectiveness lies in its simple concision, as seen in Laura Jones's script:

17. *Janet's hand slides into Dad's best trousers hanging on a hook behind the bedroom door. There is the chink of coins.*
18. *Janet stands at the door of the Infants room. She hands each child who comes in a pillow of chewing-gum, naming them: Marjorie, Joy, Billy, and so on.*

19. *The children sit at desks in rows, all chewing gum. Two monitors walk*
    up and down the aisles giving out green-covered copy books.
      Miss Botting turns from the board where she has lettered the day
    and date. Not all the children stop chewing as she turns.
                                   (*An Angel at My Table: The Screenplay from the*
                                    Three-Volume Autobiography of Janet Frame,
                                       London: Pandora, 1990, pp. 4–5)

Both 17 and 18 create only partial meaning in themselves. The cutting is
severe and quick. Viewed in isolation the scenes would mean little, but their
juxtaposition provides a synthesis of meaning: Janet is stealing money from
her father in order to buy friendship and popularity. We do not see her going
to buy chewing gum with the stolen money (though this detail is included in
Frame's account). Janet's shock when her lie – that her father gave her the
money to buy the chewing gum – is not believed becomes tangible in the
ensuing close-up. Shock turns to guilt, turns to shame; and finally comes the
realisation that words have got her into this mess and words somehow have
got to get her out of it. Yet no words are used to show this.

More recent advocates of montage such as David Mamet suggest that the ideal
film would be wordless (*On Directing Film*, London: Faber, 1991, p. 72), and *An
Angel at My Table* is relatively silent. The events in the classroom provide the
only extended dramatic scene in the early part of the film, and surprisingly the
dialogue is taken almost verbatim from a mimetic passage in Frame's autobiography. Frame's text otherwise contains what might be considered to be non-
filmic qualities: a level of interiority that often pauses to scrutinise the ways in
which language is used. In the book her childhood is illustrated by her reading
– quoted songs, poems and described magazines (only sometimes films), arte-
facts that are shared with others and which in combination form an intertextual thread. Frame points out her estrangement from the world, her difference,
as she announces these linguistic curiosities. She misreads a story's title, enun-
ciating the silent 's', Is- land, and this becomes seen as New Zealand's North
Island. She inadvertently personalises the anthems of Empire: having a favourite kerosene tin, she is convinced the song runs 'God save our gracious tin'.

In the film, Frame's difference is represented without this linguistic detail.
Though Jones's early scripts contained voice-overs using passages from the
autobiography, attempts to translate Frame's poetic, interiorised and sometimes
literary voice, these don't survive in Campion's final version. The intertextuality of Frame's early reading is subsumed in the film version by an ongoing dialogic relationship with the original autobiography; the film's audience
appreciates what Linda Hutcheon terms the 'multilaminated' storytelling (*A*

Theory of Adaptation, London: Routledge, 2006, p. 21), in this instance the layers provided by Frame's œuvre as well as her memoir. Hutcheon suggests that the power of close-up unravels the assumption that diegetic literary 'telling' is exclusively effective at revealing interiority; and that, conversely, close-up also unwraps the assertion that the kind of mimetic 'showing' found in films can only reveal exteriority and action (p. 58). This is especially true in the Miss Botting scene, where the silent close-up of young Jean facing the blackboard could not be more revealing of her inner dilemma. Frame's 'difference' is symbolised in the film by her hair, a striking ginger mop which clashes with the predominant greens and browns of her home town, Oamaru. Gone are the poems, songs and idiosyncratic phrases. We see from Frame's perspective but this viewpoint is understated; the interiority, the cogitation and import of those perceptions, exists largely in the gaps between explicit shots. Besides the use of silence, close-up and viewpoint, an interior life is created via the other key method: montage and the use of visually contrasting, partial images which, when viewed in combination, create a new meaning. Such juxtapositions allow the audience to think alongside a character and, as Eisenstein suggested, offer a 'personage in "close-up"' in a way that translates, without reproducing, some of the intrinsic qualities of the verbal text.

QUESTIONS AND EXERCISES

1   Choose an example from your own reading of a passage where allusion to another medium makes it particularly memorable. Why?

2   Can you think of an adaptation into another medium that has influenced you as a reader and critic of a literary text?

3   Is there a technical or theoretical aspect to a medium that you think might enhance your literary research? Identify the resources to improve your knowledge of such aspects.

4   How do you think adaptation studies might contribute to, or veer away from, poststructuralist theorising of intertextuality and its 'challenge to dominant post-Romantic notions of originality, uniqueness, and autonomy' (Hutcheon, *A Theory of Adaptation*, p. 21)?

SELECTED READING

Daniel Albright, *Untwisting the Serpent: Modernism in Music, Literature, and Other Arts* (Chicago: University of Chicago Press, 2000).

Stephen Benson, *Literary Music: Writing Music in Contemporary Fiction* (Aldershot: Ashgate, 2006).

Delia da Sousa Correa, *George Eliot, Music and Victorian Culture* (Basingstoke: Palgrave Macmillan, 2003).

—— (ed.), *Phrase and Subject: Studies in Literature and Music* (Oxford: Legenda, MHRA/Maney Publishing, 2006).

Peter Dayan, *Music Writing Literature, from Sand via Debussy to Derrida* (Aldershot: Ashgate, 2006).

Kate Flint, *The Victorians and the Visual Imagination* (Cambridge: Cambridge University Press, 2000).

William S. Heckscher, *Art and Literature: Studies in Relationship* (Durham: Duke University Press: 1985).

Linda Hutcheon, *A Theory of Adaptation* (London: Routledge, 2006).

Lawrence Kramer, *Music and Poetry: The Nineteenth Century and After* (Berkeley: University of California Press, 1984).

Brian McFarlane, *Novel to Film: An introduction to the theory of adaptation* (Oxford: Clarendon, 1996).

John Picker, *Victorian Soundscapes* (Oxford: Oxford University Press, 2003).

Mario Praz, *Mnemosyne: the Parallel between Literature and the Visual Arts* (London: Oxford University Press, 1970).

Julie Sanders, *Adaptation and Appropriation* (London and New York: Routledge, 2006).

Robert Stam, and Alessandra Raengo (eds), *A Companion to Literature and Film* (Oxford: Blackwell, 2004).

10

Literary research and translation

Susan Bassnett

TRANSLATION AND GLOBALISATION

The twenty-first century is a time of unprecedented movement for vast numbers of people all around the planet. Some are driven to leave their homelands by war, political oppression, famine, natural disasters or economic crisis; others set out in search of a better life for themselves and their families and choose their destination proactively. Millions now travel for leisure purposes: since the early 1990s citizens of states that had previously restricted travel, such as China, the former Soviet Union and countries across Eastern Europe now jostle in airport check-in queues with citizens of the more affluent Western states. This mass movement of people constitutes one of what globalisation theorists have characterised as the circulation of global flows, along with the movement of capital, commodities, information and, as communications increase in speed, images (see Arjun Appadurai, *Modernity at Large: Cultural Dimensions of Globalization*, Minneapolis: University of Minneapolis Press, 1996). In less than two decades we have moved into an age of intercultural communication and global mobility, into an age of interconnectedness undreamed of by previous generations.

Since language is an inevitable aspect of global movement, it is not surprising that there should also be unprecedented interest around the world in translation, conceived of both as a linguistic process and as a metaphor for explaining the flow of creative ideas. Literary theorists such as Homi Bhabha have developed a notion of 'cultural translation' which expands the idea of translation as linguistic transfer to describe the processes and the condition of global migration and exchange. Bhabha defines translation as 'the performative nature of cultural communication', and points out that translation continually reminds us of difference, for there is always in translation a starting point and a point of arrival that are never the same (Homi Bhabha, *The Location of Culture*, London and New York: Routledge, 1994, p. 228). Translation, as he sees it, reflects the intrinsic condition of the millions of people flowing around the world, for they are engaged in a constant process of translating and being translated, taking their own languages with them, learning new languages, striving to make contact with people from other cultures who have other communication systems.

What translation involves

I have begun with Bhabha to underline the signal importance of translation in our time for literary and cultural theorists who are endeavouring to articulate a new phenomenon in terms that can be widely understood. At the same time, it is important not to lose sight of what the actual activity of translation comprises, to focus on the physical dimension of this ancient form of textual practice. Put simply, translation involves the transposition of a text that has come into being in one context into a different one, a process that necessarily involves reshaping that text, indeed, rewriting it, as Andre Lefevere has argued (*Translation, Rewriting and the Manipulation of Literary Fame*, London and New York: Routledge, 1992), from which it is easy to see why cultural theorists like Bhabha should choose translation as a metaphor through which to discuss the linked issues of originality and hybridity. Translation involves intercultural transfer, it implies negotiation between the original, the *source*, and its destination, the *target*, to use the terminology current among translation studies scholars.

The task facing any translator is how best to render a work produced for one set of readers for another, totally different set of readers, who may (almost certainly will) have different expectations, different tastes, different aesthetic concepts, different needs. It is an extremely demanding task, for the translator has first to read the original with the utmost care, and then has to take decisions on how to set about reconstructing it in the target language, for since no two languages are identical, no translation is ever going to be identical to its original. Moreover, because a language is embedded in a cultural context, the translator has to take into account not only the linguistic dimensions but the problem of diverse layers of meaning that come from acquired cultural knowledge extraneous to the text itself. How, for example, might a translator tackle the multilayered complexity of the following, the opening lines of Carol Ann Duffy's 'The Kray Sisters', taken from her collection of poems about the female relatives of famous, or in this case, infamous men, *The World's Wife* (London: Picador, 1999, p. 63):

> *There go the twins!* Geezers would say
> When we walked down the frog and toad

In our Savile Row whistle and flutes, tailored
To flatter our thr'penny bits, which were big,
Like our East End hearts.

The poem is an extended joke, as the imaginary sisters of the Kray twins, con-
victed London East End criminals of the post-war period tell their life stories,
in similar terms to the versions recounted by their brothers that had so dominated the tabloid press at the time of their trial. Readers, therefore, first have
to understand the context that frames the poem, and then need to be familiar
to some extent with the mythology of the East End, which Duffy is satirising
in lines 4 and 5, with the reference to the old cliché about Eastenders being
big-hearted. These five opening lines will sink without trace unless readers can
grasp the fact that the sisters are using Cockney rhyming slang: frog and toad
= road; whistle and flutes = suits; thr'penny bits (coin long since vanished
from circulation but preserved in the language) = tits, which supplies another
layer of humour.

In a case like this, the translator has different options. A translation for a
scholarly readership would include explanatory notes; another strategy would
involve reworking the poem in terms of the target culture's expectations,
which could involve abandoning the Krays and the East End altogether and
substituting characters who would be known to readers from their own
context. This is what often happens in the theatre, and recent examples
include translating the work of the French-Canadian playwright, Michel
Tremblay into Glaswegian Scots dialect or the Neapolitan playwright Edoardo
de Filippo transposed into Scouse. Edwin Morgan, a major poet and translator
from many languages has chosen to render the Russian poet Vladimir Mayakowsky in colloquial Glaswegian, which he justifies by arguing that there is a
strain of fantastical satire in the Scottish tradition that comes close to the
mood and tone of Mayakowsky's anarchic humour (see Edwin Morgan, *Collected Translations*, Manchester: Carcanet, 1996).

Brian Holton has translated a fifteenth-century classic vernacular Chinese
novel, *Shuihu Zhuan* into Scots and in an essay where he explains not only
how he did this, but also why he undertook what might to some appear an
absurdly complicated task, he makes a powerful case for the importance of
translation as a bridge between cultures that are separated both in space and
time. He quotes the famous essay by Walter Benjamin, 'The Task of the Translator', in which Benjamin argues that translation does not conceal the original, but allows it to shine through, for translation effectively ensures the
survival of a text (Walter Benjamin, 'The Task of the Translator', trans. Harry
Zohn, in *Theories of Translation: An Anthology of Essays from Dryden to
Derrida*, Chicago: University of Chicago Press, 1992, pp. 71–82). Then he

reminds us of an account of the joys of reading by Robert Henryson, the Scots Renaissance writer and translator:

> You may sit in your study … lost in your books, but unless … you take your book in hand like Robert Henryson did, and tell those for whom the book is eternally shut, 'Look, here's a story, boys, here's something that might change your life' – then what is the good of your knowing, of your reading, if no one but you knows the tale? Hence the need for folk like us – owresetters, takers-over: translators.
>
> (Brian Holton, 'Wale a Leid an Wale a Warld: *Shuihu Zhuan* into Scots', in *Frae Ither Tongues: Essays on Modern Translations into Scots*, ed. Bill Findlay, Clevedon: Multilingual Matters, 2004, pp. 15–37 (p. 36))

Holton's point is wittily made, and is fundamental to any understanding of translation: the translator has an advantage over the target readers for whom he/she is translating, because he/she has access to the original language, but the translator also has a responsibility. Holton plays with the Scots word *owresetter*, which is similar to the German word for translator, *übersetzer* which rendered literally into English would be 'someone who places over'. Holton's owresetter is also someone who takes over, a phrase with a double meaning in English. The translator does indeed take a text over a linguistic frontier, but in so doing he/she also takes over the text, transforms it and makes it his/her own.

Assessing translation

The earliest European conceptualisation of translation is generally attributed to the Roman orator and philosopher, Marcus Tullius Cicero, in his *De oratore* ('About the Orator') in 55 BC, in which he explains how he worked:

> I decided to take speeches written in Greek by great orators and to translate them freely, and I obtained the following results: by giving a Latin form to the text I had read I could not only make use of the best expressions in common usage with us, but I could also coin new expressions, analogous to those used in Greek.
>
> (Cicero, in *Translation/History/Culture: A Sourcebook*, ed. Andre Lefevere, London and New York: Routledge, 1992, pp. 46–7)

Here Cicero refers to the freedom he exercised to translate Greek masters, and argues that this meant that not only could he avail himself of the best Latin style, but could also introduce stylistic innovations. Four centuries later, in another classic work setting out the parameters of translation, his 'Letter to Pammachius', St Jerome declared that Cicero had been his teacher in enabling him to formulate a theory of translation that distinguished between word for word and sense for sense:

> I admit and confess most freely that I have not translated word for word in my translations of Greek texts, but sense for sense, except in the case of the scriptures in which even the order of the words is a mystery.
>
> (St Jerome, in *Translation/History/Culture: A Sourcebook*, ed. Andre Lefevere, London and New York: Routledge, 1992, p. 47)

St Jerome goes on to condemn literal translation, which he claims smothers meaning in the same way that weeds choke the life out of seedlings. This distinction, between the literal or word for word and the more creative, or sense for sense form of translation has dominated debates about translation over the centuries and to some extent still continues. The fundamental issue is the extent to which the translator is free to restructure another writer's work, and at different moments in time translators and literary critics have argued for and against different degrees of freedom. What is at stake, of course, is a profound ethical question: since the target readers are dependent on the translator to bring the original text across to them, the burden of responsibility on the translator is therefore doubly onerous. It is not accidental that the terminology of faithfulness and betrayal should have dominated translation discourse. A bad translation betrays both the original author and the expectations of the new set of readers. The problem for literary scholars, however, is to determine what constitutes a good or a bad translation. One way of proceeding is to compare different translations of the same work, which exposes the strategies and aims of the translators.

The two texts selected here for comparison are E.F. Watling's translation of Sophocles' *Antigone* in the Penguin Classics series, which was first published in 1947, and the more recent version by David Franklin and John Harrison in the Cambridge Translations from Greek Drama series, published in 2003.

If we compare just two passages, the different strategies employed by the translators are immediately foregrounded. When Haemon comes to speak to his father Creon, he makes a powerful speech defending the woman he loves, while at the same time endeavouring to show the respect he owes to his father. Here is the Penguin version of the opening lines:

> Father, man's wisdom is the gift of heaven,
> The greatest gift of all. I neither am
> Nor wish to be clever enough to prove you wrong.
> Though all men might not think the same as you.
> Nevertheless, I have to be your watchdog,
> To know what others say and what they do,

And what they find to praise and what to blame.
Your frown is a sufficient silencer
Of any word that is not for your ears.
But *I* hear whispers spoken in the dark;
On every side I hear voices of pity
For this poor girl, doomed to the cruellest death
And most unjust, that ever woman suffered
For an honourable action...

(*Sophocles: The Theban Plays*, trans. E.F. Watling,
Harmondsworth: Penguin Books, 1947, pp. 144–5)

Contrast it with the Cambridge version:

Father, the gods plant wisdom in mankind, and it is the greatest of all our possessions. I cannot say that you are not right to speak as you do, and I would not know how. (And yet it could be that another view is right). It is not your nature to pay attention to everything that people say or do or find to criticize; and your look frightens the citizens and prevents them saying things you would not like to hear. But I can hear under cover of darkness how the city mourns for this girl; they say that of all women she least deserves to die in disgrace for such glorious deeds.

(*Antigone*, trans. David Franklin and John Harrison, Cambridge:
Cambridge University Press, 2004, p. 51)

The most obvious difference is that one is in verse, the other in prose. Both follow the same line of argument, beginning with Haemon's reference to wisdom being a divine gift, then moving through to expose the gap between what Creon might think and what the citizens are saying. Where striking differences emerge is in the characterisation of Haemon. In the Watling version he describes himself as his father's watchdog, someone whose duty it is to find out what is happening and report back. This is an image that does not appear in the Franklin and Harrison, where Haemon comes across as gentler and more passive. Their version suggests that 'they' are saying that she does not deserve to die, while Watling's version is more ambiguous and the phrase 'most unjust' could be Haemon's own opinion, indeed, the way the lines are structured and punctuated suggests that this is the case. More broadly, the overall effect is that the character of Haemon acquires greater prominence in the earlier version, where he is a heroic figure in the Shakespearian mould, as opposed to being a decent young man with a logical mind in the later version. Heroes, after all, are constructed according to the norms of their age.

It could be argued that without Ancient Greek, a reader cannot know which of these versions may be more accurate than the other, but the point is that the translators have interpreted the original differently, so that slight and subtle clues encoded in their versions lead to different conclusions. Comparing translations exposes the translators' different interpretations. Such differences make the concept of the single, perfect equivalent translation impossible.

TRANSLATION STUDIES

In the 1970s a distinctive field of research into translation practices began to emerge. James Holmes, an American poet and translator wrote a seminal paper entitled 'The Name and Nature of Translation Studies' where he argued that after centuries of desultory interest in translation as a literary activity, the subject of translation had grown in importance in the aftermath of the Second World War (reprinted in *The Translation Studies Reader*, ed. Lawrence Venuti, London and New York: Routledge, 2000, pp. 172–85). Holmes and a group of young researchers with an interest in interdisciplinary studies came together, and Translation Studies came into being as a distinct area, linked in different ways to literary studies, sociolinguistics and other emergent fields such as cultural and media studies, gender studies, postcolonial studies. What all these fields shared was a dissatisfaction with more traditional modes of studying texts, and a desire to challenge established ideas of canonicity. Significantly, all embarked in different ways on a review of literary history: where feminist critics brought to light hundreds of neglected women writers, translation studies researchers worked on showing how significant translation had always been in the shaping of literary systems. Far from being a marginal literary activity, what was proposed was that translation had been a major shaping force in literary and cultural history, a means of bringing in new forms, genres and ideas.

Itamar Even-Zohar was the first of the translation studies group to pull together research in the history of translation and theories of culture. He devised the term 'polysystem' to describe all the elements that might be studied under the heading of 'literature', including what he called high or canonised forms, and non-canonised forms, such as children's literature or detective fiction, and stressed the role played by translation in the development of a polysystem. He drew attention to the differing role of translation at different historical moments and in different cultures, asking why some cultures translate more extensively than others, why there are boom periods for translation, why translation is seen as a high-status activity at certain times, and as a marginal low-status activity at others. His hypothesis, set out in an essay that appeared in 1978, was that there are distinct social circumstances that affect the production of translations. Translation, he suggested, is significant when a literature is in its early stages of development, 'young', as he terms it, when a literature perceives itself as marginal or 'weak' and when a literature is going through a period of extreme change (Itamar Even-Zohar, 'The Position of Translated Literature within the Literary Polysystem', 1978; reprinted in *The Translation Studies Reader*, 2000, pp. 192–7).

The emergence of 'young' national literatures across Europe in the nineteenth century was characterised by massive translation activity. This was the time when Shakespeare became so thoroughly integrated into European literatures through translation that Tolstoy could remark ironically that Shakespeare's fame originated in Germany and only later spread to England (Tolstoy, cited in Susan Bassnett, *Shakespeare: The Elizabethan Plays*, London: Macmillan, 1993, p. 3). The high number of published translations (frequently over 50 per cent of the market) in many of the less well-known European languages, such as Dutch, Swedish or Italian compared to the minute percentage of books translated into English (less than 3 per cent of the total UK market) exemplifies Even-Zohar's theory of 'weak' or lesser-known literatures engaging more energetically in translation activity. The case of China today, which is experiencing a translation explosion as it builds contacts with the rest of the world is an example of a literature that is remaking itself in a period of extreme change by importing of works produced in other languages.

TRANSLATION EQUIVALENCE

The polysystems group of translation studies researchers challenged two long-established shibboleths: they refuted the well-established view that translation was a marginal literary activity that did not deserve critical attention, and they refused to go on engaging in what they perceived as arid debates among linguists about definitions of equivalence. These debates, as unresolvable as the old literary arguments about whether it is possible to separate form from content in the analysis of a poem, revolved around attempts to define equivalence in terms that would accommodate language, meaning, style and function. Suggestions that equivalence could be conceived of as either formal or dynamic had been around for some time, though attempts at clear distinctions between these two aspects remained unresolved.

James Holmes pointed out that no translation can ever be equivalent to the original, if equivalence is conceptualised in terms of being 'the same as'. In an essay that appeared in 1973–4, he argued that if five translators are set the task of translating the same poem, the chances of any two of those five versions being identical is remote. There are likely to be as many translations of any text as there are translators, hence any attempt to theorise equivalence in terms of sameness is not only idealistic, it is impossible or, as Holmes himself put it, 'perverse' (Holmes, 'On Matching and Making Maps:

From a Translator's Notebook', 1973–4; in James Holmes, *Translated! Papers on Literary Translation and Translation Studies*, Amsterdam: Rodopi, 1988, pp. 53–64).

The reason why equivalence should have been such a fraught topic in the study of translation is because translation, unlike other literary forms, has a dual dimension: there is always an original somewhere else, hence any discussion of translation involves the analysis of an intertextual relationship. While we can analyse a poem or a novel in their own right, when we consider a translated poem or novel, we are engaging with that text and its original, regardless of whether we are able to access that original or not. This then has an impact on the evaluation of a translation: if equivalence is conceived of in terms of sameness, then a translation can be condemned for having diverged too far from the original, hence the freedom of the translator to exercise creativity is curtailed.

In the 1980s German translation scholars such as Hans Vermeer and Katharina Reiss took the equivalence debate much further and proposed *skopos* theory, which posited that it is the function a text is destined to have in the target system that determines the strategies employed by the translator (see Hans Vermeer, 'Skopos and Commission in Translational Action', trans. Andrew Chesterman, 1989; in *The Translation Studies Reader*, 2000, pp. 221–32). This made a great deal of sense, particularly for translators of non-literary texts, and it has come increasingly to be utilised by researchers in theatre, media and news translation, Internet and blog translation. In this conceptualisation of translation, it is the purpose and objective that determines how a translator will proceed – what to leave out, what to gloss, what to restructure in terms of target conventions. The emphasis is firmly on what the text is destined to do for the readers for whom it is intended.

Umberto Eco has provocatively argued that nobody can really understand translation unless they have tried their hand at it and seen what happens to their own work when someone else translates it. In his essay 'Translating and Being Translated', he declares:

> Equivalence in meaning cannot be taken as a satisfactory criterion for a correct translation, first of all because in order to define the still undefined notion of translation one would have to employ a notion as obscure as equivalence of meaning, and some people think that meaning is that which remains unchanged in the process of translation.
>
> (Umberto Eco, 'Translating and Being Translated', in *Experiences in Translation*, ed. A. McEwen, Toronto: University of Toronto Press, 2001, p. 9)

Eco homes in on one of the most fundamental questions about translation: whether meaning can ever remain unchanged or whether meaning is culturally and hence linguistically determined.

NORMS AND ETHICS

The translation theorists who emerged in the 1970s shifted the emphasis from the source onto the target literary systems. Where earlier writings about translation had concentrated on what happened to the original text when it was translated, focusing especially on what elements were lost or damaged in the process, the group that emerged from polysystems research chose to focus on relationships between literary systems, on the fortunes of a translation in the target culture, on the impact a translation might have at a given moment. Their emphasis was on the reception of a translation and on the strategies employed by translators as they brought in texts from outside a literature. This led to an investigation by such scholars as Gideon Toury, Theo Hermans and Andrew Chesterman of the role played by cultural and literary norms in translation, which remains an important field of research, that also reflects the importance of studying the history of translation (see Toury's 1978 essay 'A Handful of Paragraphs on "Translation" and "Norms"', in *Translation and Norms*, ed. Christina Schaeffner, Clevedon: Multilingual Matters, 1999, pp. 9–31, and his book *Descriptive Translation Studies and Beyond*, Amsterdam and Philadelphia: John Benjamins, 1995; Hermans, *Translation in Systems: Descriptive Translation and Systems-Oriented Approaches Explained*, Manchester: St Jerome, 1999, and *Translating Others*, Manchester: St Jerome, 2006; and Andrew Chesterman, *Memes of Translation: The Spread of Ideas in Translation Theory*, Amsterdam: John Benjamins, 1997; and Andrew Chesterman and Emma Wagner, *Can Theory Help Translators? A Dialogue between the Ivory Tower and the Wordface*, Manchester: St Jerome, 2002).

Translation studies developed rapidly in the 1980s and 1990s, with the emergence of books, journals, international conferences and associations. In his *Contemporary Translation Theories*, Edwin Gentzler claims that the two most important theoretical shifts in translation in the latter years of the twentieth century were:

> 1) the shift from source-oriented theories to target-text-oriented theories and 2) the shift to include cultural factors as well as linguistic elements in the translation training models. Those advocating functionalist approaches have been pioneers in both areas.
>
> (Genztler, *Contemporary Translation Theories*, second edn, Clevedon: Multilingual Matters, 2001, p. 70)

Translation studies is generally held to have undergone a 'cultural turn' in the early 1990s, with the collection of essays edited by Susan Bassnett and Andre Lefevere, *Translation, History and Culture* (London: Pinter, 1990) seen as one of the definitive books marking this shift of emphasis. Literary studies had for some time been adopting methodologies developed under the umbrella of cultural studies, while history had expanded its reach to include fields that had once been marginal, such as history of the family, history of science, social history generally and history of medicine. That translation studies should move in a similar direction was unsurprising, particularly since the field had established itself through a redefinition of its relationship with other literary, linguistic and sociohistorical disciplines.

ANCIENT AND MODERN

Central to the new approaches to translation was a rethinking of the ideological issues that underpin translation. The transfer of texts does not happen in a vacuum, it takes place in a continuum, and there is always a context from which a text emerges and into which a text is recreated. Walter Benjamin proposed the life-enhancing theory of translation as survival, as the afterlife of a text that may have all but vanished in its original context, and his work has been extremely influential for translators working with ancient texts (Benjamin, 'The Task of the Translator', in *Theories of Translation: An Anthology of Essays from Dryden to Derrida*, ed. Rainer Schulte and John Biguenet, Chicago: University of Chicago Press, 1992, pp. 71–82). Indeed, some of the most interesting research into translation at the present time is coming from classicists. Writing about Seamus Heaney's description of Virgil as his hedge-schoolmaster, a direct reference to the history of British repression in Ireland, Lorna Hardwick notes that the borders between ancient and modern, dominant and marginalised, imperialist and colonised are constantly shifting:

> The cultural politics of the debates surrounding translations and the shift in norms which they reveal hinge on changing perceptions of fidelity, equivalence and appropriation. These open up the whole question of the kinds of cultural operations which are involved when writing moves across the borders between the cultural authority of the ancient text and the modern positions and practices with which translation must engage.
>
> (Lorna Hardwick, *Translating Words, Translating Cultures*, London: Duckworth, 2000, p. 79)

Hardwick rightly draws attention to changing perceptions, for just as there is no consensus as to what constitutes equivalence, so ideas as to what is faithful translation vary enormously. In her introduction to her translations of poems by Catullus, Josephine Balmer discusses the difficulties she had in translating the Roman poet's explicitly sexual puns, and then explains her decision to break with tradition and reorder the poems according to themes. Her justification is based on sound scholarship and meticulous research into the history of the editing of Catullus' poetry, while her decision to add modern titles to the poems derives from her recognition of the expectations of contemporary readers (see *Catullus: Poems of Love and Hate*, trans. Josephine Balmer, Tarset: Bloodaxe, 2004).

One of the most continually contentious questions in the history of translation concerns the way in which ancient texts are brought to contemporary readers. George Steiner, in his *After Babel*, suggests that when a translator renders an ancient work in the language and forms of the present, claiming that this is how the writer would have written had he/she been writing now, what that translator is doing is introducing an alternative existence, 'a "might have been" or "is yet to come" into the substance and historical condition of one's own language and legacy of sensibility', meeting the needs of readers of his own time (Steiner, *After Babel: Aspects of Language and Translation*, second edn, Oxford: Oxford University Press, 1998, p. 334).

POSTCOLONIAL TRANSLATION

Balmer's reworking of classical authors may still offend readers who have more traditional expectations. Lorna Hardwick, an advocate of making the ancients accessible, reminds us that the history of translation is also a history of cultural appropriation, an issue that has disturbed some postcolonial translation theorists such as Tejaswini Niranjana (*Siting Translation: History, Post-Structuralism and the Colonial Text*, Berkeley: University of California Press, 1992) or Anuradha Dingwaney, who sums up the dilemma: 'The processes of translation involved in making another culture comprehensible entail varying degrees of violence, especially when the culture being translated is constituted as that of the "other"' (*Between Languages and Cultures: Translation and Cross-Cultural Texts*, ed. A. Dingwaney and Carol Meier, Pittsburgh: University of Pittsburgh Press, 1995, p. 4). Balmer's strategy can be justified by citing Walter Benjamin, for she provides a 2,000-year-old poet, writing in a language that few people can read, with a new lease of life in the twenty-first century. However, if translation is perceived as an appropriative act, whereby a dominant culture prevails over a less powerful one, the ethical position of the translator becomes questionable. A quotation much cited in translation studies is the statement by the nineteenth-century translator Edward Fitzgerald, who published a version of the Persian *Rubaiyat of Omar Khayyam*, when he declared that

It is an amusement to me to take what liberties I like with these Persians, who, (as I think) are not Poets enough to frighten one from such excursions, and who really do want a little Art to shape them.

(Cited in Susan Bassnett, Translation Studies, third edn, London and New York: Routledge, 2002, p. 13)

Here Fitzgerald makes no attempt to hide his belief in the superiority of English writing over the Persian; he will take what liberties he likes with the work of a writer who needs his artistic help. The irony, however, is that Fitzgerald's appropriation of the Persian text became the most successful translation ever made into English, and has entered the English literary canon.

Lawrence Venuti discusses ethical issues in his several books on translation (see his *Rethinking Translation*, London and New York: Routledge, 1992; *The Translator's Invisibility: A History of Translation*, London and New York: Routledge, 1995; *The Scandals of Translation: Towards an Ethics of Difference*, London and New York, Routledge, 1998). He stresses the need for translators to become more visible, while questioning the difference between translation strategies. Adapting the German Romantic theories of Friedrich Schleiermacher, he distinguishes two kinds of translation technique: foreignising and domesticating, also referred to as acculturation. This latter, which is the dominant model in the English-speaking world, means that the translation is shaped so that it reads as though it had been written in the target language in the first instance, with traces of its foreign origins erased. Venuti questions the political implications of such a strategy, and proposes instead that translators should seek to retain those foreign traces so as to highlight the Otherness of the original. Gentzler notes that Venuti's theory has been important in that it shows

that the manipulations of translation in terms of faithfulness to some sort of essential core have resulted in vast distortions – foreign syntax and styles sublated to appear the same as English, metaphors and images altered to fit our conceptual system, cultural values either omitted or adapted to fit our ways of thinking, and especially, innovative forms made to appear as forms commonly practised in the United States.

(Edwin Genztler, Contemporary Translation Theories, second edn, Clevedon: Multilingual Matters, 2002, p. 42)

Reassessment of translation from a postcolonial perspective involves a revaluation of the freedom of the translator. The Brazilian writer Haraldo de Campos has formulated a theory of translation as 'cannibalisation', that has received a great deal of attention by postcolonial translations scholars. De Campos proposes that a translator can justifiably devour an original and use it freely in new ways:

Any past which is an 'other' for us deserves to be negated. We could say that it deserves to be eaten, devoured ... the cannibal ... devoured only the enemies he considered strong, to take from them the marrow and protein to fortify and renew his own natural energies.

(Cited in Else Ribeiro Pires Vieira, 'Liberating Calibans: Readings of *Antropofagia* and Haroldo de Campos' Poetics of Transcreation', in *Post-Colonial Translation: Theory and Practice*, London and New York: Routledge, 1999, pp. 95–114 (p. 103))

The postcolonial translator will therefore take the source, acknowledge its power and then respectfully devour it, in order to gain strength and renewal. This will lead to a translation practice wherein the translator has the freedom to do whatever he or she chooses with the text; de Campos himself reduced Goethe's vast *Faust* to just 40 pages of Portuguese and transformed William Blake's poem 'To a Sick Rose' into a piece of concrete poetry.

The most important essay on translation in the post-colonial context is the Mexican writer Octavio Paz's 'Translation: Literature and Letters' (1971, trans. Irene del Corral; reprinted in *Theories of Translation: An Anthology of Essays from Dryden to Derrida*, ed. Rainer Schulte and John Biguenet, Chicago: University of Chicago Press, 1992, pp. 152–62). In this essay, Paz proposes that we look at writing and translating as twin processes, engaged in constant interaction. The history of Western literature should be conceived not in terms of national traditions, but in terms of styles and trends that cross linguistic boundaries through translation. Styles, Paz argues, are translinguistic.

In his vision, the original writer's task is to fix words as signs in an immutable form, consolidating the fluidity of language into a desired shape. The translator, on the contrary, does not start with language in movement but with the fixed language of the text waiting to be translated. What the translator then does is to dismantle the elements of the text, 'freeing the signs into circulation, then returning them to language' (Paz, in Schulte and Biguenet, *Theories of Translation*, p. 159). This can be termed a liberationist theory of translation, for the translator frees the text from the shape into which the original writer has placed it, and recreates it elsewhere. The postcolonial implications are obvious: translation is an act of liberation, a means of talking back, a process of reconciliation.

TRANSLATION AS MEMORIALISATION

Walter Benjamin introduced the important concept of translation as a means of ensuring the survival of a text. This has been taken up in different ways by literary theorists concerned to show how texts move in time and space, most recently by theorists working in the field of cultural memory studies. In *The*

Translation Zone, Emily Apter tackles the issue head on, writing in the aftermath of 9/11, when she points out that translation studies has always had to confront the problem 'of whether it best serves the ends of perpetuating cultural memory or advancing its effacement' (Apter, *The Translation Zone: A New Comparative Literature*, Princeton: Princeton University Press, 2006, p. 4). She argues that translation is both an act of disruption and a means of repositioning the subject in the world and history. Translation for Apter is 'the source of an ambitious mandate for literary and social analysis' (p. 11).

This view is shared by Sherry Simon, who physicalises translation in her book, *Translating Montreal: Episodes in the Life of a Divided City* (Montreal: McGill-Queen's University Press, 2006). Simon takes up the idea of translation as a journey, in this case round the city she loves, but also through time. 'Translation', she insists, 'is part of the evolving history of the cultures it links' (p. 6).

Both Simon and Apter draw upon research in translation studies to develop their ideas about comparative and world literature, and both are concerned to show the way in which contemporary human social and aesthetic interaction can be conceived of in terms of translation. This point is succinctly made by Bella Brodski in her *Can These Bones Live?*, subtitled *Translation, Survival and Cultural Memory* (Stanford: Stanford University Press, 2007). Where Apter starts with reflections on the linguistic politics of a post-9/11 world and Simon starts with a journey around her own bilingual city, Brodski starts with literature. She acknowledges her indebtedness to Benjamin on the very first page, and suggests that the rise of interest in translation globally is linked to paradigm shifts in critical and cultural theory across disciplines. Translation, Brodski argues, is not a marginal activity, it does not belong to a separate sphere of literary production, rather it is at the heart of everything. Translations contribute to and reflect changing literary-historical contexts, translation is a function of every cognitive and communication operation, translation is transformative. When we remember, we translate, when we express our thoughts or retell our dreams, we translate, when we engage with the global and the local simultaneously, we translate. Brodski makes a huge claim for the fundamental importance of translation in contemporary culture:

> More than ever, translation is now understood to be a politics as well as a poetics, an ethics as well as an aesthetics. Translation is no longer seen to involve only narrowly circumscribed technical procedures of specialised or local interest, but rather to underwrite all cultural translations, from the most benign to the most venal.
>
> (*Can These Bones Live?*, p. 2)

This chapter began with Homi Bhabha's use of translation as a metaphoric means of talking about the movement of peoples around the planet, endlessly translating and being translated. We have looked at some of the fundamental issues involved in the translation process itself, at the impossibility of having a single perfect translation for all time, at the futility of seeking exact equivalence between texts. The emergence of translation studies as a distinct field was extremely important in the 1980s and 1990s because it raised awareness across the disciplines of the need to think more scientifically about translation, and to theorise translation in a more sophisticated way, more fitting to the needs of a rapidly changing intellectual landscape. Today, thinking about translation is entering a new phase; comparative literary theorists, cultural geographers, globalisation researchers, writers and theorists concerned with history and the cultural politics of remembering and forgetting are all using translation as a means of talking about intercultural, transnational communication. Translation is no longer seen as a narrowly circumscribed technical field; in the twenty-first century it is recognisably right at the centre of human communication, and the paradigm shift in literary studies towards a growing concern with translation both in practice, in theory and metaphorically, reflects this exciting and long-overdue recognition.

QUESTIONS AND EXERCISES

1   Compare and contrast any two passages from two translations of the same text. What can you deduce from this about the translators' priorities?

2   Do you agree that translation should be seen as unpinning all cultural transactions?

3   To what extent can a translation be seen as just one person's individual reading of a text?

4   Can there ever be a definitive translation of any text?

5   What factors might ensure the survival of a text? Is its translatability crucial?

SELECTED READING

Susan Bassnett, *Translation Studies*, third edn, London and New York: Routledge, 2002.
Susan Bassnett and Harish Trivedi (eds), *Postcolonial Translation: Theory and Practice*, London and New York: Routledge, 1999.
Bella Brodski, *Can These Bones Live? Translation, Survival and Cultural Memory*, Stanford: Stanford University Press, 2007.
Michael Cronin, *Translation and Globalization*, London and New York: Routledge, 2006.

Andre Lefevere, *Translation, Rewriting and the Manipulation of Literary Fame*, London and New York: Routledge, 1992.

Jeremy Munday, *Introducing Translation Studies: Theories and Applications*, London and New York: Routledge, 2001.

Mary Snell-Hornby, *The Turns of Translation Studies: New Paradigms or Shifting Viewpoints?*, Amsterdam/Philadelphia: John Benjamins, 2006.

Lawrence Venuti (ed.), *The Translation Studies Reader*, London and New York: Routledge, 2000.

Part 4

Planning and completing a research project

Deciding on a topic
Turning a topic into an argument
Working out a structure
Preparing a research proposal
Writing your dissertation or thesis
Presenting your dissertation or thesis

11

Planning, writing and presenting a dissertation or thesis

W.R. Owens

To gain a postgraduate qualification in literature, you will have to complete a research project on a topic you have devised for yourself, and will have to present this for examination. The name given to the piece of work you present varies from country to country, and for which qualification it is submitted. In the UK, the final document you submit for an MA is usually known as a 'dissertation' and what you submit for a PhD is known as a 'thesis'. These terms are reversed in the USA, where work for an MA is known as a 'thesis' and for a PhD is known as a 'dissertation'. Since much of what I will be saying in this chapter applies equally to MAs and PhDs, I will use both terms.

Generally speaking, the length of an MA dissertation/thesis will be set somewhere between 10,000 and 20,000 words. The purpose is to enable you to demonstrate (a) that you know how to use libraries effectively to locate relevant materials, (b) that you can prepare and write up a sustained and logically structured academic argument in clear prose, and (c) that you can present your work well, using appropriate scholarly conventions. In short, an MA dissertation/thesis gives you the opportunity to show that you are capable of undertaking further independent work at postgraduate level.

A PhD is a much longer piece of work, usually running to between 70,000 and 100,000 words. As with an MA, it needs to be well-written and presented in an appropriately scholarly fashion, but it differs in that it must not only advance a coherent argument, but must represent an original and substantial contribution to knowledge in its field. Unlike an MA, a copy of a PhD will be placed in the library of the awarding institution, and made available on request to other scholars, who may cite its findings in the way a published book or article would be cited.

To a very large extent, the principles involved in planning and bringing to completion any research project in literature are the same, whatever the length of the piece of work being produced. However, we will return to the question of what distinguishes a PhD from an MA. More comprehensive treatment of all the issues in this chapter can be found in the books recommended at the end.

DECIDING ON A TOPIC

One of the points to stress at the outset is that the range of possible research topics in literature is very wide indeed. Despite this, or perhaps because of this, students occasionally find it difficult to make up their minds what it is they want to investigate. If you feel, momentarily, that you can't decide what might interest you, you could try making a list of things that you would like to learn more about. Once you have a list of up to five or six things, you should take some time to read around each of them a bit, trying to think not only which seems most enticing and likely to hold your interest, but which of them your previous study has best equipped you to pursue. By 'reading around' I don't mean reading aimlessly, or in a desultory fashion. On the contrary, you should be reading quickly and purposively, with questions in your mind, scanning material that seems potentially relevant to your areas of interest and getting an overview of it. The questions you should be asking include:

- What are some of the key studies in this field?

- What kinds of approaches have been taken to the subject?

- What are the key issues and questions in this field?

- Are there any possible gaps, or approaches yet to be explored?

Whatever your area of interest may be, it is likely that you can follow it up – providing only that the materials you need are available to you. This is a crucial early part of deciding on a topic. Indeed, if you discover that you can't obtain easy access to the necessary materials, you may need to switch to another topic. Thus, for example, it is no use deciding to work on a little-known writer unless you are certain that you can borrow or buy copies of the key primary texts, or have easy access to electronic copies of them, or live close enough to a non-lending research library to be able to do intensive reading and note-taking there.

Some students want to explore some aspect of the work of a particular author, whether well-known or not. Others are interested in an interdisciplinary theme or issue, or may want to address some historical or literary-historical problem, tracing it through the writings of selected authors. Others, again, want to test how a given theoretical approach may be applied to a particular text or group of texts, or may indeed want to focus on a theoretical issue itself.

In order to turn any one of these broad areas of interest into a viable research topic, it must be focused on a particular, manageable body of material. Nothing is more fatal than to attempt blanket coverage of a large field – let's say a topic such as 'Narrative Technique in the Eighteenth-Century Novel', or 'The Representation of Women in Nineteenth-Century Poetry'. The objection to such a topic is not merely that you could not hope to cover it effectively in the time and space at your disposal, but also that it would be difficult to achieve much that would be of interest (either in terms of original ideas or of factual discovery) in such a broad field.

A good general tip is: *choose a relatively narrow and sharply defined topic which nevertheless opens out into large and important issues.* Thus, for example, 'The Use of Parallel Narrations as a Narrative Technique in Richardson's Novels' or 'Tennyson and the Education of Women', would be more suitable topics than the larger ones just cited. Remember, too, that there are many lesser-known authors whose works would repay study. Indeed an out-of-the-way topic, provided it offers serious interest and the materials are available to carry it through, has certain advantages over a well-worn or middle-of-the-road one.

TURNING A TOPIC INTO AN ARGUMENT

Having decided on your topic and limited its scope, the next step is to *give it a direction.* The way to do this is to develop out of your topic a set of *questions* you want to answer, or *problems* that you want to solve. Doing research is not about gathering information or data for its own sake: the information or data is presented in order to answer questions, in order to try to change what is thought about something. Virtually every good dissertation will take the form of an *argument,* of an attempt to prove or establish something by means of presentation and analysis of *evidence.*

There are many possible ways of turning a topic into an argument. To give some examples, your dissertation might be one of the following:

- an argument for or against an existing critic (or critical position) in relation to the author or group of works you are studying;

- an argument about the importance of a particular influence on a writer, or influence exerted by him or her;

- an argument for the importance of some hitherto little-regarded piece of evidence to the discussion of the work of some author or group of authors;

- an argument about the value of a new theoretical approach to a text or set of texts;

- an argument turning upon the nature of the genre of a work or group of works;

- an argument about the significance of a little-known or undervalued author or work;

- an argument about some historical or literary-historical aspect of literature;

- an argument about the adequacy of existing scholarly texts of a particular work;

- an argument showing how a particular theme or concept may be related to a group of texts;

- an argument bringing together some aspect of a well-known literary text with a lesser-known text or with other media.

By framing your topic in some way such as this, you will find it easier to move on to the next stage, which is finding a way of structuring your dissertation or thesis.

WORKING OUT A STRUCTURE

The first principle here is related to one we have already discussed: choose a topic which is capable of being dealt with adequately within the allocated word limit. This may seem like a counsel of perfection; partly because it is hard to know at the outset what 'being dealt with adequately' means, but also because any work on any worthwhile research topic is liable to develop once it is under way. One way of dealing with this problem is to look for areas where you might need to be flexible, areas which might be cut back or even omitted altogether if other, more relevant, material needed to be included.

You might think that 15,000 words sounds like a lot, or, if you are embarking on a PhD that it would hardly be possible ever to reach the vast number of 80,000 words. You would be wrong. Of one thing you can be certain: any topic you choose will be subject to a version of Parkinson's Law whereby it will expand to fill, and more than fill, your word allowance.

Thinking carefully at the outset about the question of length is one of the best ways of helping you to structure your dissertation or thesis. Any dissertation or thesis will have, at least, an introduction, middle and conclusion. Obviously an introduction is important: you need to tell your reader what you are intending to do, and why. A conclusion is equally important: it should briefly summarise the significance of what you have done and, if appropriate, suggest how the subject might be extended.

Between the introduction and the conclusion comes the body of work in which you *assemble* the evidence, *analyse* it and put forward your *argument* based on that analysis. This middle section will need to be divided into chapters, each of which would represent a major step in the development of the argument, and each of which would be long enough to accommodate the amount of evidence and the detailed analysis required. If you are aiming to produce, say, a 15,000-word MA, you would have no more than three, or at the most four, 3,000–4,000 word chapters available to you, assuming your introduction and conclusion take up no more than 1,500 words each. For a PhD of 80,000 words, you might plan to devote about 4,000 words each to an introduction and conclusion, with something like seven or eight chapters of 8,000–10,000 words each.

PREPARING A RESEARCH PROPOSAL

Assuming that you have an idea for a possible research project that is sufficiently tightly defined so that it is do-able in the time and space available, and further assuming that you have checked that you can get access to the necessary materials, you will usually need to write a research proposal for approval by your tutor or supervisor. Although some of the elements of a proposal document will be the same, there will be some differences depending on whether you are embarking on an MA or a PhD. I'll begin by outlining what an MA proposal should contain, and then say something further about a PhD proposal.

An MA research proposal should probably be not more than 1,000 words in length. Its purpose is to show that you have a promising line of research and to indicate how you hope it will develop. Think of it as an exercise in persuasion: you are trying to convince your tutor or supervisor that you have evidence (although as yet unexploited) to support the argument you propose to advance. You should present it in continuous prose, but arranged under a set of headings such as the following.

Title	Do not feel bound by this: it is important to have a title that is clear and informative, but a first attempt can be altered in the finished product.
Argument	State as concisely as possible what your subject is and what your argument will be.
Materials	Go into more detail about your materials, i.e. the chief primary and secondary sources you will use and discuss, giving some

indication as to their aptness for your project, and how easy it will be to get hold of them.

Chapters   Show how you think your discussion of your topic may be organised, chapter by chapter, in the final product. This provisional chapter structure is very important, so make sure it is clear to the reader how many chapters there are going to be, what is going to go into each, how they will connect with each other, and how long each is planned to be. If possible, give provisional chapter titles.

You should be alluding throughout this section to the main secondary literature on your subject (historical, critical, theoretical, etc.), not just to demonstrate that you are aware of it, but to indicate how you might use it. So, for example, you might be planning to take issue with what some critic has said, or you may want to show how your work relates to, and perhaps extends or qualifies, some existing scholarship on your subject.

Conclusion   Clearly this will be provisional at this stage. You have not yet argued your case, merely outlined the materials and likely directions of your argument. You might also like to indicate at this stage what problems you think you might encounter along the way.

Bibliography   A list of the key primary and secondary texts you intend using should be appended to the proposal – though, again, this list will be provisional and will certainly expand once you begin serious work.

A PhD proposal could very well be structured in a similar way, and under similar headings. However, it would be a longer document, running, perhaps, to 2,000 or 3,000 words. The key thing about a PhD proposal is that *it needs to indicate how the research findings or argument will add significantly to what is already known about the subject.* To do this it needs to set out in more detail what relevant work already exists, and how what is proposed will add to, modify or challenge the work of other scholars – in other words, how it will contribute to knowledge.

In very broad terms, there are two ways in which a thesis on a literary topic may be said to 'contribute to knowledge'. One is by finding and analysing texts or documents that have not previously been known about or studied. Finding such material in literary studies is perhaps less common than it might be in a subject like history, where vast untapped archives remain to be explored, but it is certainly not unheard of. There is much to be done in the field of publishing history, for example, or in tracing the circulation of texts and their reception histories. Similarly, there are writers who for one reason or another have dropped from sight, or have not yet attracted scholarly interest, but whose works are well worth study.

The other, and more common way of contributing to knowledge in literary studies is by presenting a new argument about a given writer, or set of literary works, or about some historical or theoretical issue, or some theme that is relevant to literature. The argument needs to be 'new' in the sense that it has not been put forward in these terms previously. How you present it will demonstrate your ability to engage productively with the work of other scholars in the field, and your ability to exercise independent critical judgement. You will need to be able to marshal and explicate existing theoretical, literary-critical or historical arguments in a coherent way, but even more importantly to explore and analyse them from your own distinctive perspective.

The concept of 'independence' is crucial to research at the level of a PhD. Even at the stage of your proposal you will need to demonstrate that you have a good preliminary knowledge of some of the main existing work in your field, and be able to indicate where you think your work could make an original contribution. Your thesis will show how your work relates to and builds upon that of other scholars in your field, but without seeming derivative, or merely repeating the work of others. In short, by the time you have completed a PhD you will be able to convince a reader that your work changes (or has the potential to change) the way in which we think about the subject.

WRITING YOUR DISSERTATION OR THESIS

Once your research proposal has been approved, you are ready to begin work in earnest. All your previous study has been leading up to and preparing you for this moment, but you will need stamina to keep going on a lengthy project, and you need to be organised about such practical matters as note-taking and developing a filing system. Most of all, you will need to start writing early, and keep writing all the way through.

What follows is a brief list of Dos and Don'ts – mainly Dos – to help you with the business of writing your dissertation or thesis.

1 *Do* make sure that you have a clear timetable of contacts with your tutor or supervisor.

2 *Do* plan well ahead. Organise library visits and things like inter-library loans in advance. It is an infallible rule that everything (research, writing

up, typing and correcting) will take longer than you expect, so *do* plan in some spare time.

3 *Do* start compiling a bibliography as soon as you start work. Record only one book or article on each sheet of paper or card, or in bibliographic management software such as EndNote or RefWorks (see p. 16), so that later you can shuffle entries around. If you store notes on your PC make sure that you have a back-up disk that is kept up to date: never store important electronic information in only one place. To be safe from disaster such as theft, have a copy of your bibliography and draft dissertation or thesis both on the hard disk in your machine and on a memory stick or CD that you store away from your PC.

4 *Do* keep a weather-eye open for new publications in your own field, checking current abstracts, indexes and specialist bibliographies.

5 *Do* write as you go along. *Don't* get so carried away by research that you only write notes (or even nothing at all) for weeks on end. Writing drafts is scarcely ever a distraction from research. When writing, make sure that from the very beginning you use the proper scholarly conventions: getting it right from the start will save you an awful lot of time later on.

6 *Do* write clearly and crisply and avoid jargon wherever possible. Short sentences are more easily controlled than long ones.

7 *Do* take time to work out a clear and effective way to *structure* your ideas, to make sure that they are being presented in a logical order of progression, and that connections and transitions are signposted.

8 *Do* keep in mind that a dissertation or a thesis should take the form of an *argument* in which the writer must attempt to convince the reader of his or her case. Be honest with yourself, and make sure that you understand your own argument – and that it *is* an argument and not just an unsubstantiated speculation.

9 *Do* remember also that an argument is not the same as an assertion. You must make sure that you prove, or justify, or offer evidence for whatever you say – by including properly referenced citations from primary sources (texts contemporary with those you are discussing) and/or from secondary sources (critical books, articles, historical studies, etc.). Remember, too, that your argument will be greatly strengthened if you recognise the force of points that might be made against – or that qualify – the case you are advancing. Try to suggest ways in which these objections or qualifications might be answered.

10 *Do* aim to have the first rough draft of your dissertation or thesis complete so that you have plenty of time to refine and revise it before the final dead-

line. Unless you've been very restrained, your first draft is likely to be over-length and you will need to slim it down. You will also need some time to add any introduction and/or conclusion necessary. As a general rule, you should always leave both the introduction and the conclusion until the bulk of the research has been written up.

PRESENTING YOUR DISSERTATION OR THESIS

Each university will have its own regulations governing the format and submission arrangements for MAs and PhDs, and you will need to check carefully whether there are any special requirements about the style of references, layout of bibliography, etc. to which you will have to conform. What follows is some *general* guidance on the presentation of a dissertation or thesis in literature.

Format of text

Your work will have to be printed out in letter-quality print, on white paper of good quality. Some institutions allow you to use both sides of the paper, but it is better to use one side only. (This is partly because you can then take out single pages for correction more easily, but also because it is usually more convenient for an examiner to work with text printed on only one side.) The main text should be in double spacing throughout. The only exceptions to this are that inset quotations and footnotes should be in single spacing, and items listed in a bibliography should be in single spacing, with a line space between items. It is important to leave good margins. The *minimum* widths should be 40 mm at the inside margin (to allow for binding), 15 mm for the top and outside margins, and 20 mm for the bottom. You should choose a font such as Times New Roman, in a size of about 12 point. Italic font should be used for titles of books, foreign words and phrases, etc.

As regards the layout of paragraphs, the first line of the opening paragraph of a chapter or section should always begin 'flush left'. There are two methods of presenting subsequent paragraphs. One method (in some ways preferable) is to indent first lines by four or five spaces. In this case there is no need to insert extra space between paragraphs: the usual double spacing is sufficient. The other method is to set the first line of every paragraph 'flush left'. In this case an extra line space must be inserted between paragraphs (but with double spacing this tends to open up unsightly gaps in the text).

The pages of the dissertation or thesis should be numbered consecutively throughout, and each chapter should begin on a new page. The titles of chapters should be in capital letters, and be centred on the page. Section headings (if any) within chapters should be in italics as a general rule, and aligned with the left-hand margin. A table of contents should be provided, listing all the parts of the dissertation or thesis, with page references. Check that the wording of the chapter titles is identical with that in the body of the work.

You should make sure that you leave time to proof-read your work thoroughly before submission. Punctuation and grammar, as well as spelling, should be checked carefully, and particular attention should be paid to quotations to ensure that you have transcribed them accurately. These are all matters to which examiners will pay close attention.

Setting out references

It is an absolute rule in scholarship that when a source is quoted or referred to or otherwise drawn upon in any extended piece of academic writing, it must be acknowledged and full details provided. By acknowledging your sources you are first and foremost giving proper credit to the author or authors of the source you have used (and if you did not do this you would stand accused of plagiarism). Second, you are enabling anyone reading your work to check back on how you have used or interpreted a source, so that they can decide whether they agree with the conclusions you have drawn from it. They should be able to 'repeat the experiment', so to speak. You need to provide citations or references in all of the following cases:

- when you quote from a source;
- when you paraphrase a source;
- when you refer directly to a source (but not actually quoting it);
- when your ideas are heavily indebted to the work of another scholar (whether quoted directly or not);
- when you wish to cross-refer to a source relevant to a point you are making.

It goes without saying that your citations or references must be full and accurate in every respect, so that they can be identified and traced with ease by any reader of your work.

There is more than one set of scholarly conventions about how to provide 'citations' or 'references', and my purpose here is not to give a comprehensive survey of these, but simply to provide an account of two of the systems most widely used in literary studies. One is known as the running notes or numerical referencing system, which uses superscript numbers in the text keyed to footnotes or endnotes. The other is the author–page system, which uses citations in the text giving the name(s) of authors with the page reference keyed to an alphabetical list of 'works cited' given at the end of the work. The 'running notes' system is recommended by the Modern Humanities Research Association (MHRA) in the UK. The 'author–page' system is recommended by the Modern Language Association of America (MLA). The author–page system is similar to the 'author–date' system (also known as the 'Harvard' system) which is widely used in the sciences, where the date of a published paper or book is highly important and is therefore given prominence in the in-text reference. In humanities disciplines, the date of publication of a work does not usually have the same importance (though it is of course included in the full citation).

The 'running notes' referencing system

In this system, a superscript number is placed in the text itself at the relevant point, like this.[1] It is usually best to place the note reference number at the end of the sentence (or the quotation) and it should follow any punctuation except a dash. The note (single-spaced) is placed either at the foot of that page as a 'footnote', or at the end of a chapter or at the end of the main text as an 'endnote'. If you have a choice as to whether to have footnotes or endnotes, it is worth opting for the former. This is primarily for the convenience of your most important readers, your examiners, who will be interested to see what sources you are using, and who may want to check some of your references. It is distracting for them to have to keep flicking to the end of a chapter to look at notes. But *any* reader of your work will benefit from having ready access to the sources of the evidence, argument and discoveries you are presenting. This is the primary function of footnotes. They should not normally be used to amplify points made in the main text; if amplification is needed, it should be worked into the text or, exceptionally, added as an appendix.

The examples below will show you how to present footnote (or endnote) references to a variety of books (including edited works, multi-volume works, translated works and works in series), articles and online publications. (For further details of how to refer to other kinds of material, such as manuscripts or unpublished theses, you should consult the more specialised works listed below in 'Selected reading'.) The presentation below follows that recommended in the *MHRA Style Guide*. You should note carefully the order in which information is presented and the punctuation used. Note too that these are examples of *first* references to a given work. I will come on to ways of abbreviating and limiting footnotes when making subsequent references.

Examples of first references to books
[1] Michael Dobson, *The Making of the National Poet: Shakespeare, Adaptation and Authorship, 1660–1769* (Oxford: Oxford University Press, 1992), p. 95.

[2] *The Letters of Robert Louis Stevenson*, ed. by Bradford A. Booth and Ernest Mehew, 8 vols (New Haven and London: Yale University Press, 1994–5), II, 189–90.

[3] Althea Hayter, *Elizabeth Barrett Browning*, Writers and their Work Series, 192 (London: Longman, 1965), p. 18.

[4] F.A. Wolf, *Prolegomena to Homer (1795)*, trans. and ed. by Anthony Grafton, Glenn W. Most and James E.G. Zetzel (Princeton: Princeton University Press, 1985), pp. 45–67.

[5] *Authorship: From Plato to the Postmodern. A Reader*, ed. by Seán Burke (Edinburgh: Edinburgh University Press, 1995), p. xiv.

[6] James Joyce, *Ulysses*, ed. by Jeri Johnson (Oxford: Oxford University Press, 1993), p. 247.

[7] Livia Veneziani Svevo, *Memoir of Italo Svevo*, trans. by Isabel Quigley (London: Libris, 1989), pp. 100–10.

[8] William Shakespeare, *Hamlet: a New Variorium Edition*, ed. by Horace Howard Furness, 2 vols (1877; rep. New York: Dover, 1963), I, 146–50.

[9] Aphra Behn, 'The Disappointment', in *The Works of Aphra Behn*, ed. by Janet Todd, 7 vols (London: Pickering and Chatto, 1992–6), I: *Poetry* (1992), pp. 65–9.

As you can see from 2 and 8 above, it is not necessary to insert 'p.' or 'pp.' immediately after a volume number.

Examples of references to chapters or articles in books
[10] Penelope Wilson, 'Classic Poetry and the Eighteenth-Century Reader', in *Books and their Readers in Eighteenth-Century England*, ed. by Isabel Rivers (Leicester: Leicester University Press, 1982), pp. 97–126.

[11] G. Thomas Tanselle, 'Textual Study and Literary Judgment', in his *Textual Criticism and Scholarly Editing* (Charlottesville and London: University Press of Virginia, 1990), pp. 325–37 (first publ. in *Papers of the Bibliographical Society of America*, 65 (1971), 109–22).

The second example indicates that an article has been previously published elsewhere.

Examples of references to articles in journals

[12] Alice Walker, 'Principles of Annotation: Some Suggestions for Editors of Shakespeare', *Studies in Bibliography*, 9 (1957), 95–105 (p. 99).

[13] Anne McDermott, 'The Defining Language: Johnson's *Dictionary* and *Macbeth*', *RES*, n.s., 44 (1993), 521–38.

[14] Grace Ioppolo, '"Old" and "New" Revisionists: Shakespeare's Eighteenth-Century Editors', *Huntington Library Quarterly*, 52 (1989), 347–61 (p. 350).

Note that it is not necessary to precede the page span of articles in journals by 'pp.'; nor is it necessary to precede the volume number by 'vol.'. The full page range of the article should be given, but, as in 12 and 14, the specific page on which the quotation is found is given in parentheses. The inclusion of 'n.s.' (i.e. 'new series') in footnote 13 indicates that the journal had begun a new sequence of numbering. When abbreviating a journal title to initials, full stops are not used: see footnote 13 above, where *RES* is short for *Review of English Studies*.

Examples of references to online publications

As far as possible, references to online publications should present information in the order used for printed publications: author's name(s), title of work, any publication details (such as volume, issue, date), full address (the Universal Resource Locator (URL) or Digital Object Identifier (DOI) of the source (in angle brackets), the date at which the source was consulted (in square brackets), and the location of the passage quoted or cited (in parentheses).

The following is an example of a reference to an article published in a Web-based journal:

[15] Matthew Steggle, '*Paradise Lost* and the Acoustics of Hell', *Early Modern Literary Studies*, 7.2 (2001) <http://extra.shu.ac.uk/emls/07–1/stegmil2.htm> [accessed 27 September 2008] (para. 3 of 17).

A reference to an article published online and with a DOI is given as follows:

[16] Heather Walton, 'Staging John Coetzee/Elizabeth Costello', *Literature and Theology*, 22 (2008), 280–94 <doi: 10.1093/lithe/frno36> (p. 286).

Note that if an URL cannot be given on one line, it should be broken at a forward slash, and without introducing an end-of-line hyphen.

Limiting and abbreviating references

All the examples given in 1–16 above are for the *first* reference to a book or article: at that point, details need to be presented in full. It is not necessary to keep repeating all the bibliographical information in later references, and subsequent references should be abbreviated. They can be shortened to the author's surname, or surname and brief title, or brief title, depending on which will be more intelligible to readers.

So, in relation to our first example, if no other work by Michael Dobson was being referred to, subsequent references could be shortened to:

[17] Dobson, p. 72.

But if this was one of several works by Dobson, second and subsequent references would be:

[17] Dobson, *Making of the National Poet*, p. 72.

Second and subsequent references to articles in books and journals can be shortened in a similar way:

[18] Walker, 'Principles of Annotation', p. 100.

It is also possible to limit the number of footnotes by incorporating a very brief reference in parentheses in the main text. For example, if you were writing a chapter which included frequent quotations from Virginia Woolf's novel *The Voyage Out*, your first reference could be given in full as a footnote, but explaining that all future page references would be to this edition and would be included in the text:

[1] Virginia Woolf, *The Voyage Out*, ed. by Lorna Sage (Oxford: Oxford University Press, 1992), pp. 128–9. Future page references are to this edition, and are included in parentheses in the text.

Thereafter, you would simply include '(p. 75)' after quotations in your text, without any need for footnote reference numbers.

Another way of limiting the number of separate footnotes is by putting a single reference number at the end of a paragraph and grouping, in one footnote, all the references for that paragraph. Care should be taken that there is no ambiguity, however, and a footnote should not cover more than a single paragraph.

If you are using the 'running notes' referencing system, your dissertation/thesis will need to conclude with a bibliography. This should contain details of *all* the books and articles you have consulted, not just the ones from which you have actually quoted. It is usually helpful to subdivide it in some way. For example, if your dissertation/thesis is on a particular author or group of authors, a list of the editions of their works which you have used should come first. This section might be followed by a list of other primary sources used (i.e. other works from the period of the subject or author(s)), and then by a list of all the *secondary* books and articles consulted.

Works in each section of the bibliography should be listed alphabetically under the surname of the author or editor (which is therefore placed first), with the full reference following. Note that where there is more than one author or editor, only the first has the surname preceding the forename(s), as in the example of the book edited by Booth and Mehew below:

Booth, Bradford A. and Ernest Mehew (eds), *The Letters of Robert Louis Stevenson*, 8 vols (New Haven and London: Yale University Press, 1994–5)

Note that the full stop is not included at the end of items listed in a bibliography.

The 'author–page' system

In the MLA version of this system, superscript numbers and footnotes/endnotes are not used. Instead, the surname or page number(s), or both, are placed inside parentheses at the appropriate point in the text, and the reader then knows to turn to the list of 'Works Cited' for the full bibliographical reference. What is placed in parentheses will depend on the wording of the sentence. So, for example, if the author's name is mentioned in the sentence, the name is not repeated in the parenthetical page citation. The following list gives some examples of citations and references, followed by the list of 'Works Cited' to which they refer. Note in the 'Works Cited' list that the MLA style is to underline main source titles, rather than italicising them, articles are placed within double quotation marks, and the second and subsequent lines of each entry are indented five spaces.

> Roth's *American Pastoral* trilogy 'consciously alludes, both thematically and formally, to Milton's epic poem *Paradise Lost*' (Morley 180).

> John Richetti argues that *Robinson Crusoe* is 'as much a novel of ideas as of personal experience' (203).

> Scholars have generally regarded the first two editions of *Paradise Lost* as well printed and containing few significant errors (Moyles 31; Lewalski 455–6).

> Norton's two-volume study provides the fullest account to date of the history of translations of the Bible in English.

In her *Vindication of the Rights of Woman*, Mary Wollstonecraft argued that 'Women are, in common with men, rendered weak and luxurious by the relaxing pleasures which wealth procures' (145).

Saint Jerome said that a translator 'takes over words like prisoners and conqueror' (qtd. in Apter 99).

Works Cited

Apter, Emily, "Global *Translatio*: The 'Invention' of Comparative Literature, Istanbul, 1933." In <u>Debating World Literature.</u> Ed. Christopher Prendergast London: Verso, 2004. 76–109.

Lewalski, Barbara Kiefer. <u>The Life of John Milton</u>. Oxford: Blackwell Publishing, 2000.

Morley, Catherine. "Bardic Aspirations: Philip Roth's *Epic of America*." <u>English</u> 57 (2008): 171–98.

Moyles, R.G. <u>The Text of Paradise Lost: A Study in Editorial Procedure</u>. Toronto: University Press of Toronto, 1985.

Norton, David. <u>A History of the Bible as Literature</u>. 2 vols. Cambridge: Cambridge University Press, 1993.

Richetti, John. <u>The Life of Daniel Defoe</u>. Oxford: Blackwell Publishing, 2005.

Wollstonecraft, Mary. <u>A Vindication of the Rights of Woman</u>. Ed. Carol H. Poston. New York: Norton, 1975.

OTHER PARTS OF THE DISSERTATION OR THESIS

There are three other important parts of your dissertation/thesis that will require attention. First of all, you will almost certainly be required to supply an abstract, or synopsis, of the contents. This is usually no more than about 400 words in length, and a copy should be placed at the front of the dissertation, immediately following the cover and before the contents page. The purpose of the abstract is to provide the reader with a brief but accurate summary of the content and structure of the dissertation – a bit like the description often provided on the flap or back cover of the dust-jacket of a book. You should try to describe clearly and concisely what your dissertation/thesis is about, giving an indication of the main divisions or chapters, how your argument is developed, and the conclusions reached.

Second, you must of course provide a title page. On both the title page and the cover, you should give the following information:

- the full title of the dissertation/thesis;

- your full name and first degree (and any subsequent degree);

- the degree for which the work is submitted (for example, MA in English, or Doctor of Philosophy in English);

- the date (month and year) of submission.

Finally, you should include a statement making clear whether any part of the dissertation/thesis has previously been submitted for a degree or other qualification of any university or other institution. Where this is not the case, you should say so explicitly. You should also include a sentence making clear that the entire work has been prepared by you alone or, if this is not the case, what part of it is your independent contribution.

SELECTED READING

Wayne C. Booth, Gregory G. Colomb and Joseph M. Williams, *The Craft of Research*, third edn (Chicago and London: University of Chicago Press, 2008).

Patrick Dunleavy, *Authoring a PhD: How to Plan, Draft, Write and Finish a Doctoral Thesis or Dissertation* (Basingstoke and New York: Palgrave Macmillan, 2003).

Joseph Gibaldi, *MLA Handbook for Writers of Research Papers*, sixth edn (New York: The Modern Language Association of America, 2003).

Xia Li and Nancy B. Crane, *Electronic Styles: A Handbook for Citing Electronic Information*, second edn (Medford: Information Today, 1996).

MHRA Style Guide: A Handbook for Authors, Editors and Writers of Theses, second edn (London: Modern Humanities Research Association, 2008). Available, free of charge, online at www.style.mhra.org.uk.

Colin Neville, *The Complete Guide to Referencing and Avoiding Plagiarism* (Maidenhead and New York: Open University Press and McGraw-Hill Education, 2007).

Part 5
Reference

Glossary
Checklist of libraries, print, online and
other research resources

12
Glossary

W.R. Owens

This is a brief list of words and abbreviations used in this Handbook together with some others that you are likely to come across when doing research in literature. It does not cover anything like a full range of literary, theoretical or bibliographical terms. For more detailed and/or more comprehensive coverage, see the reference books listed at the end.

A

ABELL	*Annual Bibliography of English Language and Literature.*
ABES	*Annotated Bibliography of English Studies.*
accidentals	term in textual editing, referring to the elements that determine a text's appearance on the page (for example, spelling, capitalisation, word-division and punctuation). The words themselves are commonly referred to as 'substantives'.
acculturation	term (from anthropology) used in analysis of the manner of adoption or assimilation of a different culture brought about by contact between two or more cultures or groups.
ACLA	American Comparative Literature Association.
allegory	figurative description or narrative with hidden as well as overt meaning – for instance, John Bunyan's *The Pilgrim's Progress*, in which the vicissitudes of a Christian's religious experience are represented under the guise of the adventures and mishaps of a pilgrim.
allusion	a reference made in one work to another work, or to some event, person, etc. Whether made explicitly, or only implied or made in passing, it depends for

its effect on the reader's knowledge of what is being alluded to. There are various kinds of allusion, including *literary* (to other literary works), *topical* (to current events, as often in satire), *personal* (to the writer's own life and experience), *imitative* (as in parody), and *structural* (where a whole work refers to another, as in Tennyson's poem *Ulysses*).

anxiety of influence   a phrase derived from the work of the critic Harold Bloom, who has argued that 'the covert subject of most poetry for the last three centuries has been the anxiety of influence, each poet's fear that no proper work remains for him to perform' (see his *The Anxiety of Influence*, New York: Oxford University Press, 1973, p. 148).

ARCHON   Archive Online.

B

bibliographical codes   term used by the textual scholar Jerome McGann to refer to the format, typography, layout, paper, etc. of a text. *See also* **linguistic codes**.

bibliography   in textual scholarship, the term used for the study of the material production and transmission of books and other documents. It has been subdivided into the following specific areas:

analytical bibliography, the study of all the technical and manufacturing aspects of printing, from the manufacture of paper, ink, type, etc. through to the working practices of compositors, bookbinders, etc., that help explain how a particular book has reached its present physical form;

descriptive bibliography, the use of the techniques of analytical bibliography to describe the **format** and printing history of a specific book or books;

enumerative bibliography, the recording and enumeration of all known editions (and sometimes impressions) printed during a defined period or in a specific region or country; the entries are usually listed alphabetically by author or title and frequently contain information on the location of copies;

historical bibliography, the study of the book as a product of material resources and technical processes which are themselves changing over time; as the materials change and processes evolve, so do the nature and form of the book;

textual bibliography, the application of information from analytical and descriptive bibliography to a study of texts themselves, particularly where questions of meaning are involved and usually in the process of critical editing.

BFI   British Film Institute

BL   British Library.

BLAISE   British Library Automated Information Service.

BLC   *British Library General Catalogue of Printed Books*, originally only in printed form, now freely available on the Web.

BM   British Museum (the former location of the British Library).

BUCOP   *British Union Catalogue of Periodicals.*

C

c.   abbreviation of the Latin *circa* ('around [date]').

canon   on the analogy of the biblical 'canon' (i.e. the books of the Bible regarded as Holy Scripture, as opposed to the Apocrypha), the term 'the literary canon' means those works of literature regarded as possessing especial authority or literary merit.

catachresis   rhetorical term for the misuse of language, especially where a word is misapplied; also used of a strictly illogical **metaphor**, such as Hamlet's 'take arms against a sea of troubles'.

catchword   first word of the next page printed at the foot of the preceding page; catchwords were a common feature of books until the nineteenth century, and were used by printers as a means of telling which page followed which during imposition.

CBEL   *Cambridge Bibliography of English Literature*; superseded in 1971 by the *NCBEL*, which was in turn to be replaced by a third edition, but of which only one volume has been published (Vol. 4, 1800–1900, published in 1999).

CHAL   *Cambridge History of American Literature.*

CHEL   *Cambridge History of English Literature*; in the process of being superseded by *The New Cambridge History of English Literature*.

codex the name given to a flat book made up of bound leaves (as opposed to a roll, or scroll). It originally referred to a set of wooden (or ivory) tablets with holes bored through and bound together. These were replaced in Ancient Rome by codices made up of bound parchment leaves, which could receive writing on both sides, could be cited and referred to easily, were compact but could hold large amounts of text and were easily stored.

collate to compare (usually) a **copy-text** with other available versions of a text in order to detect **variants** in the text; this is usually done to establish the best or most likely reading of a given word or line, and to plot the bibliographic history of a text as it underwent revisions by the author and reprintings by the publisher(s).

communication circuit the name given by the book historian Robert Darnton to his model of the production and circulation of books within society.

comparative literature the combined study of literary works composed in several languages and from different cultures, usually in the original languages, but sometimes also in translation.

Copac the name by which the UK and Irish Academic and National Library catalogue is known.

copy-text the copy of a manuscript or printed version of a text that is chosen by an editor as the basis for a critical edition. The choice and nature of a copy-text are highly contentious issues.

cultural materialism a mode of analysis of literature and other cultural forms which emphasises the social, political and economic contexts within which they are produced and received. It is derived from the Marxist theory of materialism, according to which modes of economic production and material conditions determine cultural (and other) practices in society.

D

DAB *Dictionary of American Biography*.
death of the author the title of a famous article published in 1967 by the

French literary theorist Roland Barthes, in which he sought to undermine the habit of invoking authorial intention in interpretation, which he regarded as a way of imposing limits on the meanings of texts.

defamiliarisation the usual translation of *ostranenie* ('making strange'), a term used by the Russian Formalist critic Viktor Shklovsky to refer to what he argued was the distinctive function and effect of literary works in making the familiar unfamiliar, or making the habitual seem fresh or strange.

diachronic occurring in historical succession, or over time, as opposed to **synchronic**.

dialogic a term given currency by the Russian scholar Mikhail Bakhtin, according to whom language is always social in that by its nature it presupposes dialogue with others. He sees the novel as the most dialogical of literary forms in its capacity to subvert the single (monological) voice of the author.

diegesis term used in film studies and narratology to distinguish the narrated events or 'story' from the manner of their narration or presentation. The diegetic level of a work is the main story, and the 'higher' level at which it is told is extradiegetic (or outside the main story).

discourse a term associated particularly with the French cultural historian Michel Foucault, now widely used to denote 'any coherent body of statements that produces a self-confirming account of reality by defining an object of attention and generating concepts with which to analyse it (e.g. medical discourse, legal discourse, aesthetic discourse)' (Chris Baldick, *The Concise Oxford Dictionary of Literary Terms*, second edn, Oxford: Oxford University Press, 2001, p. 68).

DNB *Dictionary of National Biography*; now replaced by the *Oxford Dictionary of National Biography* (**ODNB**).

DOI Digital Object Identifier.

duodecimo book **format** produced when the original **sheet** has been folded so as to produce 12 leaves (24 pages). Because the sheet has been folded so many times, this format tends to be very small. Commonly abbreviated to *12mo*, and hence referred to as 'twelvemo'.

E

ECCO	*Eighteenth Century Collections Online.*
écriture feminine	literally 'feminine writing', a term used by the feminist critic Hélène Cixous to refer to a new or experimental kind of writing (not restricted to women) in which phallocentric divisions between nature and culture, man and woman, etc. would be broken down.
edition	'all the copies of a book printed at any time (or times) from substantially the same setting of type, and includes all the various impressions, issues, and states which may have derived from that setting' (Philip Gaskell, *A New Introduction to Bibliography*, Oxford: Oxford University Press, 1972, p. 313).
edition (critical)	scholarly edition of a given work, whose aim is to present a text as close as possible to the author's original or ultimate intentions (so far as they are ascertainable). Such an edition is based on a **copy-text**, lists textual **variants** and is often extensively annotated.
edition (variorum)	can refer to an edition that lists all the **variants** in the author's manuscript and in editions other than the **copy-text**, or to an edition that includes some of the annotations and commentaries of previous editors. Some variorum editions do both, for example *The New Variorum Shakespeare.*
EEBO	*Early English Books Online.*
emendation	a correction made to a text by an editor to remove error or corruption and restore the author's original wording or punctuation. (Not to be confused with 'amendment', which would be the creation of a new wording, or with 'revision', which is an alteration made by the author.)
ESTC	originally the *Eighteenth Century Short Title Catalogue*; now stands for the *English Short Title Catalogue*. (Access to *ESTC* is provided free of charge on the Web by the **BL**.)
et al.	abbreviation of the Latin *et alia* ('and others').
et seq.	abbreviation of the Latin *et sequens* ('and the following').
exegesis	originally a commentary on a particular biblical text; now used to mean a rigorous analysis and explication of any text. *See also* **hermeneutics**.

external evidence any evidence – not derived from the text itself – for the authorship, intended meaning, circumstances of production, or date, of a particular work; it includes biographical information, as well as evidence from analytical and other bibliographical studies, and from publishing history. *See also* **internal evidence**.

F

fidelity criticism name given in adaptation studies to an approach by which the 'fidelity' of an adaptation to the adapted text is regarded as the main criterion of judgement or focus of analysis.

fl. abbreviation of the Latin *floruit* ('he [or she] flourished'); used of a writer whose birth and/or death dates are not known, but who was alive and active around the time specified.

focalisation in **narratology**, the term used for the perspective within the narrative from which the events of a narrative are witnessed. Someone who witnesses events is known as a 'focaliser'.

folio large book **format** produced when the printed **sheet** is folded only once; commonly abbreviated to *fol.*

format size and shape of a book. Standard formats are **folio, quarto, octavo, duodecimo**; these are relative sizes, as the exact dimensions of a book depend on the size of the original **sheets** on which it is printed. Some of the most common traditional (imperial dimensions) sheet sizes were: Foolscap (17 × 13 in.), Post (19 × 15 in.), Crown (20 × 15 in.), Demy (22 × 17 in.), Royal (25 × 20 in.).

free indirect style or **free indirect discourse** refers to the way in which, in reporting what a character says or thinks about a situation, novelists may merge or combine the 'indirect' report of the narrator with the 'direct speech' of the character, but without using quotation marks or other devices to indicate that the point of view has become more personal.

G

gathering a pamphlet-like section of a book produced when the printer folds and cuts the original printed **sheet**. A gathering is usually of two, four, eight, 12 or 16 leaves, depending on the number of the folds made; the number of folds determines the **format** of the book. In the case of **folios** and **quartos**, the gatherings are sometimes made up of more than one sheet (often one and a half sheets). A number of gatherings are sewn together to make the final book. Approximate synonyms for gathering are **quire** and **signature**.

globalisation   'a term that encompasses a number of theories concerning the international extension of political, technological, and economic capital, in association with a form of cultural imperialism that seeks a universalized consumer culture' (Gregory Castle, *The Blackwell Guide to Literary Theory*, Oxford: Blackwell Publishing, 2007, p. 311).

gynocriticism   a term adapted from 'gynocritics', which had been invented by the critic Elaine Showalter to distinguish feminist study of writings by women, as opposed to feminist studies of writings by men.

H

hermeneutics   originally referring to the art or science of biblical interpretation (as distinct from **exegesis** or exposition of specific texts), but now used for the nature and theory of interpretation more generally. From the Greek *hermenus* ('an interpreter').

HERO   Higher Education and Research Opportunities (in the UK).

heteroglossia   a term used by the Russian literary theorist Mikhail Bakhtin to refer to the multiplicity and variety of voices or languages within a novel, often extended to include the mixing of heterogeneous discourses within a national language. It is contrasted to monoglossia, as dialogism is contrasted to monologism.

holograph   a document wholly in the author's own handwriting.

homophonic   term used of music which is characterised by the predominance of one part or melody (as opposed to polyphony). Also the adjectival form of homophone, the name for a word pronounced the same as one that is spelt differently.

horizon of expectations   the term used by the reception theorist Hans Robert Jauss to refer to the sets of criteria by which readers in specific historical periods understand and evaluate literary works. These 'horizons' change over time, so that later generations read and respond to works differently; indeed for Jauss it is a mark of a great work, such as Flaubert's *Madame Bovary*, that it will run counter to the 'expectations' of its initial readers, and will shock and disturb them.

hybridity, hybridisation   terms used particularly in Postcolonial Studies to refer to the pluralised and ever-changing multiethnic and multilingual identities resulting from colonialism, exile, migration and diaspora.

hypermedia archive   the name used by Jerome McGann to describe an electronic edition which is capable of including audial and/or visual documents as well as text.

hypertext   a form of electronic text which contains links to other texts and multimedia, and which, it has been argued, facilitates a different kind of reading experience from 'linear' printed books. The term is also used by some theorists of **intertextuality**, such as Gérard Genette, for whom 'hypertextuality' refers to the relationship between one text, a 'hypertext', and an earlier text, a 'hypotext'.

I

ibid.   abbreviation of the Latin *ibidem* ('in the same place') used when making a second or subsequent reference to the same work where there is no intervening reference to another work.

ICLA   International Comparative Literature Association.

implied reader   a term used by the reader-response theorist Wolfgang Iser to denote the hypothetical reader addressed by a literary work (and to be distinguished from a 'real' reader).

imposition   creation of a composed area of type large enough to print a whole **sheet** of paper at one time. This was done by taking the required number of pages of movable type and locking them firmly, in the correct order for printing, in a rectangular iron frame (or 'chase') by means of wooden blocks and wedges ('furniture'). The locked-up chase with type was known as a 'forme'.

impression   all those copies of an edition printed at one time.

infra	Latin for 'below' as in *vide infra* ('see below').
intentional fallacy	the name given by the critics W.K. Wimsatt, Jr and Monroe C. Beardsley to what they saw as the mistaken assumption that a literary work can or should be interpreted by reference to the supposed intentions of its author.
inter alia	Latin for 'among other things'.
intermediality	a field of study devoted to analysis of interrelationships between literature, art, music, film and other artistic media.
internal evidence	any evidence for the authorship, intended meaning, circumstances of production or date of a particular work derived from the text itself (for example, stylistic features and references to events contemporary with the writing). *See also* **external evidence**.
intertextuality	in its broadest sense, a term used to describe the great variety of ways in which texts interact with and are in relationship with other texts. These interactions and relationships are much wider than is implied by the notion of 'influence', including all kinds of direct and indirect allusion, imitation, parody, adaptation, etc., so much so that some theorists hold that meaning exists not within an independent text, but in its whole network of textual relations.
ISBN	International Standard Book Number.

J

JSTOR	short for Journal Storage, the name of an organisation dedicated to the conversion of printed scholarly journals into electronic form and their storage in digital archives.

K

knowledge sites	the name used for electronic editions by the textual scholar Peter L. Shillingsburg.

L

LC	The Library of Congress, the most comprehensive library in the USA.
leaf	a single piece of paper, being two pages back to back.

letterpress	can refer to the text of a book (including any line illustrations) but not its plates (if any), or to printing from raised type or blocks (as opposed to printing from lithographic plates).
linguistic codes	term used by the textual scholar Jerome McGann to refer to the words, punctuation, etc., of a text. *See also* **bibliographical codes**.
LION	short for Literature Online.
literary field	term derived from the French philosopher Pierre Bourdieu's theory of 'social field' by which he means the complex interrelations and interconnections that constitute systems of social power. The 'literary field' is the interlinking network of relations between the producers of literary works (authors, publishers, etc.), the products themselves (books, periodicals, etc.), and the consumers of these products (the readers).
loc. cit.	abbreviation of the Latin *loco citato* ('in the place cited').
logocentrism	term used by the philosopher Jacques Derrida to cover 'that form of rationalism that presupposes a "presence" behind language and text – a "presence" such as an idea, an intention, a truth, a meaning or a reference for which language acts as a subservient and convenient vehicle of expression' (*Modern Literary Theory: A Reader*, ed. Philip Rice and Patricia Waugh, fourth edn, London: Arnold, 2001, p. 182).

M

metaphor	naming or describing something in terms of something else, as for instance speaking of the 'neck' of a bottle or of 'swallowing' an insult. In a broad sense it includes **metonymy**, **synecdoche** and **simile**. *See also* **catachresis**.
metonymy	rhetorical figure by which the name of an attribute is substituted for the thing itself, as for instance the use of the word 'throne' to signify monarchy.
MHRA	Modern Humanities Research Association.
mimesis	the Greek word for 'imitation', used to express the idea that literature 'imitates' life.
MLA	Modern Language Association of America.

montage   in film editing, the technique of juxtaposing apparently unrelated shots or scenes which, when combined in sequence, produces a meaning beyond that of the individual shots or scenes.

MS, MSS   manuscript, manuscripts.

multilaminated   term (usually meaning having many laminae or layers) applied by the literary theorist Linda Hutcheon to the ways in which certain adaptations are 'directly and openly connected to recognisable other works, and that connection is part of their formal identity' (*A Theory of Adaptation*, New York: Routledge, 2006, p. 21).

N

narratology   theoretical study of the various forms of narrative, narration and narrators.

NCBEL   *see* **CBEL**.

n.d.   no known date (or 'not dated'). Any date in brackets that follows this can be assumed to be the product of an educated guess. If the date of publication of a book is known but not given on the title page, it should be given in square brackets thus: [1719].

New Historicism   the name given to a school of literary criticism that is concerned not only with the historical nature of literary texts but with the textual nature of history, and which seeks to demonstrate how literary texts are implicated in power-relations in society.

n.p.   no known place of publication. Any place in brackets that follows this can be assumed to be the product of an educated guess.

NUC   *National Union Catalog* (USA). *See also* **union catalogue**.

O

octavo   book **format** produced when the original **sheet** is folded three times to produce a gathering of eight leaves; commonly abbreviated to '8vo' or '8°'. The majority of modern books are octavo format.

ODNB   *Oxford Dictionary of National Biography* (60 vols, published in 2004; replaces the original **DNB**, published 1885–1901).

OED	*The Oxford English Dictionary*, first published 1884–1928, now in a second, revised edition.
OHEL	*The Oxford History of English Literature*, now being superseded by *The Oxford English Literary History*.
OPAC	Open Public Access Catalogue; this system allows a user to access and search an electronic library catalogue via the Internet and the web.
op. cit.	abbreviation of the Latin *opera citato* ('in the work [already] cited').
Orientalism	term identified with the work of the literary critic Edward Said, who used it to refer to Western literary, historical, linguistic and other discourses by which the East (Orient) was represented in a stereotyped, exoticised and imperialistic manner.

P

page	can refer to one side of a **leaf**, or to type arranged for the printing of one side of a leaf.
paratext	all those parts of a book except the main contents, i.e. book covers, blurbs, forewords and prefaces, apparatus such as footnotes, indexes, etc.
passim	Latin for 'everywhere' (or throughout'). In other words, 'references to this subject are found throughout the work'.
periodical	serial normally issued at regular intervals; *see also* **serial**.
phenomenology	in philosophy, the investigation of 'phenomena', or things apprehended by consciousness. Phenomenological criticism is the application of the phenomenological method to literary works, and has been influential in the development of reader-response criticism.
polyphonic	a term meaning 'many-voiced', used by Mikhail Bakhtin to convey the idea that a literary text is not 'univocal' (or 'single-voiced'), but has multiple voices. *See also* **dialogic**. The term is used to describe music in which independent melodies sound simultaneously (in contrast to homophonic music).
press-mark	numbers and/or letters indicating the location of a given book in a library that has fixed locations (i.e. the book is always to be found in a set range of shelves,

and is not moved around to accommodate additional or new books). Sometimes called 'shelf-mark' or 'call-number' (USA).

PRO   Public Record Office; now known as the National Archives (NA).

Q

quarto   book **format** produced when the original **sheet** is folded twice to produce a gathering of four leaves. Commonly abbreviated to '4to' or '4°'.

quire   the pamphlet-like group of leaves produced when the printer folds and cuts his original **sheet**. *See also* **gathering** and **signature**.

q.v., q.v.v.   abbreviation of the Latin *quod vide* and *quae vide*, meaning (respectively) 'which see' and 'all of which see'; in other words: 'refer to this other entry [or entries]'. Commonly used in dictionaries and encyclopaedias.

R

recto   front of a leaf (i.e. the right-hand (odd-numbered) page); opposite of **verso**.

REED   *Records of Early English Drama.*

roman à clef   French for 'novel with a key', one in which real people appear as characters under fictitious names, but remain recognisable.

S

samizdat   Russian word for 'self-publishing' which in the 1960s and 1970s came to be applied to banned 'dissident' writings circulated in the Soviet Union in photocopied typescript form.

semiology   science of signs. It studies signs as a form of language and, like **structuralism**, is influenced by the linguistic theories of Ferdinand de Saussure, who defined a linguistic sign as the combination of a 'signifier' and 'a signified'.

serial   any work issued at intervals in successive parts, sometimes irregularly and frequently with no expected limit on the number of parts; *see also* **periodical**.

sheet	large piece of paper which, when printed and folded, goes to make up a **gathering**, **quire** or **signature**. Every book is composed of a series of such gatherings sewn or stuck together. The number of pages printed is determined by the number of times the sheet is to be folded. If folded once (thus producing two leaves or four pages), two pages are printed on one side of the sheet and two pages on the other (once this is complete, the sheet is said to have been 'perfected'). If folded twice (thus producing four leaves or eight pages), four pages are printed on each side of the sheet. Sheets vary in size, so **format** names (for example, **folio**) are only an approximate indication of size.
sign, signifier, signified	terms used by the Swiss linguist Ferdinand de Saussure, for whom *signifier* is the written or spoken word within a linguistic system, and *signified* is the concept designated by a signifier. The two together constitute a *sign*. According to Saussure, the relationship between signifier and signified is entirely arbitrary: there is nothing about a tree that requires it to be called 'tree' (as is proved by the fact that the German word for tree is 'Baum', the French is 'arbre', etc.)
signature	can mean (a) a printed **sheet** folded and cut; there are two synonyms for this – **gathering** and **quire**, or (b) a printer's mark (usually a letter or a number, or a combination of the two) that appears at the foot of the **recto** of the first **leaf** of a **gathering** (and sometimes on the second leaf as well); these marks are used by the binder to make sure that the gatherings are assembled in the correct order. **Catchwords** were used for the same purpose.
STC	*Short Title Catalogue*.
structuralism	theory that human activities are structured like a language. (Thus, for instance, the structuralist critic Roland Barthes analysed the 'grammar' and 'syntax' of women's fashions.) The movement was inspired by the theories put forward by the linguist Ferdinand de Saussure in his *Cours de linguistique générale* (1916), according to which language is a system of differences, its terms conveying meaning only in relation to other terms. The structural anthropologist Claude

	Levi-Strauss represents the culture of primitive societies as organised around binary differences or oppositions, such as raw versus cooked. *See also* **semiology**.
substantives	*see* **accidentals**.
SUNCAT	Serials Union Catalogue (for the UK).
supra	Latin for 'above', as in *vide supra* ('see above').
synchronic	occurring simultaneously, as opposed to **diachronic**.
synecdoche	figure of speech in which a part is used for a whole (for example, 'all *hands* on deck'), or a whole for a part (for example, '*Pakistan* won the test').

T

| **trope** | figure of speech in which words are used in senses other than their usual ones. The most widely used tropes include **metaphor**, simile, **metonymy**, **synecdoche**, etc. |

U

ULS	*Union List of Serials.*
union catalogue	catalogue that lists the holdings of two or more libraries.
URL	Universal Resource Locator.

V

variant	alternative reading of a given word or passage in a text; for example, in the line from the Folio text of *Hamlet*, 'O that this too, too solid flesh would melt', a variant for 'solid' found in other editions is 'sallied', a possible spelling for 'sullied'.
variorum	*see* **edition (variorum)**.
verso	back of a leaf (i.e. the left-hand (even-numbered) page); opposite of **recto**.
vide	Latin for 'see'.
viz.	abbreviation of the Latin *videlicet* ('namely').

W

| **Web** | the World Wide Web or WWW; that part of the Internet which allows the easy transmission not just of text but also of graphics, audio and video. It is also |

| | characterised by the use of hypertext, which allows a user to jump from one piece of information to a related piece by means of 'hot' links between words or phrases in different documents, or in different parts of the same document. |
| WorldCat | a union catalogue offering online access to the collections of over 10,000 libraries worldwide. |

Y

| YWCCT | *The Year's Work in Critical and Cultural Theory.* |
| YWES | *The Year's Work in English Studies.* |

SELECTED READING

M.H. Abrams and Geoffrey Harpham, *A Glossary of Literary Terms*, ninth edn (Belmont: Wadsworth Publishing, 2009).

Chris Baldick, *The Concise Oxford Dictionary of Literary Terms*, second edn (Oxford: Oxford University Press, 2001).

J.A. Cuddon, *The Penguin Dictionary of Literary Terms and Literary Theory*, fourth edn, rev. C.E. Preston (London: Penguin, 1999).

Dictionary of World Literary Terms, ed. Joseph T. Shipley, second rev. edn (London: Allen and Unwin, 1970).

G.A. Glaister, *Encyclopedia of the Book*, second edn (New Castle, DE and London: Oak Knoll Press and The British Library, 1996).

Heinrich Lausberg, *Handbook of Literary Rhetoric*, trans. Matthew T. Bliss, Annemiek Jansen and David E. Orton (Leiden and Boston: Brill, 1998).

The New Fontana Dictionary of Modern Thought, ed. Alan Bullock and Stephen Trombley, third edn (London: HarperCollins, 1999).

The New Oxford Dictionary for Writers and Editors, ed. R.M. Ritter (Oxford: Oxford University Press, 2005).

The New Princeton Encyclopedia of Poetry and Poetics, ed. Alex Preminger and others, second edn (Princeton: Princeton University Press, 1993).

13

Checklist of libraries, print, online and other research resources

M.A. Katritzky

HOW TO USE THE CHECKLIST

This checklist is designed to help you with two fundamental aspects of literary research: (a) identifying and locating appropriate primary and secondary texts, and (b) checking and elucidating facts and points of detail.

It has been planned to support a wide range of research enquiries – far more than any individual project will need. You are encouraged to read the whole checklist right through fairly quickly at an early stage, to give yourself an overview of its range and structure. By doing this you will discover which types of resources exist to help with particular enquiries. This will help you decide at an early stage which resources you are likely to need most, where they are located, and how you can most efficiently access them. The most widely used of these resources are discussed in greater depth in Chapter 2 of the Handbook.

Part 1, 'Finding and using libraries and collections', identifies resources providing details of collections that may be useful/available for research.

Part 2, 'Finding and searching literary texts', surveys databases of medieval through to contemporary literary publications and manuscripts.

Part 3, 'Finding and searching reference resources and critical texts', introduces a wide range of electronic and hard-copy bibliographies, indexes, directories, surveys and guides that help to locate specific published and (some) unpublished secondary sources relating to the vast field of literary and related studies.

Part 4, 'Information resources for facts and details', presents useful reference tools and other sources and possibilities for checking points of fact (such as biographical and general data, meanings of words) and details (such as allusions and quotations) and for gaining an overview of the field.

The Internet has heightened our awareness of the extent to which even the most authoritative and reliable reference works, printed as well as Web-based, contain inaccuracies such as misprints, misquotes, 'guesstimates', or mistakes perpetuated from incorrectly interpreted, faulty or indiscriminately 'borrowed' sources/evidence. Although generally un-refereed, under-edited and insufficiently referenced, Web-based information sources, search engines and commercial sites such as **Google, Wikipedia** and **Amazon** have an increasingly useful place in academic research. Most valuably, they provide quick short cuts to locating facts for which there are often more reliable scholarly sources.

Effective researchers approach all information, especially if it is inadequately acknowledged, with a healthy helping of scepticism. Wherever possible, rather than citing at second or third hand from unstable Web-based or other sources, they track quotations and other specific points of information back to their original or most authoritative source before using and referencing them, and consult multiple unrelated information sources in order to double check the accuracy of key 'facts'.

For any research resource you consult, find out how it is organised by taking the time to read the introduction and experiment with the options, either on your own initiative or in consultation with a librarian. Most of the resources in the Checklist have their own quirks and distinctive structures. Before plunging into any reference resource that is unfamiliar, it is *always* sensible to familiarise yourself with its key features. For reference books, invest a little time in examining their introduction, contents page and index. Find out, in particular:

- how the information is set out and organised;

- why the information is presented in this particular way;

- the rationale for including certain types of information and excluding others (most works *are* selective).

For electronic databases, investigate:

- their scope. Identifying and using appropriate databases for your field of enquiry is an essential part of graduate research;

- their search criteria. Help pages and library tutorials provide useful guides;

- their reliability. Is the resource you are consulting affected or biased by commercial, political or personal agendas? Is the author qualified in the field, and aware of current developments? Is the information appropriately referenced and dated?

- their long-term stability. However good the resources it offers, unless a website or database offers a stable, predictable and long-term environment for checking and rechecking them, its scholarly validity is seriously devalued.

Being clear in advance about these points, and so being aware of the potential strengths and limitations of individual resources, makes it easier to use complex reference resources in a time-efficient and productive way. This makes for a better research experience, and better research.

For detailed support on many aspects of the effective use of hard-copy and electronic research resources, including time-effective browsing and searching of Web-based library databases, you should consult Thomas Mann, *The Oxford Guide to Library Research*, third edn (Oxford: Oxford University Press, 2005).

PART 1: FINDING AND USING LIBRARIES AND COLLECTIONS

Locating research library holdings

Useful websites (some discussed in greater detail in Chapter 2) of research libraries in the UK, USA and worldwide include:

COPAC. Online at http://copac.ac.uk.

COPAC provides access to online catalogues of some of the largest UK research libraries, including the British Library and the National Library of Scotland.

The European Library. Online at www.theeuropeanlibrary.org.

Provides access to the combined resources of the 43 national libraries of Europe, including the Bibliothèque Nationale.

HERO. Online at www.hero.ac.uk.

Provides links to the online catalogues of selected UK academic libraries.

The Library Index (Libdex). Online at www.libdex.com.

Offers links to national, academic, specialist and public libraries in an A to Z of countries worldwide. The collection can be browsed by country, or searched by keyword, including the extremely useful Library of Congress catalogue, which is also directly accessible on the Web (see below, p. 235).

LIBWEB. Online at http://lists.webjunction.org/libweb.

Links to US national, state, academic and public library homepages, including the Library of Congress, and also to selected academic and public library homepages worldwide.

National Library Catalogues Worldwide. Online at www.library.uq.edu.au/natlibs.

Global collection of links to national library websites and online catalogues.

National Library of Ireland. Online at www.nli.ie.

Includes Gaelic manuscripts, political and literary papers, music scores and visual material as well as published books, journals and newspapers.

National Library of Wales. Online at www.llgc.org.uk.

Includes the 'Wales on the web' portal to websites on Welsh culture, history and art.

SUNCAT. Online at www.suncat.ac.uk.

Details of serials held in UK academic, specialist and national libraries.

Locating museums, archives and other collections

Details of collections of specific relevance to literary, cultural and historical studies are available in the following:

Access to Archives (A2A). Online at www.nationalarchives.gov.uk/a2a.

Covers, and in some cases catalogues, 400 repositories in England and Wales.

Archives Hub. Online at www.archiveshub.ac.uk.

Provides a single point of access to thousands of individual archives and manuscript collections, on many subjects, held in repositories in over 80 UK universities and colleges.

ArchivesUSA. Online at www.archives.gov.

Directory of 5,600 US repositories and over 150,000 US collections of primary-source materials, including contact information.

The Archives of British Publishers (Cambridge: Chadwyck-Healey, 1975–). Microform.

Includes the archives of Cambridge University Press (1696–1902), Longman (1794–1914), Macmillan (1854–1924) and Routledge (1853–1902).

> *Archives of the Royal Literary Fund 1790–1918*, compiled by Nigel Cross (London: University Microfilms, 1982). Microfilm.

Case studies from this charity set up in 1790 for the support of impoverished late-eighteenth- and nineteenth-century writers.

> Alexis Weedon and Michael Bott, *British Book Trade Archives, 1830–1939: A Location Register* (Reading: History of the Book on Demand Series, 1996). Online (at www.meanwhile.beds.ac.uk/dav/britishbooks) and print.

Reliable guide to UK publishers' archives.

> *Directory of Literary Societies and Author Collections*, ed. Roger Sheppard (London: Library Association, 1994). Print only.

Describes over 500 societies and collections.

> *The Europa World of Learning.* Online at www.worldoflearning.com.

Regularly updated searchable database providing a concise worldwide guide to the contact details and scope of learned societies, research institutes, libraries, archives, museums, universities and colleges.

> Janet Foster and Julia Sheppard, *A Guide to Archive Resources in the United Kingdom*, fourth edn (Basingstoke: Palgrave, 2002). Print only.

Comprehensive single-volume guide to UK archives.

> *National Archives.* Online at www.nationalarchives.gov.uk.

This detailed guide to the UK's publicly available archival resources includes the National Register of Archives (www.nationalarchives.gov.uk/nra), a searchable index to over 44,000 unpublished lists and catalogues of UK and other archives, and the British National Archives' Documents Online site, providing access to a range of digitised UK public records. It also includes the ARCHON directory, which provides links to archival repositories worldwide, including the National Archives of Australia, the Archives Nationales (France), the Bundesarchiv (Germany), the National Archives of India, the Amministrazione Archivistica Italiana and the National Archives and Records Administration (USA). For further details, see Chapter 2.

PART 2: FINDING AND SEARCHING LITERARY TEXTS

In this section, you will find details of some online and printed reference resources that support you in:

- finding specific references and passages and checking them for accuracy and context;

- comparing different editions;

- contextualising works of literature, for example within the framework of their author's production;

- conducting full-text word or phrase searches.

You should note that some online resources may need to be accessed through your institutional gateway. As indicated, others are freely available.

Pre-1800 publications

EEBO (Early English Books Online). Online at www.eebo.chadwyck.com/ home. Pre-1700 publications.

ECCO (Eighteenth Century Collections Online). Online at www.galeuk. com/ecco. Eighteenth-century publications.

Between them covering many editions of most titles published in the UK before 1800, these full-text searchable databases represent two extremely powerful tools for researchers of literature in any historical period or geographical region. At the time of writing, EEBO and ECCO are both being continually expanded.

Literary conventions shape and influence publications, writings and oral output of every type. All writers read previous authors, whose influences are reflected in their own and subsequent work. The full-text search and print facilities of EEBO and ECCO offer researchers the opportunity to throw light on the texts that are their own main focus of enquiry by, for example, tracking down specific concepts, words or phrases, names, or direct 'quotations', whether in texts that are contemporary with each other, or in those separated by many centuries.

Set up and run by two different initiatives, EEBO and ECCO do not share the same search and print criteria. But their importance is such that, regardless of whether your main research focus pre- or post-dates 1800, you should consider it an excellent investment of a few hours to thoroughly familiarise yourself with the full range of possibilities offered by both databases. Note that you can now include ECCO records in your EEBO searches and link to the corresponding records in ECCO. This is especially beneficial if you are researching authors who published works both before and after 1700.

Burney Collection Newspaper Archive. The online full-text resource is by subscription only at www.bl.uk/reshelp/findthe/prestype/news/burneynews.

Bibliographic details are freely available online via the BL integrated catalogue.

Searchable full-text database of London and UK newspapers and pamphlets dating from the seventeenth and eighteenth centuries collected by the Rev. Charles Burney and held in the British Library newspaper collections.

Eighteenth Century Parliamentary Publications. Online at www.parl18c. soton.ac.uk/parl18c/digbib/home.

Searchable database of parliamentary proceedings, reports, acts, bills and registers dating from 1688 to 1834.

English Reports. Online at www.justis.com/titles/titles.html.

Searchable database of reports on over 100,000 court cases, dating from 1220 to 1873.

Internet Library of Early Journals. Online at www.bodley.ox.ac.uk/ilej.

Substantial runs of digitised eighteenth- and nineteenth-century journals.

Justis State Trials and *Justis UK Acts.* Online at www.justis.com/titles/titles. html.

Searchable full-text databases for UK trial reports dating from 1163 to 1858, and UK primary legislation dating back to the Magna Carta.

John Johnson Collection. Online at www.bodley.ox.ac.uk/johnson.

Freely available, searchable database of thousands of items, mostly illustrated, from the Bodleian Library's John Johnson Collection of Printed Ephemera, mainly dating from the eighteenth to early twentieth centuries.

LION (Literature Online). Online at http://lion.chadwyck.co.uk.

Bibliographies of specific literary forms, author biographies and full-text search facilities for a representative selection of UK and US poetry, drama and prose dating from the sixteenth to the twenty-first centuries. Selected critical and reference resources are also provided.

Nineteenth-century publications

A wide variety of searchable online databases offer everything from a helpful but limited selection of full-text nineteenth-century prose, poetry and drama (*LION*), to all UK government working documents from 1801 onwards (*HCPP* – *House of Commons Parliamentary Papers*, at http://parlipapers.chadwyck.co.uk/ marketing/index.jsp), or a comprehensive collection of tens of thousands of pages of full-text publications and manuscripts by and about one particular writer

(*Charles Darwin Online*, at http://darwin-online.org.uk – freely available).

Basic bibliographical details of most nineteenth-century titles in the UK national collections are available in:

> *The Nineteenth Century Short Title Catalogue, Series I, 1801–15, Series II, 1816–70, Series III, 1871–1919* (Newcastle upon Tyne, Avero Publications, 1984–). Print, and online at http://nstc.chadwyck.com/marketing/index.jsp.

The listing is based on the holdings of the British Library, Bodleian, University Library Cambridge, National Library of Scotland, Trinity College Library (Dublin), the University Library of Newcastle upon Tyne and (from 1816 onwards) Harvard University and the Library of Congress. It offers a subject index. At the time of writing, students of nineteenth-century literature still await a full-text resource for the publications listed by this catalogue.

Pre-1900 periodicals

> *Nineteenth century British Library newspapers*. Online at www.gale.cengage.com/DigitalCollections/products/britlib.

Fully searchable facsimile text selection of digitised daily and weekly UK regional and national newspapers representative of the Victorian era.

> *Nineteenth-Century Serials Edition*. Online at www.ncse.ac.uk/index.html.

Fully searchable facsimile digitisations of six UK nineteenth-century serials, including *Publishers' Circular* (1880–90).

> *ProQuest Historical Newspapers*. Online at www.proquest.com/en-us/catalogs/databases/detail/pq-hist-news.shtml.

Fully searchable facsimile digitisations of some leading US and UK newspapers, including the *New York Times* (1851–2005), the *Wall Street Journal* (1889–1991), the *Hartford Courant* (1764–1984), the *Guardian* (1821–2003) and the *Observer* (1791–2003).

> *Times Digital Archive* 1785–1985. Online at http://archive.timesonline.co.uk.

Searchable full-text facsimiles for the *Times*, from 1785 to 1985. (Less-comprehensive coverage in *Palmer's Index to the Times, 1790–1905* and *Palmer's Full Text Online, 1800–1870*, both available via *History Online*).

> *Wellesley Index to Victorian Periodicals 1824–1900*. Online at http://wellesley.chadwyck.com/marketing/index.jsp.

Indexes 50 literary journals.

The Waterloo Directory of Victorian Periodicals 1824–1900, ed. Michael Wolff, John S. North and Dorothy Deering (Waterloo, Ontario: North Waterloo Academic Press, 1982). Print only.

Provides accurate lists of the large body of nineteenth-century newspapers and journals.

Poole's Index of Periodical Literature (Chicago: Poole, rep. by Peter Smith, Gloucester, MA, 1963): vol. 1, *1802–81*; vol. 2, *1882–7*; vol. 3 *1887–92*; vol. 4, *1892–6*; vol. 5, *1897–1902*; vol. 6, *1902–6*; with supplements. Print and microfiche only.

An accessible index of earlier periodicals.

The Nineteenth-Century Periodical Press in Britain: A Bibliography of Modern Studies 1972–87, ed. Larry K. Uffelman, Lionel Madden and Diana Dixon (Niwot: University of Colorado Press for Victorian Periodicals Review, 1992).

Surveys modern research in this field up to 1987.

Victorian Periodicals Review (Niwot: University of Colorado Press for Edwardsville, Research Society for Victorian Periodicals, 1968–, quarterly). Print, and online available via Project Muse at http;//www.muse.jhu.edu.

One of several journals covering current research on Victorian periodicals.

Post-1900 publications

Numerous online subscription databases (such as *LION* and *Times Digital Archive*, see above) offer helpful but limited resources.

By their very nature, freely available unfunded Web-based sources cannot be relied upon to remain as constant, updated and comprehensive as subscription databases. Some have interface and downloading issues, or may be unreliable as long-term scholarly resources. Even so, depending on your research topic, you may well find it worth checking them out. At the time of writing, freely available literature-related databases considered significant enough to be given their own links on many university library database pages include **Bartleby** (http://bartleby.com), **Bibliomania** (http://bibliomania.com), **Electronic Literature Directory** (http://directory.eliterature.org), **Fiction Connection** (http://fictionconnection.com), **Poetry Archive** (www.poetryarchive.org), **Project Gutenberg** (http://gutenberg.org) and **Read Print** (www.readprint.com). Other potential research resources include the websites of commercial publishers and contemporary writers.

Manuscripts

Seek advice specific to your own research needs from your graduate advisors and from librarians. Many specialist collections have catalogues of their own manuscript material that can only be consulted on site. As well as **Archives Hub** (see above, p. 228), other useful online and print resources include:

> *British Library Manuscripts Catalogue* and *British Library Catalogue of Illuminated Manuscripts*. Online at http://catalogue.bl.uk.

Comprehensive online searchable guides to the largest UK collection of manuscripts, and a representative selection of their images.

> *Catalogue of English Literary Manuscripts 1450–1700 (CELM)*, ed. Peter Beal. Online information at http://ies.sas.ac.uk/cmps/Projects/CELM/index. htm.

This open-access resource will supersede volumes I and II of *Index to Literary Manuscripts* (see below).

> *Documents Online*. Online at www.nationalarchives.gov.uk/ documentsonline.

The digitised public records of the UK National Archives, including both academic and family history sources.

> *Index of English Literary Manuscripts* (London: Mansell, 1980–93, 4 vols), compiled by Peter Beal *et al.* Print.

A census of major UK literary manuscripts, 1450–1900. For online version of vols. I and II, see CELM, above. At the time of writing, there are also plans to make Vol. III, 1700–1800 (Barbara Rosenbaum and Pamela White) available online.

PART 3: FINDING AND SEARCHING REFERENCE RESOURCES AND CRITICAL TEXTS

By becoming familiar with these reference resources, you can

- check the details of a particular book or journal reference for accuracy and context;
- find out what else an author has written;
- identify other publications on a topic.

General bibliographic guides to published work

The following online resources include coverage of publications from the start of the print age to the present:

WorldCat. Online at http://firstsearch.oclc.org.

Despite endemic typos and multiple entries, an excellent first stop for identifying and searching the bibliographical and location details of over 50 million publications. *OCLC First Search* member libraries holding a particular edition are individually identified for each publication. This data enables researchers to track down copies of rare editions, and supports quantitative book-history researches.

British Library Integrated Catalogue. Online at http://catalogue.bl.uk.

Fully searchable catalogue of 13 million items in the British Library's collections in London and Boston Spa (Document Supply Centre). The newspapers subset catalogues over 52,000 titles held at the Newspapers Reading Room in Colindale, including every UK national daily and Sunday paper from 1801 to the present. The manuscript collection is separately catalogued (see above, p. 234).

National Union Catalog (Library of Congress). Online direct or via LIBWEB at http://lists.webjunction.org/libweb.

Freely accessible database to bibliographical details of the holdings in the world's largest library.

EEBO and *ECCO*. Online (see also above, p. 230)

Effective bibliographical guides to pre-1700 and eighteenth-century publications.

Global books in print. Online at http://globalbooksinprint.com.

Cross-searchable database including Bowker's *Books in Print* and Book Data's *British Books in Print* databases, with access to over five million titles available, or previously available, in the USA and UK.

Commercial websites.

Amazon (www.amazon.co.uk), **Abebooks** (www.abebooks.co.uk), **Google Scholar** (http://scholar.google.co.uk) and other commercial websites offer valuable support in tracing very recent titles, or publication details that may not be available on subscription sites. For instance, by supporting time-effective one-stop full-text searches of the contents of hundreds of thousands of the most recently published books, the Amazon 'search within' facility has useful scholarly applications.

Literary bibliographies, surveys

Important basic survey works that are wholly or partially searchable online include:

> The Annual Bibliography of English Language and Literature (ABELL, London: Modern Humanities Research Association, 1967–). Online via LION at http://lion.chadwyck.co.uk.

Searchable database of 860,000 records.

> The Routledge Annotated Bibliography of English Studies (ABES). Online at http://abe.informaworld.com.

Searchable bibliography of publications in literary studies, language and linguistics, cultural and film studies.

> Review of English Studies. Online via JSTOR (www.jstor.org), LION (http://lion.chadwyck.co.uk) and Oxford Journals Online (www.oxfordjournals.org).

Review articles, notes, articles, and regular summaries of periodical literature, featuring details of the contents of some 30 major literary journals.

> SEL (Studies in English Literature). Online via JSTOR (www.jstor.org), LION (http://lion.chadwyck.co.uk) and Project Muse (www.muse.jhu.edu).

Reviews historical and critical literary studies in the post-medieval to pre-1900 periods.

> The Year's Work in English Studies. Online via Oxford Journals Online (www.oxfordjournals.org).

Oldest evaluative periodical of literary criticism. Provides critical surveys of scholarly periodicals, essays and monographs in particular historical periods, on an annual basis.

Journals, periodicals, book reviews

Previous generations of literary researchers often found it helpful to trace the development of particular interests, related writing and even controversies through the links provided by the references and footnotes of publications. Now, online full-text searching has transformed this laborious slog into a speedy and creative operation that represents an essential skill for all serious literary researchers. Online journals also represent accessible sources of detailed review articles and book reviews of recent work, and again, their search facilities greatly simplify the process of locating these.

Not all important reviews are yet readily available online. Literary researchers need to keep in touch with essential publications such as:

> *The London Review of Books* (1979–); fortnightly. Print, and online (individual subscription only) at http://.lrb.co.uk.

University libraries offer links to numerous individual online journals, many with full-text search and print facilities. Also available through many good research library database pages are useful online resources that cut down on the time required to search individual journal titles, by offering search facilities across larger collections of journals. Those of particular significance for literary research include:

> *Academic Search Complete.* Online at http://search.ebscohost.com.

Full-text search and print facility for over 5,100 peer-reviewed scholarly journals in many areas of academic study.

> *Arts and Humanities Citation Index.* Online via *ISI Web of Knowledge* at http://work.mimas.ac.uk.

Based on the analysis of footnotes and references contained in articles and papers published in over 6,400 journals and some books. It offers title, keyword and citation searching of articles, book reviews and other entries in some 1,400 journals, dating from 1975 onwards.

> *Directory of Open Access Journals (DOAJ).* Online at http://doaj.org.

Growing resource coordinating access to freely available scholarly electronic journals in many academic areas.

> *JSTOR.* Online at www.jstor.org.

Searchable full-text database of 460 key scholarly journals in many academic disciplines, providing good coverage (including some nineteenth-century material) for all but the most recent years of publication.

> *Literature Online (LION)* at http://lion.chadwyck.co.uk.

Includes full-text search facility for many key literary journals.

> *Modern Language Association International Bibliography of Books and Articles on the Modern Languages and Literatures (MLA).* Online at http://mla.org.bibliography.

Comprehensive indexing of two million monographs, proceedings, bibliographies and articles in the fields of literature, language and linguistics since 1926, from over 7,000 journals worldwide. No full-text facility.

Nexis UK. Online at http://lexisnexis.com/uk/nexis.

Full-text searchable access to content drawn from a wide range of the most important newspapers worldwide, including many (such as *The Times Higher*) with book reviews and other content of interest to literary researchers.

Periodicals Index Online (http://pio.cadwyck.co.uk) and *Periodicals Archive Online* (http:/pao.chadwyck.co.uk).

Periodicals Index Online indexes bibliographical details of articles from over 4,500 journals in the humanities and social sciences; Periodicals Archive Online provides full-text searching for 200 of them.

Project Muse. Online at http://muse.jhu.edu.

Full-text searching of post-2000 issues of 145 key humanities journals

The Times Literary Supplement. Online via *TLS Centenary Archive* at http://tls.psmedia.com.

Full-text search facility for the years 1902 to 1990.

Commercial online databases.

At the time of writing, various academic publishers offer searchable subscription databases of their journals. They generally include basic bibliographical information for all their journals, with the option to purchase individual articles. Their full-text contents will vary from one library to another, according to exactly which journal titles each individual library subscribes to. Databases that include significant literature journals, and are available through many good university library Web-pages, include *Cambridge Journals* (http://journals.cambridge.org), *IngentaConnect* (http://ingentaconnect.com) and *Oxford Journals* (www.oxfordjournals.org).

Theses, research documents, conference papers

Conference proceedings are the reports of conferences and other academic meetings, such as symposia, congresses and workshops. Contributions to conference proceedings are less easily traced than journal articles, because they are not always catalogued by individual author. A useful starting point for tracing them is the catalogue to the collection built up by the British Library, accessible online via the *BL Integrated Catalogue* (http://catalogue.bl.uk) or the *ProceedingsFirst* database (http://ock.org.uk/firstsearch).

Much valuable research appears in theses before being formally published in books or journals. Some of this work is never published at all. Bibliographical details, and in some cases full-text, of many recent theses and dissertations submitted for higher degrees can be searched through online databases, and copies can sometimes be made available for reference and research on library premises, via inter-library loan. Earlier theses, if available, may have to be consulted in the form of a microfilm or photocopy if they are not available for loan. When you need to study particular theses, ask a librarian at your university library for advice, and details of formalities and conditions. Useful guides to theses include

> *Index to Theses with Abstracts Accepted for Higher Degrees by The Universities of Great Britain and Ireland and the Council for National Academic Awards.* Online at www.theses.com.

Fully searchable bibliographical details of well over half-a-million theses submitted at UK and Irish universities from 1716 to the present, and of abstracts since 1987.

> *Proquest dissertations and theses.* Online at www.proquest.com/en-us/catalogs/databases/detail/pqdt.shtml.

Indexes bibliographical details of 2.4 million mostly US dissertations dating from 1861 onwards. Abstracts are included for doctoral dissertations since 1980 and Master's theses since 1988. Depending on subscription level, full-text or 24-page searchable previews are also available for dissertations since 1997.

> *Worldcat dissertations and theses.* Online at http://ock.org.

Searchable bibliographical details of five million theses held by OCLC *First Search* member libraries.

> L.F. McNamee, *Dissertations in English and American Literature: Theses accepted by American, British and German Universities 1865–1964* (New York: Bowker, 1968); with supplements 1964–8 (1969), 1696–73 (1974). Print only.

> Gernot U. Gabel and Gisela R. Gabel, *Dissertations in English and American Literature: Theses accepted by Austrian, French and Swiss Universities 1875–1970* (Basel: Editions Gemini/Saur, 1977); with supplement 1971–5, 1981. Print only.

Useful guides to older theses for literary researchers.

PART 4: INFORMATION RESOURCES FOR FACTS AND DETAILS

Dictionaries

General

Dictionaries are essential tools of the trade of literary research. The larger dictionaries of usage (as distinct from translation) are general language dictionaries providing definitions. Essential guides to historical and current usage, meaning and implication, they can be used to clarify issues of terminology, and to support enquiries into unknown or challenging concepts and expressions. The most authoritative is:

> *Oxford English Dictionary Online (OED)* at www.oed.com.

Definitions of words, with examples of different usages and meanings of individual words at various stages in their history. This searchable full-text database contains the complete contents of the 20-volume second edition (*The Oxford English Dictionary*, ed. J.A. Simpson, E.S.C. Weiner *et al.*, Oxford: Oxford University Press, 1989), and three additional volumes published between 1993 and 1997. It is updated quarterly.

Specialised dictionaries devoted to a single subject serve a useful reference function by providing greater detail and explanation. Online cross-searchable reference resources covering numerous specialist fields of literary relevance include subscription databases such as Oxford Reference Online (www.oxfordreference.com). Particularly useful individual specialised dictionaries include:

Abbreviations

For dictionaries of abbreviations see:

> *Acronyms, Initialisms & Abbreviations Dictionary* (Detroit: Gale, 1976–). Print only.

> *Abbreviations Dictionary*, ed. Ralph De Sola *et al.*, tenth edn (London: CRC Press, 2001). Print only.

Allusions, phrases, proverbs, quotations

For pre-1700 allusions, phrases, proverbs and quotations, it is worth remembering the powerful full-text variable-spelling search facilities of *EEBO* and *ECCO*. Specialised reference works helpful for identifying and studying allusions, references and quotations include:

> Robert Andrews, *The New Penguin Dictionary of Quotations* (London: Penguin, 2006). Print only.

Robert Collison and Mary Collison, *Dictionary of Foreign Quotations* (London: Macmillan, 1980). Print only.

Richard Branyon, *Latin Phrases and Quotations* (New York: Hippocrene, 1997). Print only.

John Ayto and Ebenezer Cobham Brewer, *Brewer's Dictionary of Phrase and Fable*, seventeenth edn (New York: Collins, 2005); first published 1870, numerous subsequent editions. A treasury of literary bric-a-brac that provides 19,000 definitions of typical and less well-known phrases and words, and explains their historical origins.

A.M. Hyamson, *A Dictionary of English Phrases, Phraseological Allusion, Catchwords, Stereotyped Modes of Speech and Metaphors, Nicknames, Soubriquets, Derivations from Personal Names, etc.* (London: Routledge, 1922; facsimile rep. Detroit: Gale, 1970). Print only.

Various derivative editions of some of the publications noted in this and following sections are available online. For example, *Oxford Reference Online* (www.oxfordreference.com), which offers access to the extremely authoritative *The Oxford Dictionary of Quotations*, ed. Elizabeth M. Knowles, sixth edn (Oxford: Oxford University Press, 2004). It also includes full-text access to *The Oxford Dictionary of Phrase and Fable*, *The Oxford Paperback Thesaurus* and *The Oxford American Thesaurus of Current English*.

Antonyms, synonyms, metaphor, metonymy
The most well-known dictionary of antonyms (words opposite in meaning) and synonyms (words sharing the same or overlapping meaning), widely available online and easily searchable, is:

Roget's Thesaurus of English Words and Phrases. Print, and online at http://thesaurus.com.

A freely available searchable database covering examples of metaphors (figures of speech characterising something or someone by the attribution of a name or quality that is not literally applicable), metonymy (figures of speech referring to something or someone by a symbolic component) and other figurative language, drawn from monographs, journals, dissertations and unpublished research papers, is:

Bibliography of Metaphor and Metonymy, ed. Sabine Knop (Amsterdam: John Benjamins, 1990 – annual). Online at www.benjamins.com/online/met.

Literary terms
Printed glossaries or dictionaries of literary terms that are reasonably authoritative, and have survived several editions, include:

A Glossary of Literary Terms, ed. Michael H. Abrams, ninth edn (Boston: Wadsworth, 2009).

J.A. Cuddon, *The Penguin Dictionary of Literary Terms and Literary Theory*, fourth edn (London: Penguin, 1998).

The Oxford Dictionary of Literary Terms, ed. Chris Baldick, third edn (Oxford: Oxford University Press, 2008). Online via *Oxford Reference Online* (www.oxfordreference.com).

Jeremy Hawthorn, *A Glossary of Contemporary Literary Theory*, fourth edn (London: Arnold, 2001).

For poetic terms see:

Miller Williams, *Patterns of Poetry: An Encyclopedia of Forms* (Lanham: Louisiana State University Press, 1986).

Jack Myers and Don Wukasch, *Dictionary of Poetic Terms* (Denton: University of North Texas Press, 2003).

Encyclopaedias

In practice, encyclopaedias, companions and dictionaries are often synonymous. The previous section has dealt with dictionaries that concentrate primarily on terms and their meanings. In this section, the focus is on works that attempt to satisfy an encyclopaedic need (i.e. as general collections of facts and analysis). The easiest and most convenient way to acquire a large body of information rapidly is probably by searching the major full-text searchable online encyclopaedic resources.

The most well-known online subscription encyclopaedia is:

Encyclopaedia Britannica. Print, and online at www.britannica.com.

This provides simultaneous searching of *Encyclopaedia Britannica* and several other reference resources, including an authoritative dictionary, thesaurus, yearbook and Internet directory. The nineteenth-century published editions (fourth edition of 1810 to tenth edition of 1902) are valuable reference sources for accepted contemporary viewpoints and attitudes.

Also available on many university library databases:

Credo reference. Online at www.credoreference.com.

This provides full-text search access to hundreds of specialist reference books (eg CIA – *The World Factbook*), including encyclopedias, dictionaries, thesauruses and handbooks of quotations.

Know UK. Online at www.knowuk.com.

This provides access to numerous reference books, and information on local and central UK government.

Some publishers provide fully searchable online subscription databases of their own publications that in effect represent encyclopaedic reference resources. At the time of writing, these include Cambridge Collections Online (http://cco. cambridge.org) and Oxford Reference Online (http://oxfordreference.com). General encyclopaedias and information databases provide a useful start, from which the researcher can graduate to the very wide range of specialist or subject encyclopaedias, handbooks and companions, many only available in printed form, for more detailed information.

Biographical information, diaries, autobiographies

Whether you are using print or online resources, searching for information about people is generally easier than trying to follow up ideas and concepts, because it is simpler to index and search for names. Productive online routes to locating monographs and journal articles on a particular individual could involve keyword searching for the specific name in databases such as *JSTOR* (www.jstor.org), *Project Muse* (http://muse.jhu.edu) or *WorldCat* (http://lion.chadwyck.co.uk). Some online databases primarily offering literary texts and information (such as *LION*, at http://lion.chadwyck.co.uk), or non-literary biographies (such as *The Complete Dictionary of Scientific Biography*, at www.gale.cengage.com/ndsb), also represent valuable sources for author biographies. Detailed information on major figures can be found in some general encyclopaedias, particularly those published in their countries of birth. Information on lesser-known literary figures can sometimes be traced in one or another of the remarkably comprehensive online databases primarily used by family historians, or the online UK Census Record databases.

Significant biographical resources include:

Oxford Dictionary of National Biography. Online at www.oxforddnb.com.

Full-text searchable resource based on the *Oxford Dictionary of National Biography*, ed. H.C.G. Matthew and Brian Harrison, 60 vols (Oxford: Oxford University Press, 2004). With over 56,000 entries, this is the most authoritative source of biographical information, and is regularly updated.

Who's Who. Online at www.ukwhoswho.com, or via Know UK, at www. knowuk.com.

Full-text searchable database of the current editions of *Who's Who* and *Who Was Who*.

American National Biography. Online at www.anb.org.

Database of 17,400 North Americans, updated quarterly.

Wilson Biographies Plus Illustrated. Online at http://hwwilson.com/databases/wilsbio.htm.

Cross-searchable resource based on several highly respected volumes first published by H.W. Wilson (New York). They include those authored by Stanley J. Kunitz and Howard Haycraft (among them *British Authors Before 1800: A Biographical Dictionary* (1952), *British Authors of the Nineteenth Century* (1936) and *American Authors 1600–1900, a Biographical Dictionary of American Literature* (1938)); and *Biography Index*, first edited in print by by Bea Joseph (1946–).

World Biographical Information System (WBIS). Online at http://db.saur.de/WIBIS.

Searchable database of brief biographical information on over five million people worldwide, from the eighth century BCE to the present.

Some key biographical works still have to be consulted in printed format or on microfiche. These include:

Frederic Boase, *Modern English Biography, Containing Many Thousand Concise Memoirs of Persons Who Have Died Since the Year 1850* (London: Bohn, 1892–1921). Print only.

Usefully supplements online resources with information on numerous minor nineteenth-century figures.

British and Irish Biographies, 1840–1940, ed. David Lewis Jones (Cambridge: Chadwyck-Healey, 1984–6). Microfiches.

272 biographical dictionaries with a computerised index of 700,000 names.

British Biographical Archive (London: British Library, 1984–), 16 microfiches.

An alphabetical assembly of entries from 324 biographical reference works published between 1601 and 1929, with later indexes.

The Houghton Mifflin Dictionary of Biography, intr. Justin Kaplan (Boston: Houghton Mifflin, 2003). Print only.

A concise single-volume collection of information on 18,000 noteworthy people worldwide, from all periods of history.

Samuel Austin Allibone, *A Critical Dictionary of English Literature and British and American Authors Living and Deceased, from the Earliest Accounts to The Latter Half of the Nineteenth Century* (London: Trubner, 1872); three vols with a later supplement (1891), compiled by John F. Kirk. Print only.

A huge, erratic but very useful compilation covering over 46,000 authors.

> *Dictionary of Literary Biography Yearbook* (Detroit: Gale, 1980–2002 – annual). Print only.

Comprehensive collection of author biographies.

Diaries and autobiographies are usefully indexed in three older publications:

> *British Diaries: An Annotated Bibliography of British Diaries Written between 1442 and 1942*, compiled by William Matthews (Cambridge: Cambridge University Press, 1950). Print only.

> *British Manuscript Dairies of the Nineteenth Century*, compiled J.S. Batts (Totowa: Rowman and Littlefield, 1976). Print only.

> *British Autobiographies: An Annotated Bibliography of British Autobiographies Published or Written before 1951*, compiled by William Matthews (Berkeley: University of California Press, 1968). Print only.

Further reference resources

Literature and literary theory
Useful reference books include:

> *The Oxford Companion to English Literature*, ed. Margaret Drabble, sixth edn (Oxford: Oxford University Press, 2006). Online via *Oxford Reference Online* at www.oxfordreference.com.

> *The Cambridge Guide to Literature in English*, ed. Dominic Head, third edn (Cambridge: Cambridge University Press, 2006). This edition print only.

> *A Dictionary of Literature in the English Language*, compiled by Robin Myers, two vols (Oxford: Pergamon, 1970, 1978). Print only.

> *Encyclopaedia of Literature and Criticism*, ed. Martin Coyle and others (London: Routledge, 1990). Print only.

Book history
The following reference resources provide general information on book history:

> Simon Eliot and Jonathan Rose (eds.), *The Blackwell Companion to the History of the Book* (Oxford: Blackwell, 2007, print, and e-book via *Blackwell Reference Online*, www.blackwellreference.com); and Simon Eliot, Andrew Nash and Ian Willison (eds), *Literary Cultures and the Material Book* (London: British Library Publications, 2007), print only.

Both offer broad surveys of book history, covering the 4,500 years before printing as well as the printed book.

The Book History Reader, ed. David Finkelstein and Alistair McCleery, second edn (London: Routledge, 2006). Print only.

The Bookseller, 1858–present. Print only.

Monthly lists of newly published books.

Directory of UK and Irish Book Publishers. Online at www.ukpublishers.net.

Provides contact details for print and electronic publishers, distributors and agents.

D. Foxon (ed.), *English Bibliographical Sources* (London, 1964–). Print only.

This series reprints a number of eighteenth-century periodicals and journals listing new publications.

John Tebbel, *A History of Book Publishing in the United States* (New York and London: R.R. Bowker, 1972–81, four vols). Print only.

Usefully introduces the subject.

Library History Database, compiled by Robin Alston. Online at www.r-alston.co.uk (at time of writing).

Information on more than 27,000 libraries established in the UK before 1850.

The Reading Experience Database (RED). Online at www.open.ac.uk/Arts/RED.

Records UK reading experiences, 1450–1945.

Robin Myers (ed.), *Records of the Stationers' Company 1554–1920* (Cambridge: Chadwyck-Healey, 1985–6). Microform.

An invaluable source of information on pre-nineteenth-century UK publications.

To identify books that people were likely to be reading, or books published in any particular year, it may be helpful to check:

Annals of English Literature, 1475–1950: The Principal Publications of Each Year Together with an Alphabetical Index of Authors and Their Works, Jyotish Ghosh, Elizabeth Withycombe and R.W. Chapman, second edn (Oxford: Clarendon Press, 1961). Print only.

Or the much more concise:

Michael Cox, *The Oxford Chronology of English Literature* (Oxford: Oxford University Press, 2002). Print only.

Classical
For information on classical allusions and details, see:

New Pauly Online Encyclopaedia of the Ancient World. Online at www. brillonline.nl/public/products.

James A.K. Thomson, *The Classical Background of English Literature* (London: Allen and Unwin, 1948). Print only.

Gilbert Highet, *The Classical Tradition: Greek and Roman Influences on Western Literature* (Oxford: Oxford University Press, 1949; rep. 1985). Print only.

The Oxford Classical Dictionary, ed. Simon Hornblower and Antony Spawforth, third edn rev. (Oxford: Oxford University Press, 2003).

The Oxford Companion to Classical Literature, Paul Harvey, rev. M.C. Howatson, second edn (Oxford: Oxford University Press, 1997).

Religious
For information on religious allusions and details, see:

Brill Dictionary of Religion. Online at www.brillonline.nl/public/products.

Encyclopedia of Religion. Online at www.gale cengage.com.

Routledge Reference Resources Online. Online at www.reference.routledge. com. Includes cross-searchable full-text access to R. Brownrigg, *Who's Who in the New Testament*, second edn (London: Routledge, 2002) and Joan Comay, *Who's Who in the Old Testament: Together With the Apocrypha*, second edn (London: Routledge, 2002).

W.B. Fulghum, *A Dictionary of Biblical Allusions in English Literature* (New York: Holt, Rinehart and Winston, 1965). Print only.

Abraham H. Lass, *The Dictionary of Classical, Biblical and Literary Allusions* (New York: Ballantine, 1988). Print only.

A Dictionary of the Bible, Dealing with its Language, Literature and Contents, Including Biblical Theology, ed. James Hastings (Edinburgh: T. and T. Clark, 1898–1904, five vols). Print only.

Allusions: Cultural, Literary, Biblical and Historical – A Thematic Dictionary, ed. Laurence Urdang, second edn (Detroit: Gale Research, 1986). Print only.

Media and performance: images, sound, theatre, film, TV and radio
TV and radio programmes relevant to your research can sometimes be followed up via their producer, or a dedicated website.

Image, sound and film databases of significance for interdisciplinary researches into literature and media include:

> *Backstage.* Online at www.backstage.ac.uk.

A performing arts gateway for the UK.

> *A Biographical Dictionary of Actors, Actresses, Musicians, Dancers, Managers & Other Stage Personnel in London, 1660–1800*, Philip H. Highfill, Kalman A. Burnim and Edward A. Langhans (Carbondale: Southern Illinois University Press, 1973–93, 16 vols). Print only.

Indispensible to anyone whose research concerns the stage during this period.

> *Bridgeman Education.* Online at www.bridgemaneducation.com.

Searchable digital image database of art of every type, historical period, and geographical region.

> *British Film Institute Film and TV Database (BFI).* Online at www.bfi.org. uk/filmtvinfo/ftvdb.

Searchable information on nearly one million film and TV titles.

> *British Library Images.* Online at www.imagesonline.bl.uk.

Searchable digital image database of art in BL ephemera, publications and manuscripts.

> *British Library Archival Sound Recordings.* Online at http://sounds.bl.uk.

Searchable collection of 12,000 music, voice and other recordings.

> *British Universities Newsreel Database.* Online at www.bufvc.ac.uk/ databases/newsreels/index.html.

Searchable database of 40,000 downloadable British Pathe newsreels, dating from 1910 to 1979.

> *Cecilia.* Online at www.cecilia-uk.org.

Archival register of music collections (instruments, sheet music, manuscripts, scores, ephemera, etc.) in Britain and Ireland.

> *Education Image Gallery.* Online at http://edina.ac.uk/eig.

More than 50,000 Getty Archive photographs.

Film and Sound Online. Online at www.filmandsound.ac.uk.

Hundreds of hours of downloadable film and television documentary footage, including the 'Performance Shakespeare' collection.

International Film Archive Database (FIAF). Online at www.ovid.com.

Searchable database including full coverage of the *International Index to Film Periodicals* (1972–), *International Index to Television Periodicals* (1979–) and the *Film/TV Documentation Collections.*

Library of Congress Prints and Photographs Online Catalog (PPOC). Online, direct at www.loc.gov/rr/print/catalog.html, or via *LIBWEB* at http://lists.webjunction.org.libweb.

Indexes over one million images, some downloadable.

Moving History. Online at www.movinghistory.ac.uk.

Cinema, film and television. A research guide to the UK's 12 public sector moving-image archives.

Music and Performing Arts Online (MPA). Online at http://mpaonline. chadwyck.com.

A portal allowing simultaneous searching of the databases *International Index to Music Periodicals* (IIMP) and the *International Index to the Performing Arts* (IIPA).

Poetry Archive. Online at www.poetryarchive.org.

Freely accessible database of poetry readings.

Poets on Screen (available online through *LION* at http://lion.chadwyck. co.uk).

Nearly 1,000 video clips of contemporary poetry readings.

Records of Early English Drama (REED). Print only.

County-by-county census of all pre-1642 UK theatre-related archival records.

TVTip – TV Times Project 1955–1985. Online at www.bufvc.ac.uk/ databases/tvtip.html.

Fully searchable database of *TV Times* television programme listings, 1955 to 1985.

Index

Routledge Critical Thinkers

Series Editor: Robert Eaglestone, Royal Holloway, University of London

Routledge Critical Thinkers is designed for students who need an accessible introduction to the key figures in contemporary critical thought. The books provide crucial orientation for further study and equip readers to engage with each theorist's original texts.

The volumes in the Routledge Critical Thinkers series place each key theorist in his or her historical and intellectual contexts and explain:

- why he or she is important
- what motivated his/her work
- what his/her key ideas were

- who and what influenced the thinker
- who and what the thinker has influenced
- what to read next and why.

Featuring extensively annotated guides to further reading, Routledge Critical Thinkers is the first point of reference for any student wishing to investigate the work of a specific theorist.

'These little books are certainly helpful study guides. They are clear, concise and complete. They are ideal for undergraduates studying for exams or writing essays and for lifelong learners wanting to expand their knowledge of a given author or idea.' – Beth Lord, *THES*

'This series demystifies the demigods of theory.' – Susan Bennett, University of Calgary

Available in this series:

Louis Althusser by Luke Ferretter
Theodor Adorno by Ross Wilson
Hannah Arendt by Simon Swift
Roland Barthes by Graham Allen
Jean Baudrillard by Richard J. Lane
Simone de Beauvoir by Ursula Tidd
Homi K. Bhabha by David Huddart
Maurice Blanchot by Ullrich Haase and William Large
Judith Butler by Sara Salih
Gilles Deleuze by Claire Colebrook
Jacques Derrida by Nicholas Royle
Michel Foucault by Sara Mills
Sigmund Freud by Pamela Thurschwell
Antonio Gramsci by Steve Jones
Stephen Greenblatt by Mark Robson
Stuart Hall by James Procter
Martin Heidegger by Timothy Clark
Fredric Jameson by Adam Roberts
Julia Kristeva by Noëlle McAfee
Jacques Lacan by Sean Homer
Emmanuel Levinas by Seán Hand
Jean-François Lyotard by Simon Malpas
Paul de Man by Martin McQuillan

Friedrich Nietzsche by Lee Spinks
Paul Ricoeur by Karl Simms
Edward Said by Bill Ashcroft and Pal Ahluwalia
Eve Kosofsky Sedgwick by Jason Edwards
Gayatri Chakravorty Spivak by Stephen Morton
Paul Virilio by Ian James
Slavoj Žižek by Tony Myers
American Theorists of the Novel: Henry James, Lionel Trilling & Wayne C. Booth by Peter Rawlings
Theorists of the Modernist Novel: James Joyce, Dorothy Richardson & Virginia Woolf by Deborah Parsons
Theorists of Modernist Poetry: T.S. Eliot, T.E. Hulme & Ezra Pound by Rebecca Beasley
Feminist Film Theorists: Laura Mulvey, Kaja Silverman, Teresa de Lauretis and Barbara Creed by Shohini Chaudhuri
Cyberculture Theorists: Manuel Castells and Donna Harroway by David Bell

Available at all good bookshops
For further information on individual books in the series, visit:
www.routledge.com/literature/rct/

Fifty Key Literary Theorists

Richard J. Lane

What is it that defines literary theory? Richard J. Lane explores fifty influential figures who have shaped this field over the last century. In one volume, theorists from a multitude of disciplines are brought together in order to explore literary theory in all its diversity, covering feminism to postcolonialism, postmodernism to psychoanalysis.

Each entry deals with key concepts and ideas that have informed literary studies in the twentieth and twenty-first centuries. Included in this comprehensive guide are entries on:

- Roland Barthes
- Judith Butler
- Jacques Derrida
- Sigmund Freud
- Edward W. Said

An essential resource for all students of literature, *Fifty Key Literary Theorists* explores the gamut of critical debate, offering both an excellent introduction to and a comprehensive overview of modern literary theorists.

ISBN 13: 978-0-415-33847-9 (hbk)
ISBN 13: 978-0-415-33848-6 (pbk)
ISBN 13: 978-0-203-44142-8 (ebk)

Available at all good bookshops
For ordering and further information please visit
www.routledge.com

The New Critical Idiom

Series Editor: John Drakakis, University of Stirling

The New Critical Idiom is an invaluable series of introductory guides to today's critical terminology. Each book:

- provides a handy, explanatory guide to the use (and abuse) of the term
- offers an original and distinctive overview by a leading literary and cultural critic
- relates the term to the larger field of cultural representation.

With a strong emphasis on clarity, lively debate and the widest possible breadth of examples, *The New Critical Idiom* is an indispensable approach to key topics in literary studies.

'*The New Critical Idiom* is a constant resource – essential reading for all students.'
Tom Paulin, University of Oxford

'Easily the most informative and wide-ranging series of its kind, so packed with bright ideas that it has become an indispensable resource for students of literature.'
Terry Eagleton, University of Manchester

Available in this series:

For further information on individual books in the series, visit:
www.routledgeliterature.com

Printed in Great Britain
by Amazon